Stefano Maso
Cicero's Philosophy

Trends in Classics – Key Perspectives on Classical Research

General Editors
Franco Montanari and Antonios Rengakos

Series Editors
P. J. Finglass, S. J. V. Malloch, Christos Tsagalis

Associate Editors
Anna Marmodoro and Elena Isayev

Volume 3

Stefano Maso

Cicero's Philosophy

—

DE GRUYTER

ISBN 978-3-11-065839-2
e-ISBN (PDF) 978-3-11-066183-5
e-ISBN (EPUB) 978-3-11-065866-8
ISSN 2626-1030

Library of Congress Control Number: 2021947997

Bibliographic information published by the Deutsche Nationalbibliothek
The Deutsche Nationalbibliothek lists this publication in the Deutsche Nationalbibliografie;
detailed bibliographic data are available on the Internet at http://dnb.dnb.de.

© 2022 Walter de Gruyter GmbH, Berlin/Boston
Cover image: Domenico Spinosa, Fondo Marino, courtesy of Nicola Spinosa
Printing and binding: CPI books GmbH, Leck

www.degruyter.com

MIX
Papier aus verantwor-
tungsvollen Quellen
FSC
www.fsc.org   FSC® C083411

Preface

*Disserens in utramque partem tum Graece tum Latine
et abduco parum per animum a molestiis et τῶν
προῦργου τι delibero* (ad Atticum).

The ages pass, and so do trends and interpretative parameters. The reason why classics of literature and philosophy remain classics is above all because they can influence the way new parameters arise.

So it is for Cicero. The Cicero we know today is certainly not the same of the nineteenth century, nor of the twentieth, nor the Cicero of western Humanism. We cannot say which one is the true Cicero, because the paths of criticism are linked not only to the manuscripts and testimonies we possess (which are less reliable or consistent than we might think), but also to the changing nature of the contexts in which he is studied, to the analytical tools available and to the specific training of individual scholars. In the case of Cicero, we are faced with an exceptional protagonist, fully involved in the historical and political events of his time, and also gifted with an extreme competence in the art of rhetoric. This ability allowed him both to organize in an effective and peculiar way the diffusion of his thought and to control the transmission of his own image and the moulding of his personality in the eyes of his contemporaries and, even, in ours. In this regard, the importance of the Ciceronian correspondence is undeniable.

Alongside Cicero the orator, the politician, the rhetorician, the man of letters and the lover of the Roman and Greek tradition, recently the philosopher Cicero has also emerged: an aspect of Cicero's that has been neglected, especially in the Romantic age. The legitimacy of this designation depends on the meaning that we give to 'philosopher'. In the Greek world, and also in the philosophical thought of recent centuries, the philosopher has often been identified with the theoretician; in other ages, the philosopher coincided with the scientist, and sometimes with the logician or the moralist. Someone previously considered a philosopher may very well today be excluded from the canon of philosophers; so too we can also find unexpected appearances in modern published 'Companions' of philosophy.

From the point of view of moral consistency and political choices, Cicero's image is likely to remain damaged. But that does not matter. The Cicero I am dealing with here is above all a man of high culture; a scholar who discussed a number of philosophical-theoretical issues with scholars and masters belonging to different philosophical schools; a tireless protagonist of the political scene who tried to combine the time of action with the time of thinking; a passionate and

https://doi.org/10.1515/9783110661835-202

enlightened investigator of the Roman tradition willing to confront without awe the Greek culture, whose revolutionary power he recognized.

I am especially interested in showing that we are not dealing with a mere populariser; I am convinced that if, thanks to Cicero's 'philosophical' work, we are able to reconstruct the history of the Academy in the Hellenistic era, we cannot for this reason renounce defining his personality and his purpose as a philosopher.

Following the aim of 'Key Perspectives on Classical Research', this volume focuses on relevant studies pursued in the last decades. For contingent reasons, I have favoured scholarship in English, without neglecting, though, the most significant works published in other European languages and not yet translated into English, with the awareness that they are the result of different cultural climates and schools: precisely for this reason they are a source of original suggestions and unexpected entries. Starting from these premises, I have explored and discussed the trends of scholarship on Cicero's philosophy, showing that a positive reconsideration of it has been achieved. On several occasions we will observe that the most recent studies have deepened specific or collateral aspects, examined the connection of the various themes and the stylistic innovation, and focussed on the planning that Cicero pursued. Almost always, the intent to contribute to consolidating a positive judgment of his philosophical work appears evident, a judgment which appreciates Cicero's recognized competence in dealing with the philosophical literature of the Hellenistic schools and in identifying the issues that he would try to discuss.

In planning this research, I favoured some paths over others, starting from the biographical picture that can illustrate Cicero's training as a philosopher. In addition, I have placed the more explicitly philosophical works at the centre of the inquiry, even if I have neglected neither the corpus of speeches nor the rhetorical works or the letters. I discuss how Cicero combines politics and philosophy, rhetoric and philosophy, ethics and philosophy: how he approaches epistemological topics, and why the 'sceptical' method appears to him so fertile and decisive in his philosophical commitment.

I also take into consideration the issues that are still open today as they are probably unsolvable, but whose development and implications are still evident: above all, the problem of free will and of the Ciceronian not clearly anti-deterministic (and not even convincingly deterministic) vision of reality. Such clarification of state-of-the-art research is essential in order to suggest directions for further investigations by scholars.

Cicero's philosophical engagement is finally captured in his tireless commitment to equipping the Latin language for philosophical thought. Through an analysis of eight key words, we will demonstrate Cicero's linguistic sensitivity and appreciate his ability to understand philosophical concepts. In many cases, solutions (or translation proposals) became canonical; in other cases, they appear significant for clarifying the understandable forcing or occasional misunderstandings, as well as for highlighting some surprising shortcomings. Among the latter, we consider that Cicero never invented a present participle for the verb 'to be'; an invented form, 'ens', would become fundamental only in medieval theoretical philosophy and in modern and contemporary philosophy.

I am grateful for the intelligent rereading of this work, which, in whole or in part, friends and colleagues with English as their mother tongue have done, to ensure that it can best be understood. Especially: Francesca Favino, Phoebe Garfinkel.

Special thanks also to the editors of the series, Patrick Finglass (Bristol), Simon Malloch (Nottingham), Christos Tsagalis (Thessaloniki), for welcoming this work and for the careful review they have made. Finally, thanks Anna Marmodoro (Durham), for suggesting them this new book on Cicero.

Contents

List of Abbreviations or *Sigla*

Cic.	**M. Tullius Cicero**
Acad.	*Academica*
Att.	*Epistulae ad Atticum*
Brut.	*Brutus*
Cluent.	*Pro A. Cluentio*
Deiot.	*Pro rege Deiotaro*
De Or.	*On the Orator* (*De oratore*)
Div.	*On Divination* (*De divinatione*)
Fam.	*Epistulae ad familiares*
Fat.	*On Fate* (*De fato*)
Fin.	*On the Ends of Good and Evil* (*De finibus bonorum et malorum*)
Inv.	*On Invention* (*De inventione*)
Lael.	*Laelius On Friendship* (*Laelius de amicitia*)
Leg.	*On the Laws* (*De legibus*)
Luc. / *Acad.*	
Pr. (II)	*Lucullus*
Mil.	*Pro T. A. Milone*
ND	*On the Nature of the Gods* (*De natura deorum*)
Off.	*On Duties* (*De officiis*)
Or.	*Orator*
Parad.	*Stoic Paradoxes* (*Paradoxa Stoicorum*)
Phil.	*Philippics* (*Philippicae orationes*)
Pis.	*In L. Calpurnium Pisonem*
Q. fr.	*Epistulae ad Quintum fratrem*
Rep.	*On the Republic* (*De re publica*)
Sen.	*On Old Age* (*Cato Maior de senectute*)
Sest.	*Pro P. Sestio*
Top.	*Topica*
Tusc.	*Tusculan Disputations* (*Tusculanae disputationes*)
Varr. / *Acad.*	
Post. (I)	*Varro*
Verr.	*In Verrem actio prima et actio secunda*
Aët.	**Aëtius**
Plac.	*De Placita Philosophorum*
Alex. Aphr.	**Alexander Aphrodisiensis**
Fat.	*On Fate*
Arist.	**Aristoteles**
De an.	*On the Soul* (*De anima*)
EE	*Eudemian Ethics* (*Ethica Eudemia*)
EN	*Nichomachean Ethics* (*Ethica Nicomachea*)

https://doi.org/10.1515/9783110661835-204

GE	*On Generation and Corruption (De generatione et corruptione)*
Int.	*On Interpretation (De interpretatione)*

Aug.	**M. Aurelius Augustinus**
Acad.	*Contra Academicos*
Civ.	*De civitate Dei*
Confess.	*Confessiones*

Clem.	**Clement of Alexandria = T. Flavius Clemens**
Strom.	*Stromata*

Diog. Laert.	**Diogenes Laertius**

D.C.	**Cassius Dio**

Epic.	**Epicurus**
fr.	*Fragmenta* (ed. Arrighetti)
Hrd.	*Epistula ad Herodotum*
Pyth.	*Epistula ad Pythoclem*

Gal.	**C. Galenus**
PHP	*De Placitis Hippocratis et Platonis*

Gell.	**A. Gellius**
N.A.	*Noctes Atticae*

Horat.	**Q. Horatius Flaccus**
Sat.	*Sermones (Saturae)*

Lucr.	**T. Lucretius Carus**
Rer. nat.	*On the nature of things (De rerum natura)*

Panaet.	**Panaetius**
Test.	*Testimonianze* (ed. Alesse)

Philod.	**Philodemus**
De signis	(ed. De Lacy)

Plat.	**Plato**
Grg.	*Gorgia*
Phaed.	*Phaedo*
Phaedr.	*Phaedrus*
Theaet.	*Theaetetus*
Tim.	*Timaeus*

Plut.	**Plutarchus**
Cic.	*Life of Cicero* (*Vita Ciceronis*)
Comm. not.	*De communibus notitiis adversus Stoicos*
Ps.-Plutarch	**Pseudo-Plutarchus**
Fat.	*On Fate (De fato)*
Sen.	**L. Annaeus Seneca**
Ep.	*Epistulae ad Lucilium*
Vit. b.	*De vita beata*
Sen. the Elder	**L. Annaeus Seneca the Elder**
Suas.	*Suasoriae*
Serv.	**M. Servius Honoratus**
In Verg. Aen.	*In Vergilii Aeneidem commentarii*
Sext. Emp.	**Sextus Empiricus**
Adv. Math.	*Adversus Mathematicos*
PH	*Outlines of Pyrrhonism*
Stob.	**Johannes Stobaeus**
Ecl.	*Eclogae*

CHHP	Algra K., J. Barnes, J. Mansfeld and M. Schofield (eds.) (1999). *The Cambridge History of Hellenistic Philosophy*. Cambridge: Cambridge University Press.
DPhA	*Dictionnaire des Philosophes Antiques*, publié sous la direction de R. Goulet de 1989 à 2018 par CNRS-Éditions, Paris. See the *Online version*, by Brepols Publishers n.v. (Turnhout, Belgium).
L&S	Long–Sedley 1987
OLD	Oxford Latin Dictionary, P.G.W. Glare (ed.) 2012^2, Oxford University Press.
PHA	Erler, M. and H. Flashar (eds.) (1994). *Die Philosophie der Antike*, vol. 4.2. Basel: Schwabe.
SVF	*Stoicorum Veterum Fragmenta*, collegit Io. ad Arnim, Stuttgart: Teubner, I (1905), II-III (1903), IV (conscripsit M. Adler, 1924); ed. stereotypa, *ibid.* 1978-1979.

1 Cicero's Philosophical Apprenticeship

1.1 Biographical paths

The importance of Cicero as a philosopher transcends what today we mean by 'being a philosopher' or 'studying philosophy'. To realize this, suffice it to recall his biography, that shows him as: (a) the protagonist of one of the most important phases of the history of Rome: the end of the Republic, whose problematic aspect was hinted at by Ronald Syme in the very title of his masterpiece *The Roman Revolution* (1939); (b) the tireless mediator, especially in the last ten years of his life, between Greek and Roman cultural philosophical milieu: an original task that Cicero took on himself and that Ulrich Knoche remarked in an essay of 1959, 'Cicero: Ein Mittler griechischer Geisteskultur'. To understand Cicero's philosophical apprenticeship, as well as his interest in the oratory and the rhetorical art he cultivated from an early age, we must proceed from a historical-cultural perspective.

To do so, we have three tools available:
1. Cicero's work;
2. the works of historians and scholars from antiquity (in particular Plutarch's *Life of Cicero*);
3. the great modern biographies.

The first two groups of sources constitute our fundamental tools: they are the supporting base of our research. Through Cicero's works we can try to reconstruct his inner world, his hopes, his projects. In this direction Cicero's correspondence with his friends and, among others, with Atticus can be considered a precious instrument. In this regard, two major preliminary investigations have also to be mentioned: a nineteenth-century and positive one by G. Boissier, *Cicéron et ses amis* (1865), which emphasizes 'moderation' in Cicero's political conception; the other, a twentieth-century malevolent one, by J. Carcopino, *Les secrets de la Correspondance de Cicéron* (1947), which sketches the figure of a prodigal man, a self-enriching lawyer, an interested husband, a bully, a doctrinaire without doctrine, an over-ambitious man, and a coward. To justify this portrait, Carcopino argues that those who published Cicero's correspondence aimed to discredit and dishonour the author. As for a recent look at the Ciceronian epistolary and its topics, see the work of J. Hall, *Politeness and Politics in Cicero's Letters* (2009); P. White, *Cicero in Letters. Epistolary Relations of the Late Republic* (2010); S. McConnell, *Philosophical Life in Cicero's Letters* (2014); R. Woolf, *Cicero: the Philosophy of a Roman Sceptic* (2015); M. Rühl, *Ciceros Korrespondenz als Medium literarischen und gesellschaftlichen Handelns* (2018). In particular McConnell and

https://doi.org/10.1515/9783110661835-001

Woolf focus on the meaning of philosophical life and Sceptical philosophy in Cicero's correspondence.

In addition to Cicero's correspondence, *Brutus* is indispensable; thanks to it we can understand important elements concerning his intellectual and oratory education. *Brutus* was composed in 46, two years after Caesar's decisive defeat of Pompey at the Battle of Pharsalus. The main interlocutor is the orator M. Junius Brutus (nephew of M. Porcius Cato), who later participated in the conspiracy against Caesar. Another important interlocutor is T. Pomponius Atticus. *Brutus* is a dialogue in which Cicero traces the history of Roman eloquence, aware that it has now reached its sunset, coinciding with the definitive crisis of the Republic. Under the stifling atmosphere of Caesar's domination there were not many opportunities left for those who still wanted to use the instrument of political mediation: Cicero had in mind precisely that, and wrote his dialogue so that the ancient values would not be completely lost.

More precisely, in *Brutus* Cicero addresses the Rome of the period of its origins, then Cato the Elder, and finally M. Antonius and L. Licinius Crassus, both of whom he had met and whom he considered master orators. As he approaches the age of his contemporaries, Cicero insists on his polemic against the Attic style as being too concise and sober. He considers this style of oratory to be archaic, and unable to express emotional tensions. In the concluding part Cicero praises his recently dead friend and adversary Hortensius Hortalus; then (§§ 305 and following) he tells us about himself and those who were the idol orators of his youth. However, to begin with, he tells us about the philosopher Philo of Larissa, head since 110 of the New Academy, the school of Sceptical orientation that Cicero preferred, who – having fled from Athens at the time of the Mithridatic War – had taken refuge in Rome.

Cicero says he completely devoted himself to Philo at that time, animated as he was by an extraordinary enthusiasm for the study of philosophy (*totum ei me tradidi admirabili quodam ad philosophiam studio concitatus*, 306). Then it is the turn of the Stoic Diodotus, who lived at Cicero's house until 59, the year of his death. His educational journey to Athens and Asia, begun in 79, and study with Molon of Rhodes would be decisive. He tells us about his careful study of the Greek language (so thorough that it allowed him to fashion an oration directly in that language) and how he has improved his ability to endure physical exertion during a speaking performance:

> Thus, after a two-year tour, I returned to Italy, having not only greatly improved, but almost changed into a new man. The vehemence of my voice and action was considerably abated;

the excessive ardour of my language was corrected; my lungs were strengthened; and my whole constitution confirmed and settled.[1]

Brutus gives us (§ 322) an image of Cicero as committed to improving and reaching a 'mature' form of eloquence: supported by literary studies (*studuisse litteris*), embracing philosophy (*complexus philosophiae*), rooted in the study of law (*ius civile didicisset*); making him the master of Roman history (*memoriam rerum Romanarum teneret*), capable of embarrassing the adversary with brief and witty arguments (*breviter arguteque*), so as to favourably impress the judges; an eloquence that foresees the possibility of 'extending' the discourse (*dilatare*) when it is necessary, of inserting any problem in a general context (*ad communem quaestionem universi generis traducere*), of pushing the hearts of the listeners where the situation required (*quocumque res postularet impellere*).

Among the works of ancient historians and scholars, we must remember the biographies of Plutarch (I-II century CE) and Cassius Dio (II-III century). Both wrote their works in Greek. If the former often presents anecdotal cues, the latter (cf. *Roman History*, particularly books 38 and 45) is evidently an anti-Ciceronian writer. Moreover, if the Platonizing Plutarch conceives of Cicero as a flawed philosopher (*Cic.* 32.6–7), Cassius Dio does not seem to know Cicero's philosophical work directly. Evidently, for him, Cicero figured only as a politician and chief orator. Plutarch compares Cicero with Demosthenes, while Cassius Dio praises in an equivocal way his skill in the use of the word.[2] Livy (I century BCE – I century CE) also dealt with Cicero, but only a fragment from the book 120 of the *Ab urbe condita*, quoted in Seneca the Elder, *Suas.* 6.17.22, has survived. There the killing of the orator by Antony's assassins is described: his hands were also cut off, guilty of having written against Antony.

With regards to Plutarch's *Life*, it is necessary to specify some points:
- Plutarch, in comparing Cicero with Demosthenes, focuses on the quality of their eloquence, not on the validity or ineffectiveness of a possible political project;
- according to Plutarch, Cicero is an orator wishing above all to show his vast literary and philosophical culture, and proud of it;
- the behaviour of Cicero as a politician appears courageous and coherent, even in the most difficult moments;

---

1 *Brut.* 316.
2 See D.C. 38.19.1: "Words, as drugs, are of many varieties, and different potencies, so that it will not be surprising if you should be able to steep in some mixture of philosophy."

– Cicero's conduct as provincial administrator (he was *quaestor* in Sicily and *proconsul* in Cilicia and Cappadocia) is irreproachable and shows a virtuous trait of his character.

In conclusion, Plutarch thinks of Cicero as a powerful speaker, capable of translating his political ideal into practice thanks to eloquence and charm (*charis*) of his oratory.[3] The overall judgment is positive, even if allusions to his defects are not spared: for example, his weakness of mind in the period of exile (§ 32), his slothfulness (§ 42), his ambition, his *philotimia* (§ 45).

With regard to group 3), all biographies obviously rely on what can be derived from Cicero's works and on the biographical reconstructions by Plutarch and Cassius Dio: they do so, however, in ways that are sometimes significantly different and with the addition of further documentation. Among the biographies published in the last century, we can roughly distinguish three phases:

A) in the first, more generalist, phase we can include T. Petersson, *Cicero. A Biography* (1920); K. Büchner, *Cicero. Bestand und Wandel seiner geistige Welt* (1964); and M. Gelzer, *Cicero. Ein biographischer Versuch* (1969). However, K. Kumaniecki, *Cyceron i jego współcześni* (1959) is not negligible; it remained practically unknown to non-Polish scholars until its translation into Italian.[4] In all these works the attempt to highlight the characteristics of the Republican era is evident: Cicero, his thought and his political choices constitute one of the most coherent and brilliant expressions of this historical phase. Their approach to Cicero attempts to reconstruct his inner world, beyond the external variables, so that his attitudes to his human story are illuminated.

Petersson's book was one of the first great results of the modern US historiographical school. Accurate and reliable, after a look at the political story of Cicero, this monograph dwells on the philosophical research of the Arpinas. It constituted the reference work for the English-speaking world in the early twentieth century.

A notable step forward, however, can be identified in the work of the German school. Büchner considered Cicero's as a true 'spiritual adventure' in which, through the power of language and oratory, a singular unity between philosophy and action is achieved. Gelzer in his monograph and in his article on Cicero in *Paulys Realencyclopädie der classischen Altertumswissenschaft* (1939) tries to overcome the features characterizing the nineteenth-century historiography of Theodor Mommsen, and aims to redeem the work of the orator, the writer and the

---

3 See also Lintott 2013, 1–17.
4 *Cicerone e la crisi della repubblica romana* (1972). There is no English translation.

philosopher. No longer a 'retrospective' reading that saw Cicero as the exponent of the late Republican conservative aristocracy (like the Junkers in the context of German unification), whom Caesar was opposing. No longer Cicero as an anticipator of the Augustan regime. Above all, his work as a politician is now placed in a non-negative perspective, if compared with the positive judgment usually expressed on Caesar at the end of the nineteenth and early twentieth centuries. Indeed, Cicero's perception of the crisis of the Roman Republic and of the political action that he intended to take is well highlighted.

Finally, Kumaniecki aims to present Cicero by avoiding pre-established judgments or modern ethical or political criteria, but rather to set him again in the context of the contemporary cultural climate and morality.

B) The second phase is represented by works that are not generalist, but predominantly focused on specific aspects of Cicero's biography. These include G. Radke (ed.), *Cicero, ein Mensch seiner Zeit* (1968); D. Stockton, *A Political Biography* (1971); T.N. Mitchell, *The Ascending Years* (1979) and *Cicero the Senior Statesman* (1991); and most recently Ph. Freeman, *How to Grow Old: Ancient Wisdom for the Second Half of Life Marcus Tullius Cicero* (2016).

Radke's collection embraces eight lectures by scholars representing German historiography, including U. Knoche, Ch. Meier, and O. Seel.[5] The effort to describe Cicero's life as an authentic phenomenon of intellectual history is evident; in this perspective, even single aspects or suggestions are considered important.

Stockton's work traces the crucial moments of Cicero's entire political course; it strives to show how much the politician was aware of the institutional crisis that would lead to the affirmation of the empire, and how important it was for him to safeguard not only the moral value of the *officium* (i.e. 'duty'), but also its prominence in the political sphere.

The first biography by Mitchell focuses on the period preceding 63, the year of Cicero's consulate: through four chapters, Mitchell examines the background and education of Cicero, his apprenticeship under such figures as L. Licinius Crassus (the orator and consul), and Q. Mucius Scaevola (the jurist and consul), as well as his advancement through successive magistracies. According to Mitchell, the ideals of the senatorial oligarchy mirrored those of the nobility in general and found in Cicero a convinced exponent. However, not all interpreters today agree on this schematic reading of Cicero's personality.

---

5 See U. Knoche, 'Ciceros Verbindung der Lehre vom Naturrecht mit dem römischen Recht und Gesetz', 38–60; Ch. Meier, 'Cicero Consulat', 61–116; O. Seel, 'Cicero und das Problem des römischen Philosophierens', 136–160.

C) The third phase includes the most important recent complete biographies: D.R. Shackleton Bailey, *Cicero* (1971); P. Grimal, *Cicéron* (1986); E. Narducci, *Cicerone. La parola e la politica* (2009). To these three important biographies we can add that of W. Stroh, *Cicero: Redner, Staatsmann, Philosoph* (2008); the monograph of K. Bringmann, *Cicero* (2010), and the monograph of G.M. Müller, *Cicero* (2016). All well documented, they accompany the historical events of the late Republic with a commentary on the roles that Cicero played there. According to Shackleton Bailey, however, Cicero owes his immortality to what he wrote, rather than to what he did. His work develops through an examination of the correspondence,[6] connected to the various historical moments and to the various political decisions that Cicero took. No other Greek or Roman, Shackleton Bailey believes, has projected himself into posterity like Cicero does in his extant correspondence. Cicero deserves to be studied not so much as a statesman, moralist, author of rhetorical and philosophical works, but as the brilliant, versatile, infinitely conversable man who captivated his society and achieved immortality from his correspondence.

According to Grimal, on the other hand, it is necessary to see in Cicero a man who knows how to appreciate the traditions and the moral values derived from the past, and who knows how to combine them with Hellenism and, therefore, with the Greek world. Grimal also believes the strength of the word, and the *dignitas* (prestige) that derives from it, to be central. On this basis, Cicero represents the morally authoritative Roman ideal man, anchored to values such as *prudentia, iustitia, temperantia, fortitudo*,[7] and able to face the new problems connected with the widening of the *imperium*. Therefore, what Grimal provides us with is the image of a politician and, at the same time, of a thinker who strongly marked the history of Rome.

Finally, Narducci's work appears as a highly documented biographical story, where the politician, the orator, the philosopher and the writer integrate into a synthesis that forms an exemplary fresco of the late Republic and the intellectual world in the transition phase towards the empire. The ethical dimension of the political conception on which Cicero focuses is the foundation on which his eloquence and his social commitment rest.

---

6 Shackleton Bailey is the author of the most authoritative critical edition of Cicero's letters, published in the series "Cambridge Classical Texts and Commentaries".

7 There is an intense debate about the way the four virtues in the Hellenistic Stoa should be defined and conceptualized. As for their redefinition by Cicero and the importance of the *decorum*, see Schofield 2012a, 46–53.

As already noted, Cicero's correspondence appears fundamental to grasping the background of his decisions and political choices, to understanding the urgency of the dense web of relationships that he managed, to comprehending the moral tension supporting his entire cultural and philosophical journey, and the biography by Shackleton Bailey explicitly confirms this.

1.2 Cultural and philosophical education

Let us now go over the phases of Cicero's youth and philosophical education.

Arpinum is a village not far from Rome, towards the southeast. Until the fourth centuries BCE, the Volsci and then the Samnites had occupied this area. Then, in 303, Arpinum became a Roman city and was administered directly by a *praefectus*. Among its important citizens we find Gaius Marius (157 – 86), seven times a Roman consul, conqueror of King Jugurtha and victorious fighter against the Cimbrians and Teutons. When Marcus Tullius Cicero was born there, on 3 January 106, Arpinum had already been a *municipium* since 188 and was therefore perfectly integrated into the Roman legal system. The municipality, however, remained attached to ancient traditions, as Cicero himself testifies, recalling the old family environment and the conservative attitude of his grandfather (M. Tullius Cicero) towards social institutions and towards innovations from the Greek world.[8]

Cicero's family belonged to the equestrian rank and, on the side of his paternal grandmother Gratidia, there was a bond with the family of Gaius Marius; therefore, their members could seriously aspire to Roman magistracies.[9] However, Cicero's father, also named Marcus, a man devoted to studying and in poor health, remained in Arpinum to look after his properties, without pursuing a military career or magistracies. However, he managed to buy a house in Rome in the Carinae quarters, near the Esquiline and not far from the modern church of S. Pietro in Vincoli: a *pied-à-terre* that would be very useful, first to his son Marcus Tullius Cicero, and then to his younger brother Quintus, when they began their careers in Rome. Marcus Tullius Cicero was about ten years old when, after his elementary studies, he moved to Rome.

On the one hand, Cicero did not deny an origin linked to local traditions and the modest countryside; this would allow him, years later, to present himself as

---

8 *Leg.* 2.2–4; 3.36.
9 In the case of Cicero's relatives, the search for connections between Roman politicians and local protagonists is profitable. See Syme 2016, ch. 11: 'Rome and Arpinum'.

the *novus homo* on the political scene, one able to overcome considerable obstacles to success in public life and, thus, to show his personal merits; on the other, he was aware of belonging to a family of ancient origins, economically prosperous, that (on his mother's side) had supplied senators to Rome.

His father, and above all his uncle L. Cicero, facilitated knowledge of and access to the great speakers of the time: M. Antonius 'Orator' and L. Licinius Crassus.[10] In *Brutus*, as already noted, Cicero points out the progressive refinement of the culture of the orators, thanks also to the contribution of the Greeks. Eloquence cannot be separated from cultural preparation and should be so elaborated that it achieves an artistic form. Very probably the thirteen-year-old Cicero found some solicitation in this direction in the school of the rhetorician L. Plotius Gallus, despite the fact that only Latin was used there and the approach was mainly technical. It was a school open not only to the aristocratic elite, but also to equestrians who could afford it.

But this was not enough for Cicero. Under the tutelage of Licinius Crassus (who, however, died in 91) and then of Scaevola (*Augur* and *Pontifex Maximus*), the brilliant schoolboy began to develop an interest in the Greek world and befriended, among others, Titus Pomponius, later nicknamed Atticus, because of his long stay in Greece. With Atticus he attended the lessons of the Epicurean Phaedrus. It was a decisive moment: Atticus became an Epicurean, but Cicero distanced himself from the theses of this philosophical doctrine, even though he had scrupulously studied its contents.

Later, in 51, Cicero wrote to the orator C. Memmius:

> I admired Phaedrus so much as a philosopher when I was still a boy and before I knew Philo. Afterwards I admired his honesty, the gentleness of his ways, and his sense of duty.[11]

In *On the Ends of Good and Evil* 1.16 Cicero would remember:

> Indeed, I regularly attended those professors (Phaedrus and Zeno), in company with our friend Atticus.

Atticus was enthusiastic and showed devotion to Phaedrus. Even Cicero was fascinated by him, and the two friends discussed and debated each other on the topics dealt with in class (*cotidieque inter nos ea quae audiebamus conferebamus*, *ibid.*). However, Cicero, at the time of *On the Ends of Good and Evil*, did not want

---

10 *De Or.* 2.1–11: Cicero explains that the eloquence of both is not extemporaneous or due to natural gifts, but based on study and erudition.
11 *Fam.* 13.1.2.

to be considered an uncritical disciple or a prejudiced adversary. There was not a problem of 'understanding' the Epicurean doctrine, but of 'adherence': "there was never any dispute over my understanding, though plenty over what I could agree with" (*neque erat umquam controversia quid ego intellegerem, sed quid probarem, ibid.*). Along with Phaedrus, we find another Epicurean teacher, namely Zeno of Sidon. Cicero had the opportunity to hear him when, between 79 and 77, he was in Athens with Atticus.

At that time, however, Cicero had already heard Philo of Larissa, a student of the Academic Clitomachus, in Rome in 88. Philo had come to Rome because of the destruction of the Academy during the Mithridatic wars, and had strongly impressed the young student with his Sceptical-probabilistic approach. In Athens, Cicero also met Antiochus of Ascalon, initially a pupil of Philo, but then his adversary, since he diverged from the approach that Philo proposed.

But what exactly can be stated about his education as a youth? At the conclusion of *Tusculan Disputations* we read:

> As my own inclination and desire led me, from my earliest youth upward, to seek her protection, so, under my present misfortunes, I have had recourse to the same port from whence I set out, after having been tossed by a violent tempest. O Philosophy, thou guide of life! Thou discoverer of virtue and expeller of vices! What would not only I myself, but the whole life of man, have been without you? .... Whose assistance, then, can be of more service to me than yours, when you have bestowed on us tranquillity of life, and removed the fear of death?[12]

In the opening of *On the Nature of the Gods* we read:

> Next, as I am concerned, I have not been recently won over by philosophy, nor have I dedicated little amount of time and energy to it: rather, the less it seemed that I did, the more I was maximally committed to philosophy. This can be confirmed by the speeches, full of philosophic judgments, and the familiarity with the most learned men, from whose attendance our house has always received prestige – in particular the masters Diodotus, Philo, Antiochus, Posidonius, who were my instructors.[13]

Cicero wrote *Tusculan Disputations* and *On the Nature of the Gods* one after the other in August 45. These two passages strongly emphasize that the study of philosophy was fundamental for him in his youth. In the passage from *On the Nature of the Gods* two pairs of teachers, belonging to only two schools of philosophy, are expressly mentioned: the Stoics Diodotus and Posidonius, and the Academics

---

12 *Tusc.* 5.5. For the English translations, see the bibliography.
13 *ND* 1.6.

Philo of Larissa and Antiochus of Ascalon. Listed in a chronologically plausible order, which perhaps corresponds to Cicero's actual course of learning, all four are mentioned as direct masters and milestones in his cultural and philosophical education. The importance of the link with Philo and Antiochus has already been mentioned, but as for Diodotus and Posidonius, Cicero long hosted the former in his own home until his death; the latter – surely met in Rome because of his embassy in 86 – was his teacher for a brief period in Rhodes in 77. To this list of teachers, we also need to add Zeno of Sidon and Phaedrus, the pair of Epicureans surprisingly absent from the passage from *On the Nature of the Gods*.

In conclusion, the formation of the rhetorician Cicero depended not only on the learning of a technique, but also involved the broadening of a frame of cultural reference and above all the study of Greek philosophy.

In 81 Cicero gave his first oration, published as *Pro Quinctio*; at the end of the 80s he performed his first criminal defence (*Pro Roscio Amerino*). However, success and recognized competence were not enough for the twenty-seven-year-old lawyer. The following year he embarked for Greece. This was an educational journey, which, however, interrupted a brilliant forensic career that had only just begun. Cicero returned to Rome in 77 to marry Terentia, a rich heiress probably of noble descent;[14] that was the time to restart his career as an orator and to start his political one.

When he left for Greece, Cicero's intention was probably not simply to improve his oratorical techniques (in Smyrna he met the orator P. Rutilius Rufus, and in Rhodes attended the rhetoric lessons of Molon, whom he had already met a few years earlier in Rome); perhaps it was not even a departure for a health problem[15] or for political reasons, as Plutarch suggests.[16] More likely Cicero, in the spirit of a modern 'Journey for education' or *Bildungsreise*, wanted to perfect his education and deepen his knowledge, especially of philosophy. As already noted, in Athens he listened to the lessons of the Epicurean Zeno and the Academician Antiochus. In Rhodes he met Posidonius, the great philosopher who was the protagonist of the renewal of Stoicism. Later on, he made friends with him and referred to his works when, in the last years of his life, he personally committed himself to building the foundations of Roman philosophy.

---

14 Her name connects her to the *gens* Terentia, well-known since the times of the Second Punic War. A cousin or half-sister of Terentia was a member of the patrician *gens* Fabia.

15 Cic., *Brut.* 313–314.

16 Plut., *Life of Cicero* 3: Cicero had to avoid the revenge of the dictator Sulla, whom he opposed by defending Sextus Roscius Amerinus.

In Athens, therefore, Cicero opened up to the world of Hellenism, which allowed him to go beyond the limits of Roman culture; in Athens Cicero programmatically combined rhetoric and philosophy. He confirmed this in *Tusculan Disputations*, a few years later, when he imagined walking with his friends in his villa in Tusculum, among the arcades that evoked the Lyceum and the Academy. On that occasion he specified that:

> And therefore, as yesterday before noon we applied ourselves to declaim (*ante meridiem dictioni operam dedissemus*), in the afternoon we went down into the Academy (*scil.* to discuss, to philosophize: *disputationem habere*).[17]

Finally, Cicero perhaps thought of moving to Athens, as suggested by Plutarch, *Life of Cicero* 4: "when he had been excluded from his public career, to live away from the Forum and politics, in peace, in the company of philosophy".

1.3 Studying rhetorical art and studying philosophy

On the Orator is the great dialogue on the rhetorical and oratorical arts. The commentary by Leeman–Pinkster 1981–2008 is fundamental, a monumental work completed with the contribution of other collaborators; in addition to the style and characteristics of the Ciceronian language, it focused on the reconstruction of the rhetorical doctrines to which Cicero refers. In *On the Orator* we find as interlocutors M. Antonius and L. Licinius Crassus, the two great orators, both teachers of Cicero. Cicero wrote it in the last months of 55, during a fairly happy period of his life. In fact, he had been recently recalled to Rome, after exile to Durres and Thessaloniki; Caesar, his opponent, was far away in Britain, while in Rome there were the consuls G. Pompeius Magnus and M. Licinius Crassus, the other two leaders, who were less hostile to him. An acclaimed and influential senator, Cicero was in a position to reflect on the future of the republic and decide on his future. After the invective against L. Calpurnius Piso Caesoninus,[18] he intended to slow down his activity as a lawyer.[19]

---

17 *Tusc.* 2.9.
18 L. Calpurnius Piso Caesoninus was Caesar's father-in-law; consul in 58, he had been responsible for the exile of Cicero.
19 So he confides in a letter to his friend M. Marius: "Sometimes I am forced to take on the defence of people who have done me harm, at the request of those who have done me good. I am therefore looking for excuses for being able to live, finally, in my own way, and I fully approve of you and the norm that your secluded life dictated to you (*teque et istam rationem otii tui*)", *Fam.* 7.1.4–5 (dated October 55).

This was a moment when he could have decided to withdraw from political life and begin to practice the *otium* which he had already alluded to in the oration *Pro Sestio* the year before. He planned to devote himself to writing something that could show the Romans what the best tools were in political art. In *On the Orator* Cicero did this by inserting his personal convictions in a broader historical perspective, in which the tragic era of Sulla and the proscriptions[20] was recalled and compared with the contemporary one.

Cicero appears convinced of the importance of eloquence. He knows that its strength is ambivalent; it is necessary to learn to make good use of it, for the purpose of moral improvement of citizens. Obviously, in this enterprise he considers the support of culture and philosophy indispensable. In the first of three books Cicero distinguishes between the fluent man (*disertus*) and the eloquent man (*eloquens*). Only the latter really knows how to highlight what he is talking about, because he understands jurisdiction as deeply as historical tradition, and also because he is capable of referring to philosophy and morality. The final part of the first book is dedicated to the Academic method based on the strategy summarized in the formula *in utramque partem disserere*.[21] Hence the importance of arranging the facts according to advantages and disadvantages, so as to show, on the basis of the law, the moral validity of the conclusions reached by the speaker. In the second book Cicero deals mainly with oratorical technique: he studies the method used for the discovery of arguments (*inventio*), the system used for the organization of arguments (*dispositio*), the discipline of recalling the arguments of a discourse (*memoria*). In the third book he focuses on word and speech. It is worth remembering at what level of power and importance Cicero places eloquence and what awareness he has of his role as speaker:

> The real power of eloquence is such, that it embraces the origin, the influence, the changes of all things in the world, all virtues, duties, and all nature, so far as it affects the manners, minds, and lives of mankind. It can give an account of customs, laws, and rights, can govern a state, and speak on everything relating to any subject whatsoever with elegance and force.

---

20 The encounter between M. Antonius and L. Licinius Crassus is set in 91, when Cicero actually attended lectures by the two orators.

21 "To argue both for and against". We find this or similar formulas in *De Or.* 1.263; 3.80; 3.107; *Or.* 46; *Acad.* 1.46; *Luc.* 7; 104; 108; 124: 133; *ND* 2.168; *Fat.* 1; *Off.* 3.89; *Fam.* 11.27.8; *Att.* 9.4.3; *Tusc.* 1.8; *Fin.* 3.3; 5.10. On this fundamental approach to philosophy, which Cicero believes to be of Socratic origin, cf. Gorman 2005, 35–84; Maso 2015, 27–33.

In this pursuit I employ my talents as well, as I can, as far as I am enabled by natural capacity, moderate learning, and constant practice; nor do I conceive myself much inferior in disputation to those who have as it were pitched their tent for life in philosophy alone".[22]

The result is remarkable not only from a technical point of view, but also a philosophical one, which is what most interests us here, because Cicero shows that the control of language and the oratory art contribute *to building an opinion that likely to be assumed as truth*. In fact, eloquence implies the ability to persuade, to develop fascinating, more or less reliable scenarios and to influence the audience (or the reader). This leads on, according to what can be deduced from *On the Orator*, to recognize the legitimacy of an oratorical argument (and therefore of any literary expression) precisely in its referring to and relying on spaces of 'truth', of which the citizen is convinced and in which immerses himself.[23] Obviously, this implies the responsibility of the orator in proposing the values he has built his scenarios around and which human civil society must refer to. Precisely as a consequence of the moral implications of oratory art, Cicero wonders what the requirements for the ideal orator are.

According to Cicero, first of all the orator must have acquired familiarity with the most important subjects and disciplines:

> Oratory must blossom and flow abundantly from knowledge; if it is not supported by a content well known and mastered by the orator, the oratory boils down to an exhibition, so to speak, empty and almost childish.[24]

The second quality of the orator consists in a "profound knowledge of all the mental emotions, with which nature has endowed mankind", *De Or.* 1.17. Only by following this path is the orator able to excite or appease the human soul on the occasions that he considers appropriate. Everything must be seasoned with grace, wit and elegance of speech, readiness to reply or attack.

Cicero summarizes what is required in this way:

> In an orator we must demand the subtlety of the logician, the thought of the philosopher, a diction almost poetic, a lawyer's memory, a tragedian's voice, and the bearing almost of the consummate actor.[25]

---

22 *De Or.* 3.76–77.
23 Grimal 1986, 218–219.
24 *De Or.* 1.20.
25 *De Or.* 1.128.

The ideal orator should therefore, by virtue of these qualities and abilities, dominate the contents and organize them in view of a result that the audience must assume as valid and true. However, the issue here becomes delicate in several respects.

1) First of all, Cicero confesses that there is a *psychologically* important aspect to keep in mind: while dominating the contents and being aware of his own expressive abilities, the ideal orator should not be so sure of himself as to appear arrogant. Usually – at the moment of speaking – he should fall prey to emotion and appear troubled. Cicero, through the mouth of the rhetorician M. Antonius, notes that: "The more capable the speaker, the more worried he is" (*De Or.* 1.123). That is: this orator is aware of his task and condition. Well, there are two reasons for concern. He knows that:

a)   sometimes the outcome of an argument does not conform to what is desired;
b)   the audience is convinced that, when an orator happens to make a mistake, his intelligence and fame are compromised. Therefore, unlike all other professionals, the speaker is not allowed to fail.

Having taken note of this, it is important to reverse the situation: the orator must be able to exploit the emotional charge and dominate it so that he can take over the listener's soul. On this ability, and on the theatricality and transgressive aesthetics developed in the *On the Orator* see Dugan (2005), 75–171.

2) But there is a second, more directly *philosophical* aspect, that needs to be highlighted: what is the relationship between the effective outcome of an artificial construction (oration or literary text) and justice and ethics? This question is not solved only by referring to adequate knowledge of the contents and jurisprudence: a certain ideal model of orator is the consequence of a certain social context – that is, of a certain political and moral experience – and depends on a certain philosophical elaboration of law. In this regard, after Görler's (1988), 215–235, work, those of Fantham (2004) and Blom (2010) are fundamental; they aim to confirm not only the adoption of Greek culture in Rome, but also to show the role of *exempla* in the construction of the models necessary for the formation of the orator and, in general, of the citizen.

The references to the Platonic environment are explicit: compared to the manuals that were beginning to spread in the schools of rhetoric, in *On the Orator* we find an absolutely original structure in proposing the scheme of the Platonic dialogue and in evoking its plot.[26] Moreover, Plato is mentioned several times in reference precisely to moral and political problems. But it is not enough: it immediately appears inevitable for any reader to link the ideal of orator to the ideal of politician outlined in *On the Republic*,[27] i.e. in the ambitious attempt to re-propose Plato's political masterpiece, adapting it to the Roman environment.

In the background there lies a totalizing thought, according to which the very meaning of man's natural social propensity is translated into theoretical political commitment and consequent political action. Since Cicero, as an authentic intellectual, feels as a personal task the transmission of the ethical values of the *maiores* and the *res publica* to the society of his time, then the acquisition of the perfect oratory art becomes for him not only the main tool to be used, but also the very foundation of his profile as a 'politician'. Furthermore, since the perfect orator is the man who practices the *eloquentia philosophica*, and since the latter includes the imitation of behaviours and values adopted as a moral model, then the perfect orator makes himself a model worthy of imitation. On the merits of this Ciceronian project, see above all Narducci (2009), 294–320.

In this way the typical dispute of the Hellenistic world between rhetoricians and philosophers – and, above all, between schools of rhetoric and philosophical schools, as Kennedy (1963), 321–330, points out – appears to be completely overcome. Philosophy is not only elevated to constitute the basis of citizen education (a citizen that is open to a complex and structured worldview), but it finds in rhetoric something more than a purely technical discipline: in it philosophy finds the main way to give meaning and value to the vision of the world that is itself proposing.

In order to be so trained, the orator must acquire not only the sense of duty and commitment, which entails reference to the *officium*, *dignitas* and *virtus*, but also the awareness of the importance of *otium*. Cicero achieves this awareness little by little. First of all, the word '*otium*' is strongly marked by the Epicurean interpretation. Of course, *otium* has to do with an apparently neutral condition: it is a real specific psychophysical *status*; but the moral implications related to the characteristics of this *status* are almost immediately derivable. The *otium* / *negotium* opposition, several times studied, is exemplary. Especially André

---

26 See the start of the conversation, *De Or.* 1.28: "When those older men had rested sufficiently and everyone had come into the garden-walk, Scaevola, after taking two or three turns, observed, 'Crassus, why do we not imitate Socrates as he appears in the *Phaedrus* of Plato?'". See *infra*, p. 63.

27 Cicero composed *On the Republic* in 54, the year following the *On the Orator*'s date of composition.

(1966), 279–334, tried to reconstruct the history of the contemplative impulses expressed on several occasions by Cicero. It is remarkable how these impulses clash with the drama of a withdrawal from public life, which Cicero would never have wanted to seriously think about.

Furthermore, the problem is particularly interesting in relation to Cicero, because we know of his clear departure from Epicureanism. Cicero's strategy is to make *otium* interact with *virtus*. In this sense, *otium* must pass from its denoting a pure and simple *status* (which, moreover, has a negative connotation, because it tends rather to renouncement than to civil commitment), to being the object of a morally acceptable and not negative evaluation. We have the impression of an authentic evolution that develops from 62 to 43 – that is, from the time of the oration in defence of P. Cornelius Sulla, to his death. At first the *otium* becomes *honestum*, then it combines with *dignitas* and, therefore, assumes a political value. From 56, i.e. from *pro Sestio* onwards, *otium domesticum* is recovered in a morally credible perspective. By *domesticum* we have to understand not only the territorial space within the borders of the state, but also, and perhaps in the first place, the space for private action and personal life; we deduce this from the hint of *Att.* 1.17.6 (of 61): "neither business (*non negotium*) nor personal commitments (*non otium*), not the problems of the forum (*non forenses*), nor those of the house (*non domesticae*), not public or private things can remain without your advice". This aspect becomes more explicit in *Att.* 9.10.33 (of 49): "My age, now bent over from hard work towards *otium*, has softened me in the pleasure of home life (*domesticarum rerum delectationi*)".[28] When this *otium* is gradually redeemed in the dimension of Stoic *dignitas*, it becomes *honestum*, as is precisely assured in *pro Sestio*:

> But all my speech is addressed to virtue, and not to slothfulness (*cum virtute non cum desidia*); to dignity, and not to luxury (*cum dignitate non cum voluptate*); to those men who look upon themselves as born for their country, for their fellow-citizens, for praise, for glory, not for sleep, for banquets, and soft delights.[29]

The civil and moral intention will become increasingly clear. In a letter dated 46 to his friend M. Marcellus, Cicero writes:

---

28 See, later, Horat., *Sat.* 1.6.128: *domesticus otior.*
29 *Sest.* 138.

You are lucky (*fortuna*), because in a dignified retreat (*honesto otio*) you have managed to maintain your *status* and fame of your worth (*statum et famam dignitatis tuae*).[30]

Well: this *otium* is necessary not only for the politician and the philosopher, but it is also necessary for the orator, whenever he has to prepare his harangue.

Some recent studies have grasped the fundamental importance of combining philosophy with eloquence and oratory art. Especially:

- A. Michel, *Rhétorique et philosophie chez Cicéron. Essai sur les fondements de l'art de persuader* (1960);
- G. Kennedy, *The Art of Rhetoric in the Roman World: 300 B.C. – A.D. 300* (1972);
- J. Wisse, *Ethos and Pathos from Aristotle to Cicero* (1988);
- J. Dugan, *Making a New Man. Ciceronian Self-fashioning in the Rhetorical Works* (2005);
- W. Nicgorski, *Cicero's Skepticism and His Recovery of Political Philosophy* (2016).

Michel's work aims to reconstruct the logical evolution of Ciceronian thought with reference to his rhetorical competence and underlining the influence of Molon of Rhodes and Asianism. Furthermore, Michel considers the influence of Platonism to be central. Kennedy rather aims to reconstruct the way in which the Romans – and Cicero among them – adopted and developed the theories of the Greek speech. Rhetoric is essentially understood as the art of persuasion. Wisse focuses on the problem of emotions by comparing the way Aristotle and Cicero use them, alongside rational arguments, as a rhetorical tool. Aristotle's *Rhetoric* and Cicero's *On the Orator* are the two main works explored. Dugan, once he has studied the characteristics of the epidictic discourse in Cicero, tackles in an original way not only the fashioning of the Ideal Orator, but above all the self-fashioning process of Cicero, starting from the modelling of the *novus homo*'s ideal. As for Nicgorski, in the second chapter of his book (*The critical and rhetorical ways of philosophy*) he studies the rhetorical tools through which Cicero mediates his philosophical message. The sceptical / probabilistic strategy applied to the oratory technique is placed in the foreground.

---

30 *Fam.* 4.9.3.

2 Cicero's Philosophical Employment

2.1 Intellectual journey and historical context

48 BCE is the year of Cicero's return to Rome, after the victory of Caesar over Pompey and his followers at Pharsalus. This date constitutes a fundamental chronological point of reference, since Cicero, who had sided with Pompey, was no longer at the centre of political power. Certainly in 47 he obtained a pardon from Caesar, but his hope of collaborating with the new government vanished when Caesar, named dictator in that same year, showed the intention to modify the state structure in an anti-optimate and authoritarian direction. The further defeat of the Pompeians at Thapsus (in Africa in 46, with the suicide of Cato Uticensis), and then in Munda (in Spain in 45), definitively sanctioned the decline of Cicero's political dream: a dream built around the centrality of the Senate and the moral values of the *maiores*. Even Cicero's family life became complicated and worrying: at the end of the summer of 46 he divorced his wife Terentia and in February 45 his daughter Tullia, shortly after giving birth to her first child, died in the villa of Tusculum. Loneliness and discouragement bent him; from his villa in Astura, on the Latium coast, where he had retired, he wrote to his friend Atticus telling him all his sadness:

> In this lonely place I do not talk to a soul. Early in the day I hide myself in a thick, thorny wood, and don't emerge till evening. Apart from you solitude is my best friend. When I am alone, all my conversation is with books (*omnis sermo est cum litteris*), but it is interrupted by fits of weeping, against which I struggle as best I can. But so far it has been an unequal fight.[1]

These are very tough years for Cicero; it was very difficult to find comfort and consolation.[2] Nevertheless this situation opened new horizons for him: in particular, this was the occasion to imagine the *otium* as a new opportunity to resume the studies he had faced in his youth and neglected by the 75, the year of the *quaestura* and the start of his political career. In fact, Cicero began to realize his project of delivering to the Romans a framework, in Latin, of the cornerstones and problems of philosophy. As he himself wrote in the prologue of the second book of *On Divination*, the main steps of this great operation, starting with *Hortensius*

---

[1] *Att.* 12.15 (dated March 45).

[2] In March 45 he composed a *consolatio* for the death of Tullia. See *Att.* 12.14.3: "I have done something which I imagine no one has ever done before, consoled myself in a literary composition", *feci quod profecto ante me nemo, ut ipse me per litteras consolarer.*

https://doi.org/10.1515/9783110661835-002

and ending with *On Old Age*, were *Academica*, *On the Ends of Good and Evil*, *Tusculan Disputations*, *On the Nature of the Gods*, and also *On Divination*.[3]

Obviously, we must not consider the time frame that goes from 75 to 48 as a real interruption. This is certainly a period of almost thirty years that saw the prevalence of interest in active politics and public commitment; but during it, the support of philosophical insight did not fail. As we know,[4] at the beginning of *On the Nature of the Gods*, 1.6, written in 45, Cicero testifies to his constant admiration for philosophy and his esteem for the masters he had. We must believe in his words, because this is the only way to explain the great research activities and the frenetic production of philosophical works that mark the last period of his life: an activity that does not consist in the simple 'translation' into Latin of Academic or Stoic school works, but which reveals a great and original effort to re-work materials whose research and understanding he had always devoted a great deal of care to. Referring to the evidence that come to us from Cicero's correspondence, we can reconstruct a fairly secure chronological framework of this activity that goes from 48 to 43:

— 46: *Stoic Paradoxes*, dedicated to Marcus Brutus;[5]

— 45 (February): *Consolatio* on the occasion of the death of his daughter Tullia;

— 45 (March / April): *Hortensius*, dedicated to the orator Hortensius Hortalus or to Marcus Brutus. Of this work, known and read during the Middle Ages, only few fragments remain;

— 45 (May / June): writing in two (or three) phases of *Academica*. The first (*Academica priora*) probably included two books: *Catulus* (now lost), and *Lucullus*. Perhaps Cicero had planned to integrate *Hortensius* (now lost) into a trilogy. The final edition (*Academica posteriora*) was to include four books: *Varro* (which reached us until the 12th chapter = 46 paragraphs) and three other dialogues, now lost, where Cicero and Varro respectively attacked and defended dogmatism. Traces of a further editorial passage can be seen between the two editions. Decisive in this regard is a reference, present in the correspondence, *Att.* 13.16.1, which announces the replacement of the pro-

---

3 Regarding the philosophical catalogue in *On the Divination*, see Schofield 2013, 73–87.

4 See *supra*, pp. 2–3.

5 M. Iunius Brutus (85 BCE – 23 October 42 BCE), nephew of Cato Uticensis, sided with the *optimates* against Caesar. He participated in the Caesaricide of 44 and committed suicide after the defeat at the Battle of Philippi against Marcus Antonius and Octavian, in 42. An eloquent orator, he composed some works of moral philosophy: *On virtue*, *On Duties*, *On patience* (of Academic and Stoic tendency), now lost. Sedley 1997, 41–53, offers us an effective profile of Brutus' personality and philosophical belief.

tagonists of the first draft (Q. Lutatius Catulus, consul in 78, L. Licinius Lucullus, the famous general in the Mithridatic war, Q. Hortensius Hortalus, the eminent orator, consul in 69: certainly three *optimates*, but not philosophers) with M. Porcius Cato and M. Iunius Brutus (two authentic philosophers); only in the final edition would M. Terentius Varro enter the scene.[6] To respect the hypothetical succession of books, modern editions present, in order, *Varro* (= *Academicorum posteriorum liber primus*) and *Lucullus* (= *Academicorum priorum liber alter*);

—   45 (end of June): *On the Ends of Good and Evil*, in five books, dedicated to M. Brutus. The drafting of this work interferes with the latest edition of *Academica*;

—   45 (June / August): *Tusculan Disputations*, in five books, dedicated to M. Brutus. The work was designed at the end of May. The conclusion may have been protracted until the spring of 44, in parallel with the translation of Plato's *Timaeus*;

—   45 (July / August): *On the Nature of the Gods*, in three books, dedicated to M. Brutus. Definitely concluded at the end of summer, but not immediately published;

—   44 (before the Ides of March): *On Old Age*, in one book, dedicated to Atticus;

—   44 (around the Ides of March): *On Divination*, in two books, dedicated to Quintus Cicero. The first book was written before the Ides, the second after them;

—   44 (March / June): *On Fate*, in one book, probably dedicated to Hirtius. The ·book has reached us incomplete;

—   44 (early summer): conclusion of *On Glory*, which has not reached us;

—   44 (summer): *Laelius On Friendship*, in one book, dedicated to Atticus;

—   44 (July): *Topica*, in one book. Addressed to C. Trebatius Testa;

—   44 (October / December): *On Duties*, in three books, dedicated to his son Marcus. The first two books were completed in October. The third was finished in December.

In connection with these works, it is necessary to mention some other works related to or anticipating some philosophical questions that Cicero addresses in his subsequent philosophical research:

---

6 See Lévy 1992, 129–140; Griffin 1997a, 20–27.

1. *Aratea*.[7] Experiment of partial translation of the *Phaenomena* of Aratus, performed between 89 and 77. It is partially reported in *On the Nature of the Gods*;

2. *On Invention*.[8] Written between 87 and 81, under the influence of Molon of Rhodes' lectures. In this work rhetoric and philosophy are closely connected;

3. *On the Orator*, in three books, dedicated to Quintus Cicero.[9] This work was concluded in November 55. It deals fundamentally with three problems: what the education of an orator should be, the relationship between style and content, and between style and philosophy;

4. *On the Republic*, in six books, dedicated to Quintus Cicero. Written between 54 and 51, this is a Socratic dialogue on political theory: central is the issue of the 'best constitution', then the analysis of the evolution of the Roman state, the relationship between justice and injustice, the study of ancient institutions and of the ancient *mores*, the task of the *rector*, his training and function and his role during the revolution. The work has reached us incomplete[10] and ends with the so-called *Somnium Scipionis*, in which the reference to spiritual values, nobility of soul and homeland is crucial;

5. *On the Laws*, in three books, dedicated to Atticus. This work was begun and then interrupted in 51; resumed in 46, it was not concluded.[11] It deals with the relationship between law and justice, the meaning of the law in the context of religion and the role and duties of judges;

6. *Brutus*,[12] in one book, dedicated to M. Brutus and Hortensius Hortalus. It was written at the beginning of 46, on the occasion of the death of the rival, the lawyer Hortensius. It precedes Cato's suicide. In practice, this work is a history of the art of oratory;

---

7 See the editions by Ewbank 1933 and Soubiran 1972.

8 See the edition by Hubbell 1976.

9 See the edition by Wilkins 1990, and the translation by Wisse-May 2001.

10 The surviving sections derive from excerpts preserved in later works (see the grammarian Nonius, and the apologists Lactantius, Ambrogius, and especially Augustine in *De civitate Dei* 2.9; 2.12–13; 2.21; 3.15; 19.21) and from the incomplete palimpsest *Vat. Lat.* 5757 uncovered in 1820 by Cardinal Angelus Mai. After the fundamental critical editions by K. Ziegler 1915, 1929, 1956, 1958, 1960, see now the edition by J.G.F. Powell 2006, conspicuous for the careful rereading of the palimpsest. For the commentary on the *Somnium Scipionis*, see Boyancé 1936a and Büchner 1976. A collection of recent studies on *Republic* is edited by North–Powell 2001.

11 See the edition by Powell 2006.

12 See the edition by Hendrickson–Hubbell 1971 (with an English translation by G.L. Hendrickson).

7. *Orator*,[13] in one book, dedicated to M. Brutus. This work was written in the summer of 46. It has a didactic and at the same time historical character, but finally it is a sort of overall evaluation that Cicero himself makes of his own approach to eloquence and rhetorical technique. Together with the *On the Orator* and the *Brutus* it constitutes a veritable trilogy dedicated to the art of oratory.

From this simple list we must recognize how the intellectual journey of Cicero is consistent: the technical and theoretical insights related to the world of eloquence and the art of oratory (and, similarly, the elaborations that pertain to political philosophy and law) should be placed on an overall unitary background. Ideally and almost continuously Cicero refers to this background. Little by little he is building it, and it is also the point of connection of his moral tensions and ethical aspirations. While in his youth he was able to study the distinct solutions that the different philosophical schools proposed, in the retreat phase (or rather after 48) Cicero undertook the realization of a methodical project of restructuring Hellenistic philosophy, which should allow him to give definitive solidity and credibility to this background.

2.2 The philosophical works

The *Dictionnaire des Philosophes Antiques* provides, at the lemma *Cicéron* (*père*) edited by C. Lévy, F. Guillaumont, F. Prost, G. Moretti (vol. Suppléments 2003), an introduction to Cicero's philosophical works accompanied by a reliable bibliographic support. In this section we will limit ourselves to briefly reconstructing Cicero's theoretical-philosophical path, emphasizing his constant confrontation with Stoicism, Epicureanism and Academy.

Stoic Paradoxes

In this work Cicero deals with six *loci* – that is, 6 assertions (or arguments) held to be commonplaces – proposed by the Stoics and all presenting a paradoxical character:
1. ὅτι μόνον τὸ καλὸν ἀγαθόν ("The moral one is the only good"): *Quod honestum sit id solum bonum esse*;

---

13 See the edition by Hendrickson-Hubbell 1971 (with an English translation by H.M. Hubbell).

2. ὅτι αὐτάρκης ἡ ἀρετὴ πρὸς εὐδαιμονίαν ("Virtue is sufficient for happiness"): *In quo virtus sit ei nihil deesse ad beate vivendum*;

3. ὅτι ἴσα τὰ ἁμαρτήματα καὶ τὰ κατορθώματα ("Evil and good actions are the same"): *Quodsi virtutes sunt pares inter se, paria esse etiam vitia necesse est*;[14]

4. ὅτι πᾶς ἄφρων μαίνεται ("All those who are stupid are crazy"): *Omnes stultos insanire*;

5. ὅτι μόνος ὁ σοφὸς ἐλεύθερος καὶ πᾶς ἄφρων δοῦλος ("Only the wise is free; all fools are slaves"): *Omnes sapientes liberos esse et stultos omnes servos*;

6. ὅτι μόνος ὁ σοφὸς πλούσιος ("Only the wise man is rich"): *Quod solus sapiens dives*.

The source of these paradoxes is certainly Greek, but the great abundance of Roman *exempla* testifies that Cicero exploited materials of Roman origin. At least in part this is material from the satire of Lucilius. As for the type of argument developed, we can observe that Cicero always proceeds from a semantic analysis of what is stated in the paradox. Starting from the true meaning of 'good' or 'virtue' or 'error' or 'freedom' or 'wisdom', he demolishes what turns out to be an 'apparent' paradox. It is always a matter of passing from the apparently surprising meaning (*contra opinionem omnium*, 4) to what, through a dialectical or oratory explanation, becomes the comprehensible and convincing meaning. These *loci* (clichés or commonplaces) thus become something 'Socratic', very close to the truth (*longeque verissima*, 4).

The fourth paradox ("All those who are stupid are crazy") stands out from the others because Cicero's personal story and his challenge to Clodius, the *tribunus plebis*, are evoked: the one who, in 58 BCE, had accused him of having unjustly condemned Catiline. Clodius, as a result of his irresponsible action (as an illegal action), can only be judged crazy: for reason cannot be present in a social context where law does not reign.

Hortensius

This admired and important dialogue of Cicero only survived into the sixth century. We owe the quotations we received of the most important passages of the *Hortensius* to the prose writer Martianus Capella, to the grammarians M. Servius

---

14 Cicero does not translate this third argument into Latin and does not report it as a subtitle; for it, see *Parad.* 3.21, quoted here.

Honoratus and Nonius Marcellus, and to the Church Fathers Lactantius and Augustine of Hippo. After Plasberg's pioneering 1892 attempt to reconstruct the dialogue structure, in 1962 A. Grilli proposed what has become its standard edition. A different reorganization of the fragments is due, in 1976, to L. Straume-Zimmermann: she is content to group the fragments according to the sequence: prooemium and, in succession, discourses of Lucullus, Catulus, Hortensius and Cicero.

Cicero himself presented his work as a justification and, at the same time, as an illustration of the advantages of philosophy, which therefore deserves to be embraced.[15] In *Confess.* 3.4.7 Augustine writes:

> During my studies I had come across the work of a certain Cicero (*in librum cuiusdam Ciceronis*) of which virtually everyone admires the language, not the heart itself. But that book of his contains an exhortation to philosophy (*exhortationem continet ad philosophiam*) and is entitled *Hortensius*. That book changed my feeling and made me turn my prayer to you, Lord God, and transformed my desires and my expectations.

To the negation of the importance of philosophy (which seems to be attributed to Q. Hortensius Hortalus), Cicero replies with a sort of real introduction to philosophy; as in the case of Aristotle's *Protrepticus*, also in this work of Cicero we find at the centre the value and meaning of 'philosophy' and its place in human life. However, we do not know if the *Hortensius* was based strictly on the Aristotelian *Protrepticus* or was rather written in hortatory and general protreptic style. Certainly, Cicero underlines the vanity of external goods and, on the contrary, the significance of the contemplative life. D. Turkowska (1965) studies the relationship between Aristotle's protreptic work and Cicero's (we only possess fragments of both); M. Testard (1958) addresses the question of Augustine's reception.

Academica

Although written in just over two months, the dialogues that constitute the *Academica* appear to be the result of in-depth preparatory research and represent for us today the most important tool available to learn about events in the Academy during the I century BCE.

As mentioned previously, only two books survived: *Lucullus* (from the first edition) and *Varro* (from the final edition). In presenting them, however, all modern editors follow the logical and thematic order. Consequently, in the first book of the second edition, the *Varro*, the position of the Ancient Academy on ethics,

---

15 See *Luc.* 6; *Fin.* 1.2; *Tusc.* 2.4 and 3.6; *Div.* 2.1; *Off.* 2.5–8.

physics and dialectics is examined; the dogmatic approach which dominates it, and which is now preached by Antiochus of Ascalon, is exposed and criticized in a dialectical challenge between Varro and Cicero. However, only a brief fragment of Cicero's speech comes to us referring to Arcesilaus and the 'suspension' of assent (45). There are very few fragments of the second, third and fourth books in which the *Academica posteriora* are organized: while in the second book Cicero probably refers to the position of Carneades and to the so-called New Academy, in the third we must imagine that Varro replied to Cicero in favour of dogmatism. Finally, in the fourth book, one finds the conclusive rejoinder of Cicero.[16] In any case, we have the impression that Plato's school was considered by all to be in direct connection with Socrates' philosophical proposal and constituted the place of perfection to which everyone referred, including Aristotle and the Stoics. The thesis – later supported by the Neo-Platonists – according to which the doctrines of the Academy and of the Peripatetic school were substantially identical, is attributable to Antiochus.

In the second book, *Lucullus*, the approach of the Sceptic is fundamental. Also, in this case it is possible to distinguish (11–62) a discourse by Lucullus (who defends the doctrine of Antiochus of Ascalon and cites his contrast with the more recent 'heretical' theses of his teacher, Philo of Larissa) and (64–147) a discourse by Cicero, careful to criticize the dogmatism and to show how Antiochus first supported, but then attacked the claims of Philo of Larissa. Consequently, on the one hand the very καταληπτικὴ φαντασία of Stoic origin is questioned; on the other hand, the positions of Sceptics such as Philo and the New Academy are analysed with the aim of verifying their validity. Cicero then, under the banner of 'relativism', performs an examination of the different philosophical doctrines, from the physical-naturalists to Plato, the Stoics and Epicurus (118–128); he also reflects on the relativism connected to the concepts of true and false (95–98, 111–113) and good and evil (128–132). Cicero goes out like this: he shows the fallacy and the unreliability of absolute Scepticism, as well as that of a possible dogmatism. Thus, he comes to support the criterion of verisimilitude in the field of perception, and the criterion of probable in the field of judgment (99–105).

---

16 Perhaps the fragment from Augustine, *Acad.* 2.26, belongs to this fourth book; here it is reiterated that, beyond the names that apply, all must have clear the value and meaning of all those things that are called *probabilia vel veri similia*. On the basis of other criteria, however, this fragment is included among those belonging to the second book of the *Academica posteriora*.

But, lastly, if the 'probability' is considered a sufficient criterion on which to anchor in order to welcome representations and then act, we must not however absolutely fall into the dogmatism to which it could refer.[17]

In both books, Cicero demonstrates a great and precise knowledge of the distinct positions developed within the Academy; it is as a consequence of the freedom of thought (and of the suspension in the judgment) of which he is made defender that Cicero effectively unravels the skein of the history of the Academy up to his days and allows us to penetrate inside a story otherwise unknown. In this respect, we must remember how important the so-called *Quellenforschung* (the search for sources) was. First of all, Glucker's (1978) research tried to reconstruct, thanks to Cicero, the role of Philo of Larissa and Antiochus of Ascalon within the Academy. This is followed by the study of Ioppolo (1986), which focused on the characteristics and importance of the teaching of Arcesilaus and Carneades (exponents of the II and III Academy), with respect to the Stoic school.[18] Barnes (1989)'s study constitutes the first specific monograph dedicated to Antiochus; the work of Brittain (2001) is, instead, the first monograph dedicated to Philo. Finally, Lévy's (1992) work aims to strongly emphasize Cicero's originality in reconstructing the events of the Academy.

In the final *peroratio* of *Academica* (*Luc.* 147), Cicero announces that, after the study of the method and after focusing on the meaning of truth, the time has come to move on to face "the darkness of nature (*de obscuritate naturae*)", comparing the very different positions of the philosophers, and those that are "the goods and their opposites (*de bonis contrariisque rebus*)". This could be done in Tusculum, suggests Lucullus. In this we can see a probable allusion to *On the Nature of the Gods*, to *On the Ends of Good and Evil* and to *Tusculan Disputations* that Cicero will complete in the two months following the conclusion of the *Academica*.

On the Ends of Good and Evil

It is not easy to translate the Latin title of this work, *De finibus*, one of the most important works of Roman philosophy. Literally it could be: "The extreme limits of good and evil", or "On the chief good and evil", or "On the ends of good and evil". In the first way we emphasize the border (*finis*) that must be placed between what is good and what is bad. In the second, one can sense the contrast between

---

17 Cf. *Luc.* 105; see *infra*, p. 141.
18 A different interpretation of the relationship between Academy and the Stoic school is now proposed by Bonazzi 2017.

extreme good and extreme evil. In the third, it is pointed out that with 'finis' Cicero means the *telos*: in their philosophical language the Greeks, with *telos*, define what human nature tends to, that for which man acts and to which it is convenient to report everything. Thus, Cicero states in § 11 of the first book:

> For nothing in life is more worth investigating than philosophy in general, and the question raised in this work in particular: what is the end, what is the ultimate and final goal (*qui sit finis, quid extremum, quid ultimum*), to which all our deliberations on living well and acting rightly should be directed (*quo sint omnia bene vivendi recteque faciendi consilia referenda*)? What does nature pursue as the highest good to be sought, what does she shun as the greatest evil (*quid sequatur natura ut summum ex rebus expetendis, quid fugiat ut extremum malorum*)?[19]

As Cicero recalls, there is no agreement between the scholars and the various schools of philosophy on what should be considered the *telos* of human life. For this reason, he considers it of great importance to provide a general picture of the theses of the most authoritative philosophical schools in this regard.

Following in part the practice of *in utramque partem perpetua oratio* (that is, of the presentation of different opinions in a distinct and consequential way), Cicero compares and discusses three theses in three dialogues: the Epicurean dialog (books I and II), the Stoic dialog (books III and IV) and the Academic/Peripatetic dialog (book V). However, the *oratio perpetua* does not seem to fit perfectly with the strategy that Cicero considers most appropriate: at the beginning of the second book, after the Epicurean Torquatus expressed his opinion, Cicero says that he liked the *oratio perpetua* very much, but that he now considers more appropriate dwelling on the single points: in doing so, he can understand correctly what each one admits or rejects, and therefore to draw the desired conclusions and reach the proposed result.[20] In the background stands the classification devised by Carneades, in which nine sustainable theses were presented. According to Carneades, as Cicero sums up in *Fin.* 5.16–21,[21] the highest good could consist in:

---

19 *Fin.* 1.11.
20 Cf. *Fin.* 2.3: "I believe, however, much as I enjoyed hearing him (i.e. Torquatus) speak uninterrupted (*oratione perpetua*), that it is none the less more manageable if one stops after each individual point and ascertains what each of the listeners is happy to concede (*quid quisque concedat*), and what they would reject (*quid abnuat*). One can then draw the inferences one wishes from the points conceded and reach one's conclusion."
21 L&S 64E and G; see Algra 1997, 120–130. This so-called *Carneadea divisio* is more complex than the original *Chrysippea divisio*, which – according to Cic., *Luc.* 138 [= SVF 3.21] – included

A) *fruendi rebus*, i.e. the actual obtainment of:
1) pleasure (Aristippus and Epicurus)
2) freedom from suffering (Hieronymus)
3) the primary natural objects (Carneades *for discussion purposes*)
B) *rebus expetendis*, i.e. the pursuit of:
4) pleasure (not actually defended)
5) freedom from suffering (not actually defended)
6) the primary natural objects (the Stoics)
C) *iunctae et duplices expositiones*, i.e the union of *honestum* (that is, of virtue) to the use of:
7) pleasure (Calliphon and Dinomachus)
8) freedom from suffering (Diodorus)
9) the primary natural objects (Ancient Platonist and Peripatetics).

In practice, after a prologue in which he expresses his enthusiasm for philosophy and for the task that he himself assumed to divulge among the Romans using the Latin language (1.1–12), Cicero deals with the Epicurean doctrine. After defining it as one of the best known doctrines (*plerisque notissima est*), he gives an exposition that he considers very accurate (*non soleat accuratius explicari*, 13). He then undertakes a critical presentation of various physical, logical and ethical doctrines (14–26). After a brief intervention by G. Valerius Triarius (orator and follower of Pompey the Great), it is up to L. Manlius Torquatus to defend Epicurus. Torquatus faces the problem of ethics and pleasure. Pleasure is to be understood as the elimination of pain. Virtue is a means to pleasure. Mental pleasure and pain are connected to the body, but they have a stronger value because they also concern the past, the future and the present. The wise Epicurean man is always happy and friendship is certainly based on utility, but it sees in love for others the re-proposition of natural love for themselves. Not the dialectic, but the knowledge of nature contributes to forming the state of happiness that characterizes the existence of the wise man. Because of this, Epicurus must be recognized with the utmost gratitude (27–72).

In the second book Cicero intervenes to refute Torquatus. Cicero proceeds from a reflection of a dialectical nature: one thing is pleasure and another thing

---

at least three possible 'simple' Ends (virtue/*honestas*, pleasure/*voluptas*, freedom from suffering/*vacuitas molestiae*), and three possible 'complex' Ends (*virtue + pleasure, virtue + freedom from suffering, virtue + the primary natural objects*). Even this *diairesis* was then reduced to three options: (1) pleasure, (2) virtue, (3) a combination of pleasure and virtue.

is the absence of pain. More precisely, Epicurus' error lies in the lack of distinction between kinetic pleasure (which admits gradations) and the absence of pain (which does not admit them). Epicurus would have confused the absence of pain with pleasure, while it is only an intermediate state between pain and pleasure (2.4–30). Once this has been established, one should not worry that two ends (absence of pain and pleasure) are placed, since even Aristotle (virtuous action and happiness) and other Greek philosophers placed two ends. For Cicero it is important to also include virtue (*honestum*) among what is to be desired. Furthermore, morality is not the fruit of simple convention. From this comes a civil and social commitment; and of this are given numerous attestations (31–95). Despite everything, however, according to Cicero, Epicurus was not a bad person; on the contrary, he led his life correctly and was faithful in friendship. He did not understand, however, that man is destined for higher ends than simple physical pleasure (96–118).

The third and fourth books are dedicated to the comparison between M. Porcius Cato[22] and Cicero. In the third book the younger Cato exposes the ethics of the Stoics. The central point consists in acknowledging that only what is in agreement with nature is valid, while what is not is to be rejected. For this reason, duty must first be placed at the centre, as it enables man to preserve his own existence. Hence the ability to choose what is in accord with nature (3.16–40). Cicero underlines the importance of the 'right choice' that everyone should be making. Moreover, it signals the parallel but not identical strategy along which the Peripatetics move: for them all external goods contribute to happiness, while for the Stoics it is necessary to be able to distinguish the value of what is external to us, just as it is necessary to be aware that suffering is not bad in itself. Furthermore, the Peripatetics believe that happiness, coming from external goods, admits a different gradation, while the Stoics deny this and believe that there is no difference in virtue (41–57). According to the Stoics, what is external is indifferent, even if one can distinguish more or less positive things and more or less negative things. Furthermore, it must be remembered that for the Stoics suicide is admissible, that patriotic feeling and cosmopolitanism are important values, that political commitment is a duty, that the education of young people has a fundamental role and that friendship and justice are valid in and of themselves. Consequently, committing evil is alien to the nature of the wise man who, by definition,

---

22 An opponent of Caesar and tyranny, Cato committed suicide in Utica in 46, presenting himself as an example of a wise man who puts freedom before the evils of servitude. A believer convinced of Stoicism, he made virtue and moral rigour his goal. Cicero always admired him.

is aware of all of this. Finally, a close relationship is established between the natural order that pertains to the cosmos and the reason that man must follow (58–76).

According to Cicero, Cato's presentation shows how Stoic philosophy would be the best of all, although it involves a series of paradoxes. In book IV, rather than responding to Cato, Cicero claims that Stoicism is not independent of the Academic/Peripatetic school. Compared to the latter, the Stoics introduced very few innovations in dialectics (Cicero does not find the logic nor the syllogistic technique effective or clear) and in physics (for example: it is not a great innovation to have replaced – as a constitutive element of the soul – fire as the fifth Aristotelian essence). As for ethics, the great novelty would be the identification of faults and vices: which is only theoretically sustainable but not in practice (4.1–23). With regard to the question concerning the 'choices' that man should make 'according to nature' and which, consequently, should be virtuous, Cicero reiterates that desires cannot be neglected. Desires, at least as impulses, must be included in the global conception of 'nature'. For this reason, the intransigence and rigidity of virtue are reproached to the Stoics: they end up eliminating free will and desire, they try to identify virtuous action with natural instinct (24–48). As a result, rigorous logical formulations apparently often lead to absurd situations: in reality it is a matter of pure syllogisms (48–77). We cannot simultaneously claim that it is good only what is honest (*quod honestum sit, solum id bonum esse*) and, on the other hand, that the inclination for things that are beneficial to life is something that has a natural origin: *appetitionem rerum ad vivendum accommodaturum a natura profectam* (78).

In the fifth book Cicero presents a third dialogue in which he examines the Academic philosophy of Antiochus of Ascalon. Cicero imagines he is in Greece, in Plato's Academy; with him are M. Pupius Piso, his friend Pomponius Atticus, his brother Quintus and his cousin Lucius. In a state of strong emotion, the prologue evokes the ancient philosophical schools and their respective Roman followers (5.1–8). First of all, M. Pupius Piso[23] cites the events of the Ancient Academy and the Peripatetic school, remembering the key points of practical wisdom. Then Antiochus is evoked, who shows that he uses the *Carneadean divisio* to discuss the supreme good (15–23). Always following the Academic/Peripatetic teaching, Antiochus underlines how man (and, in reality, every living being) must realize his own nature; hence the reference to self-love and self-knowledge

---

23 As Pompey's supporter, he obtained the consulate in 61. Until then Cicero had also praised him as a Peripatetic philosopher; from that moment on, however, a strong tension emerged between the two. He died before 47.

that must be acquired step by step. From when we are children or puppies, to when we become adults (24–32). It must still be kept in mind that the perfect action, which is such as it depends on both the physical and the spiritual part of human nature, is in itself to be preferred.

> It is evident, since we are beloved by ourselves (*ipsi a nobis diligamur*), and since we wish everything both in our minds and bodies to be perfect, that those qualities are dear to us for their own sakes (*ea nobis ipsa cara esse*), and that they are of the greatest influence towards our living well. For he to whom self-preservation is proposed (*cui proposita sit conservatio sui*) as an object, must necessarily feel an affection for all the separate parts of himself; and a greater affection in proportion as they are more perfect and more praiseworthy in their separate kinds.[24]

The Academic system presented by Antiochus is the most reliable, even with respect to the question of pleasure: whether it should be considered among the things that are consonant with nature, as Peripatetics think, or whether it is right to leave it aside, as Antiochus believes, and the Stoics too (45). From § 48 onwards, attention shifts from the body to the parts of the soul. The issue of action and the pleasure of acting is addressed: "we are born to act", *nos ad agendum esse natos* (58). However, this pleasure must be directed to the *honestum*.

In the concluding part (77–96) the position of the Stoics is compared with that of the Peripatetics. Cicero debates with Piso some critical points; in particular he cannot understand how the wise man can always and with the same intensity be happy.

As for the Greek authors on whom Cicero seems to depend, scholars favour Antiochus in books IV and V; Antiochus is also probable for book II, while some scholars have mentioned Posidonius. For the first book, the reference is to Zeno, the Epicurean master, or to Philodemus of Gadara. There are no reliable hypotheses for book III, although some successors of Chrysippus have been proposed.[25]

Tusculan Disputations

Tusculan Disputations are thought of as a 'medicine' for the soul and together constitute a real educational proposal for the Roman citizen: this is the thesis supported, with excellent insights by I. Gildenhard, T. Whitmarsh, J. Warren, in *Paideia Romana* (2007). Begun in 45, immediately after the *On the Ends of Good*

---

24 *Fin.* 5.37.
25 For this summary cf. DPHA, Lévy 1994, s.v. Cicero Marcus Tullius, II, 374.

and Evil, Tusculan Disputations are also made up of five books and are always dedicated to M. Brutus. This time Cicero imagines that he is in his Tusculum villa. There, from 16 to 20 June of 45, during five days devoted to study (in the morning rhetoric, in the afternoon philosophy), by means of five imaginary discussions with a young student present, Cicero proposes to give, in the Socratic way, a precise contribution to the culture and philosophy of the Romans.

> We proceeded in this manner: when he who had proposed the subject for discussion had said what he thought proper, I spoke against him (*ego contra dicerem*); for this is, you know, the old and Socratic method of arguing against another's opinion (*contra alterius opinionem disserendi*); for Socrates thought that thus the truth would more easily be arrived at. But to give you a better notion of our disputations, I will not barely send you an account of them, but represent them to you as they were carried on (*sic eas exponam, quasi agatur res, non quasi narretur*).[26]

In this way he believes it is possible to tackle the highest philosophical questions and thus improve the knowledge of ethics, law and family morality. In fact, Cicero in *Tusculan Disputations* combines two distinct didactic models: the method of Socratic interrogation and the method of *scholae* (lectures). R. Gorman, *The Socratic Method in the Dialogues of Cicero* (2005), 64–84, showed how these two types of philosophical speech have been combined with some skill and reinforce each other to produce Cicero's desired effect.

In the first lesson Cicero addresses the problem of death: is it evil or good? To answer this question, we must understand of what it consists. If it involves is the separation of the soul from the body, then the question should be: does the soul survive after death? There is disagreement among the philosophers on both this and on where the soul resides (1.8–23). Cicero is on the side of those who support, like Plato, the immortality of the soul and its divinity: it is indivisible and resides in the head of man (1.70). Therefore, "separating the soul from the body means nothing more than learning to die", *secernere autem a corpore animum, nec quicquam aliud, est mori discere.*[27] Cicero then presents a series of examples to show how death entails the elimination of suffering, but also, on the other hand, of the possible comforts of life. However, is this unhappiness? In fact, those who have died and do not exist can lack nothing: *an potest is qui non est re ulla carere?* (87). And the 'missing' implies 'wanting' what is needed: but this is for those who live, for those who perceive something (*carere enim sentientis est*, 88). After a final reminder of the story of Socrates and of Theramen (97–100) and after a free

---

26 *Tusc.* 1.8.
27 *Tusc.* 1.75.

paraphrase taken from the *Crito* dialogue with Socrates (103)[28] on the immortality of the soul, Cicero concludes that, if death means the definitive loss of life, then even funeral rites lose their meaning. In any case: whether the soul is immortal or not, when death is decided by the gods or is natural, it cannot be bad. It should be considered as a sort of port, a refuge (118–119).

The second discussion also opens with a prologue in which Cicero reiterates his commitment to philosophy and its dissemination in Rome. The same art of oratory can benefit from this commitment. According to Cicero, the Peripatetic and Academic methodological approach is better than the others:

> I have always been pleased with the custom of the Peripatetics, and Academics, of disputing on both sides of the question (*in contrarias partis disserendi*); not solely from its being the only method of discovering what is probable on every subject (*quid in quaque re veri simile esset*), but also because it affords the greatest scope for practicing eloquence (*maxuma dicendi exercitatio*).[29]

He even proposes to deal, in his villa in Tusculum, in a complementary way with rhetoric and philosophy: rhetoric in the morning and philosophy in the afternoon. The study will thus be more effective and integrated. Furthermore, we need to worry about actually practicing what we study.

The second discussion is dedicated to pain. It pertains (14–33) to the examination of the positions of those who believe that pain is an evil and those who think otherwise (as, for example, the Stoics). In any case, in the face of pain and suffering, one can react and can resist (34–41). There are many examples of enduring torture and heroism. The decisive factor is knowing how to dominate oneself: *totum igitur in eo est, ut tibi imperes* (53). Virtue is fundamental in the endurance of pain and it is strengthened by reasoning and wisdom (65).

The third discussion is devoted to the theme of disturbances of the soul (*perturbationes animi*); in particular, fear (*formido*) and affliction/disease (*aegritudo*), and their elimination. In any case it is an alteration of the mind. Even the wise can be subject to it, but not according to the Stoics, for whom the wise man is exempt by definition. According to the Stoics, all the non-sages are unhealthy: *omnis insipientes esse non sanos* (3.10). The causes of the disturbance are therefore examined: above all it derives from the false opinion one has of reality. The opinions of the various philosophical schools are now reported (14–52), and the classification of the Stoics is resumed, distinguishing four types of passions (24–25): two derive from what one believes to be the good (exalted pleasure without

---

28 See *Phaed.* 115C–E.
29 *Tusc.* 2.9.

limits, *voluptas gestiens*, and greed, *cupiditas*). Two others derive from what is believed to be evil (fear, *metus*, and affliction/disease, *aegritudo*). But Cicero rails above all against the position of Epicurus (28–50). It is his materialism that does not work. The various sources of what can plague and worry are then examined. Among others: political ambition, fear of losing children, taking on our shoulders the problems of others thinking that this is our duty. Certainly, we can remedy the *aegritudo* and reduce it to a minimum; besides the typical *consolatio* (74–77), there are those who believe – like Epicurus – that it is sufficient to assume that it does not exist. However, it is important to keep in mind that affliction/disease can be avoided, since it depends on our bad will and our bad ability to judge reality (80). The wise man will not experience 'worry' or anxiety because it is not something rational or natural (82).

The fourth discussion addresses the issue of the irrationality of emotions. After a prologue in which Cicero tries to highlight the incipient interest of the *maiores* for philosophy – and in particular for the most affordable philosophies like Epicureanism – we arrive at the remark that the wise man is not entirely free from 'concern': he too is subject to the disturbances of the soul. In addition to topics he treats in the third book, Cicero points out that two other emotions deserve to be taken into consideration: excessive joy and pleasure. Only if the wise man is not subject to them, can he be peaceful. First of all, Cicero studies the classification of emotions developed by the Stoics (11–14). He compares the diseases of the body with those of the soul and reports the relative analogies. Referring to the Peripatetic doctrine, he then discusses the methods of control and how to cure emotions (38–64). Since all emotions are irrational, reason must be used to control them, whether in the case of limiting its negative effects or in the event that it is intended to exploit its positive energy. But how can we deal with emotions? If we are not wise, philosophy itself may be the right guide. In this regard, Cicero proposes a methodology that is mainly based on the evocation of good examples from the past and on the optimistic expectation of the future. In conclusion, any kind of disturbance, worry or fear can be eliminated because, being emotions irrational, rationality itself can be solicited to provide a remedy. Philosophy topics are the most effective tool to achieve this result: a tool that allows man to reach happiness (83–84).

The fifth and final discussion deals with a long-standing theme: is virtue sufficient for the achievement of happiness? (12–14). Cicero not only seems convinced of this, but underlines the fundamental importance of philosophy in the formation of society and civilization; in particular, it agrees with that approach to reality and to knowledge which, by method, holds itself from expressing definitive judgments, preferring discussion and comparison on opinions:

> I have principally ... argued so as to conceal my own opinion, while I deliver others from their errors, and so discover what has the greatest appearance of probability (*quid esset simillimum veri*) in every question.[30]

In any case, the Epicurean school and that of the Ancient Academy do not seem sufficiently solid because virtue, in them, is conditioned by external and physical goods / evils; indeed, a man who possesses external goods but does not possess virtue cannot be happy. Therefore, only virtuous life seems to ensure happiness.[31] Cicero, moreover, is convinced that, in one way or another, all philosophers could come to agree that virtue is sufficient for a happy life. If this could be proved even with regard to the Epicurean philosophy, then for the other philosophies there would be no problem (73–82). Cicero therefore devotes himself to an analysis of Epicurean ethics and observes that rationality is precisely the criterion that allows Epicurus to evaluate the meaning and weight of pleasure, so that a frugal life will be effective in satisfying the force of natural and necessary desires. After a series of considerations that highlight the autonomy and universality of the wise man, starting from the fact that he does not fear exile and that he can feel at home anywhere, Cicero comes to the conclusion. He points out that if Epicurus – while not appreciating virtue adequately – believes that the wise man is happy (*semper beatum censent esse sapientem*), the more this will be true for the Academicians, the Peripatetics and the Stoics who emphasize the central role of virtue (119).

On the Nature of the Gods

In this work, too – in three books, also completed in 45 BCE and once again dedicated to M. Brutus – Cicero presents the different opinions by various schools on theological issues. In the first book he reviews the opinions of ancient philosophers concerning the conception and existence of god (1.25–42). Therein, he focuses on the position of Epicurus. The Epicurean C. Velleius (43–56) explains the theological doctrine, which the Academic C. Aurelius Cotta refutes (57–124). The Atomistic conception is exhaustively studied; issues such as those relating to the isonomy, the imperturbability of the gods, the impossibility of their intervention

---

30 *Tusc.* 5.11.

31 Cicero writes, *Tusc.* 5.50: "Now, unless an honourable life is a happy life, there must of course be something preferable to a happy life", *et quidem, nisi ea vita beata est, quae est eadem honesta, sit aliud necesse est melius vita beata.*

and the uselessness of religious piety are approached with caution but with firmness. Cicero confirms his profound disagreement with materialism and Epicurean doctrine in general.

In the second book, the Stoic Q. Lucilius Balbus, a friend of Antiochus of Ascalon, presents Stoic theology. Four cardinal theses are highlighted and argued: the existence of the gods (2.4–12), their nature (45–72), the providence in their way of governing the universe (73–162), their attention for man (162–168). Lucilius Balbus discusses the reasons for which the idea of divinity would take shape in the human soul (13–19), and describes the ways in which the presence of the activity of the god is translated in all universal nature. The Stoic conclusion that makes the rational principle what dominates in everything is strongly supported:

> There is therefore a natural element that embraces the whole universe and preserves its existence: an element endowed with sensitivity and reason. The fact is that every natural being, which does not reduce itself to a single and undifferentiated nature, but is constituted by the union of several elements connected to each other, must bear within itself a directive principle (*habere aliquem in se principatum*) which in man is the reason (*in homine mentem*) and in the animal something that resembles reason (*in belua quiddam simile mentis*) and from which natural inclinations arise.[32]

In conclusion Lucilius Balbus reaffirms that supporting atheistic positions is harmful and ungodly at the same time.

In the third book the Academic G. Aurelius Cotta is again on stage, this time to criticize Stoic theology. He examines the four Stoic theses again and, on this occasion, argues against each of them. Among other things, he proposes examples in which providence is completely absent and the gods seem uninterested in the needs of humanity. The mythology is ridiculed (42–45), the variety of names and functions that should characterize the same gods deserves to be denounced (51–62). In conclusion, according to the Stoics the gods would have too much to do; according to the Epicureans, they would have too little to do. Cicero concludes by saying: "If Cotta's speech seemed more acceptable to Velleius, to me that of Balbus seemed much closer to the truth" (95): that is to say, it is the theological proposal of the Stoics rather than the criticism of Epicurus or Stoicism that is preferable, since it is constructive.

---

32 *ND* 2.29.

On Old Age

Cicero dedicates this dialogue to his friend Atticus.[33] We are now in 44 and we see Cicero's concern for the radical change of the political situation. Cicero identifies himself with the figure of Cato the Censor: a 'great old man', one of the great Roman *maiores*.[34] Like Cato, Cicero also intends to interpret his old age in a serene and constructive way, and even Atticus proposes this goal. So here is this dialogue in defence of the value of old age and a refutation of the accusations that we normally address to it.

Cicero imagines Cato in conversation with Scipio Aemilianus and with C. Laelius.[35] Various examples drawn from Roman history serve to enhance wisdom and inner goods enriching advanced age: as an alternative to the decay of the body, the joys of the spirit are available, and so should be cultivated. Cato disputes four main criticisms of old age: old age distances us from activities; makes the body weaker; deprived of almost all pleasures; brings us closer to death (15–81). The great aspiration of Cicero is always evident throughout the dialogue: *otium*, as a special moment of life, should be direct to political ends. The dialogue ends with a call to the immortality of the soul (82–85) and with an invitation to serenely wait for death:

---

33 T. Pomponius Atticus (109–32 BCE) was one of Cicero's great friends; he had a long correspondence with him from 65 to 44. A very rich and influential man, Atticus managed to stay away from politics; he formed friendships with the most representative personalities of the various political groups and always showed himself generous with everyone. His name, Atticus, derives from the adoption of his uncle Q. Caecilius Pomponianus Atticus; however, his long stay in Athens, his passion for culture and the Greek world, his preference for the Epicurean philosophy were perfectly combined with his *gentilitius* cognomen Atticus.

34 M. Porcius Cato the elder (Tusculum 234–149 BCE) – the Old – was one of the most prominent Roman politicians. He participated in the Second Punic War and was consul in 195 BCE and censor in 184: during this magistracy he distinguished himself for his struggle against the luxury and corruption of customs. Hence the nickname 'Censor'.

35 P. Cornelius Scipio Aemilianus Africanus the younger (185–129 BCE) was a Roman general, adopted by P. Cornelius Scipio. He conquered Carthage and Numantia. Educated to traditional principles, he was a friend of Panaetius and Polibius and C. Laelius: this opened him up to the Greek cultural world. C. Laelius (190–129) was a very influential Roman politician. He was consul in 140 and belonged to the so-called Scipionic cultural circle. He was a follower of Stoic philosophy and, as a 'friend' model, Cicero made him the protagonist of the dialogue on friendship.

Such, my friends, are my views on old age. May you both attain it, and thus be able to prove by experience the truth of what you have heard from me (*ut ea quae ex me audistis re experti probare possitis*).[36]

On Divination

In two books, this work is dedicated to Q. Tullius Cicero,[37] the orator's younger brother. Probably the first book was written before the death of Caesar, the second afterwords.

Cicero and Quintus are in the villa of Tusculum and compare their opinions on the subject of forecasting the future and on divination; in the background, there lies the theological debate developed in the *On the Nature of the Gods*. In the first book, Quintus explains the arguments in favour of divination; in the second, Cicero himself exposes those against it. First of all, Quintus examines the definition of divination and its characteristics: it can be artificial or natural (1.11). To the first group belong, among others, the haruspices, the augurs, the astrologers and their pronouncements. To the second, belong oracles, dreams, and wishes (12). Principally, the Stoics believe in divination, as a consequence of their organic and rational vision of the structure of the cosmos and the relationship of cause/effect that characterizes the becoming. But, in general, an ancient tradition testifies that divination is a science, that it is of divine origin and that it receives its strength and credibility from it. Quintus notes, in particular, how some clues almost never lie (*videmus haec signa numquam fere mentientia*), even if we don't see or understand why this happens (*nec tamen, cur ita fiat, videmus*) (1.15). Moreover, he wonders if there really can be a role of 'chance', even when what happens has the characteristics of truth: *quicquam potest casu esse factum, quod omnes habet in se numeros veritatis?* (1.23). Quintus pays special attention to dreams and their interpretation (1.39–61): to the objection that many dreams are false, he replies that this depends on their difficult understanding (1.60). Moreover, if during sleep the soul can wander beyond the body, the condition of well-being in which the body is found becomes fundamental to guarantee a quiet dream and a more immediate interpretation. Thus, the soul remembers the past, sees the present and foresees the future: *cum ergo est somno sevocatus animus a societate et*

---

36 *Sen.* 85.
37 Younger than Marcus Tullius (102 – 43), he was also a politician, linked first to Pompey and then to Caesar. Antonius's assassins killed him shortly after his brother was murdered. He wrote the *Commentariolum petitionis*, on the occasion of the candidacy of Marcus Tullius at the consulate.

*a contagione corporis, tum meminit praeteritorum, praesentia cernit, futura provi-
det* (1.63).

Like the dream, divination also has its importance and validity. The great objection that Quintus raises against those who do not believe it is the following: in
many cases we find that what was predicted happens, and this cannot be denied:

> For example, if I were to say that the magnet attracted iron and drew it to itself, and I could
> not tell you why, then I suppose you would utterly deny that the magnet had any such
> power. At least that is the course you pursue in regard to the existence of the power of divi-
> nation, although it is established by our own experience and that of others, by our reading
> and by the traditions of our forefathers. Why, even before the dawn of philosophy, which is
> a recent discovery, the average man had no doubt about divination, and, since its develop-
> ment, no philosopher of any sort of reputation has had any different view.[38]

In the concluding paragraphs (1.125–127) Quintus returns to the Stoic theory and
reports with great precision the scientific definition of fate (εἱμαρμένη), remembering that:

> Moreover, since, as will be shown elsewhere, all things happen by Fate (*cum fato omnia
> fiant*), if there were a man whose soul could discern the links that join each cause with every
> other cause (*qui conligationem causarum omnium perspiciat animo*), then, surely, he would
> never be mistaken in any prediction he might make. For he who knows the causes of future
> events necessarily knows what every future event will be (*qui enim teneat causas rerum fu-
> turarum, idem necesse est omnia teneat, quae futura sint*).[39]

Obviously, everything that, in the alleged reading of the signs or interpretation of
dreams, has to do with commercialization and individual economic interest does
not belong to the divination that Quintus is thinking of (1.132).

In the second book, Cicero begins by recalling in what ways he has benefited
his fellow citizens, especially in philosophy and writing works such as *On the Republic, Hortensius, Academica, On the Ends of Good and Evil, Tusculan Disputations, On the Nature of the Gods*. To these he adds *On Old Age* and precisely the
current *On Divination*; he finally promises a work on destiny: the *On Fate* (2.2–4).
As stated several times, in parallel to the studies of philosophy, Cicero deepens
his study of rhetoric, and writes the three books *On the Orator, Brutus*, and lastly
Orator. Finally, Cicero underlines his main objective: to disseminate the contents
of philosophy in Latin, so as to consent everyone to benefit from it.

---

38 *Div.* 1.86.
39 *Div.* 1.127.

At this point, he congratulates his brother on the arguments developed in favour of the Stoic perspective on divination. But then he replies to Quintus and first of all invites his brother to study the Stoic doctrine, once he has established that divination must be understood as the presentiment of events dependent on fate (*talium ergo rerum, quae in fortuna positae sunt, praesensio divinatio est*, 2.14), if there can then be a forecast of those events which there is no reason why they should happen: *potestne igitur earum rerum, quae nihil habent rationis, quare futurae sint, esse ulla praesensio?*, 2.15. Cicero strongly asserts that the 'case' exists and that, consequently, no forecast of future events is possible: *est autem fortuna; rerum igitur fortuitarum nulla praesensio est*, 2.19. Therefore, against the Stoics, he emphasizes that, if everything happens according to destiny, then divination is useless: *vultis autem omnia fato; nulla igitur est divinatio*, 2.20.

Then, however, Cicero considers it more effective to evoke the suspension of the judgment that the Sceptical Academy proposes also on this occasion (2.150). Of the divination he signals the worst drift: the hoax and the interests behind the interpretation of astronomical facts, natural portents, wishes, predictions. Dreams are interpreted as actual and subjective illusions, and it is not possible to understand from them the intention of the divinity towards us. In any case, the amount of data they offer is too varied and too complex to give a univocal and reliable meaning. We must bring back dreams and their interpretation to the same superstition that accompanies all the other phenomena or elements on which divination is based. But superstition and religion are not the same thing (2.148); while it is wise to maintain the religiosity the *maiores* relied on, it is equally wise to reject superstition. However, even in this case Cicero declares to suspend the judgment, in the Socratic manner.

On Fate

On Fate is a structured essay in the form of dialogue that has reached us without the first and last part, and with two *lacunae* within the text. Written in 44, immediately after the death of Caesar, in one book, it was probably dedicated to Hirtius.[40] In this work, Cicero presents the positions of some of the exponents of classical philosophical schools on the theme of destiny. Behind the dialogical

---

40 Aulus Hirtius (90–43 BCE) was with Caesar in Gaul and then during the civil war. He was the consul-designate for 43 on the Ides of March. After the killing of Caesar, initially Hirtius was supporter of Marcus Antonius; but then he opposed the violent intentions of Antonius. Hirtius

framework that sees Hirtius as the interlocutor of the orator, the theses of the Stoics Posidonius and Chrysippus, of the Megarians Stilpo and Diodorus Cronus are revived; then it is the turn of the Atomist Epicurus and, above all, of Carneades, the initiator of the Third Academy.

During the *disputatio*, we can see the variation in the theoretical perspectives on which Cicero relies, even if the fundamental thesis he supports – that there is an opening for individual freedom – steadily remains in the background and is firmly confirmed. Cicero attributes this thesis to the Academic Carneades, who, resorting to an argument based on the *modus tollens*, had previously shown that "not everything that happens, happens at the behest of fate" (31).[41] Cicero comes to make Carneades' thesis explicit only after a long journey that led him to face:

(a) the problem of truth and falsehood with respect to future events and, therefore, to prediction;

(b) Diodorus' conclusions concerning 'what is possible' and the truth of 'what is possible';

(c) the Atomistic thesis of Epicurus who, on the one hand, rejects the 'principle of bivalence' with respect to truth and falsehood, while, on the other hand, introducing random motion: that is to say, he conceives of an event without a cause.

Leaning on Carneades, Cicero distinguishes between events provoked by a *natural cause*, which, as such, operates from eternity, and events that are the result of a cause *sine aeternitate naturalis*, that is *occasional* (32–33). Initially Chrysippus, as *arbiter honorarius* between the rigidly deterministic[42] and libertarian thesis (39), is placed in a position of mediation; but then Cicero analyses the Stoic doctrine of assent (40) and the Stoic distinction concerning the different types of cause (41): at this point, the position of Chrysippus – even if useful to contrast Epicurus – appears again to be inadequate in the face of the problem of freedom in deciding and acting.

---

always maintained friendly relations with Cicero, but, as the *De fato* specified, he was successfully lobbied by Cicero and switched his allegiance to the senatorial party.

41 *Non igitur fato fiunt, quaecumque fiunt*, 31. Carneades' syllogistic argument (if P then Q; but ¬ Q, then ¬ P) is reported like this: "If all things come about through antecedent causes, all things come about in such a way that they are joined and woven together by a natural connection"; from this it follows that: "if that is true, nothing is in our power". But is not so: "there is something in our power". For this then: "it is not the case that whatever come about does so through fate".

42 In § 39, listing the partisans of the necessitarian thesis, Cicero places Aristotle together with Democritus, Heraclitus, Empedocles. This is a surprise for modern historiography who considers Aristotle a champion of indeterminism. On this particular point, see Donini 1989, 124–145.

The concluding paragraphs of the *disputatio* are reserved to Epicurus, whose doctrine of the *clinamen* (46–48) is openly ridiculed from a rhetorical point of view.

Laelius On Friendship

Cicero wrote this work, in one book, in the summer of 44. In it he evokes the dialogue on friendship that he imagines to have occurred among three very high-profile personalities of the previous century: C. Laelius, friend of P. Scipio Aemilianus, Q. Mucius Scaevola the Augur, teacher of Cicero, and C. Fannius, all of whom reached the consulate. Cicero imagines this dialogue to take place shortly after the death of Scipio Aemilianus. As he had devised an old man (Cato) to deal with that subject in the 'old age' dialogue, so now in the 'friendship' dialogue, it is Scipio's memorable friend, Laelius, who deals with this theme.

After a series of reflections on the immortality of the soul (13–15), the three friends enter the heart of the theme. We need to distinguish the more formal meaning of 'friendship' from the more affective one, and we must ask ourselves (17): a) what is the opinion we have of it? (*quid sentias*); b) what is its nature? (*qualem existumes*); c) what rules govern it? (*quae praecepta des*).

As for the first question, it is fundamental to observe that friendship reveals itself only among noble and virtuous men (*boni*), among those who are able to follow the true dictates of nature. It is not just a matter of the 'Stoic' *virtus*, but rather of the way of relating to others that makes a friend a true *alter ego*. For this reason, friendship cannot arise from situations of need, but from pure and natural love. Cicero (who thus answers the second question) analyses the ways in which a friendly relationship is revealed and strengthened; he also explains the reasons why it can happen to deteriorate. Finally (and this is the third question) you can follow a series of tips and rules to correctly choose a friend and to preserve friendship until the end of life, knowing that, among the *boni*, the situation will not be identical to what normally occurs among men.

In paragraph 23 Laelius gives a brief definition of 'friendship':

> Seeing that friendship includes very many and very great advantages, it undoubtedly excels all other things in this respect, that it projects the bright ray of hope into the future (*quod bonam spem praelucet in posterum*), and does not suffer the spirit to grow faint or to fall. Again, he who looks upon a true friend, looks, as it were, upon a sort of image of himself (*tamquam exemplar aliquod intuetur sui*).

Shortly afterwards, in paragraph 27, a decisive observation follows:

Wherefore it seems to me that friendship springs rather from nature than from need, and from an inclination of the soul joined with a feeling of love (*applicatione magis animi cum quodam sensu amandi quam cogitatione quantum illa res utilitatis esset habitura*), rather than from calculation of how much profit the friendship is likely to afford (*quam cogitatione quantum illa res utilitatis esset habitura*).

These are two key passages that show both Cicero's attention to the psychological as well as the moral dimension. In this way Laelius, the main character of the dialogue, is able to emphasize that it cannot be utility to promote friendship, that we must avoid hypocrisy and flattery, that a friend must have the courage to criticize his friend, that truth and constancy, in the friendship relation, are important. In the conclusion of the dialogue, virtue is undoubtedly at the centre: it is virtue that produces love and preserves true friendship, not need or utility (100). Laelius judges the friendship and memory of his friend Scipio as 'sacred', and he hopes that the same will also happen with Cicero. According to Cicero, nothing should be preferable to friendship based on virtue (102–104).

Topica

This work, written in July 44 BCE, is addressed to the jurist C. Trebatius Testa.[43] We cannot consider the *Topica* an authentic book of philosophy; certainly not the one on moral philosophy Cicero had especially thought of. However, to respond to a request from Trebatius Cicero sums up, along the lines of what Aristotle had done in his *Topics* and especially in *Rhetoric*, the key points (*loci*) of the argumentation.

As we know, Aristotle undertakes in the *Topica* a search for a secure and trustworthy method of arguing, which, starting from true statements or from opinions expressed in generally accepted propositions, makes it impossible to support a contrary position. The study of dialectical syllogism, the inductive and deductive procedures in the argumentation are the key points addressed by Aristotle. Rather, Cicero proposes an exhaustive cataloguing of the *loci* of the argumentation with particular attention to the judicial side. However, this Ciceronian work is significant precisely because it shows how the intertwining of the technical aspect of the word and language is fundamental with respect to the contents that *the philosopher* intends to propose to his audience or to his readers. In his

---

43 The lawyer C. Trebatius Testa (died in 4 CE) as well as in close relations of friendship and confidence with Caesar, Augustus, Horace, Maecenas, was a friend of Cicero, with whom he conducted an intense correspondence.

analysis of the method of arguing (*ratio disserendi*), Cicero distinguishes the *pars inveniendi* and the *pars iudicandi* (6), i.e. what concerns (a) the search for materials and (b) the reduction to schemes of these materials and the decision concerning their use.

Then, he distinguishes (8) between internal arguments (*alii in eo ipso de quo agitur haerent*) and external ones (*alii assumuntur extrinsecus*, i.e. those related to the external context), and verifies the characteristics that allow their identification and classification on the level of grammar (in a broad sense) and of logic. The way in which the orator will be able to take advantage of his knowledge of the *loci* to solicit or to reassure the audience is fundamental.

It should be noted that, with regard to the causal relationship between the entities (causality is understood here as one of the *loci* of the argumentation), Cicero takes up the case studies he had already analysed in *On Fate* regarding 'destiny' (58–66). As for the expository method, Cicero shows, in the *Topics*, a lot of attention in distinguishing and defining the various aspects of what he is examining. For example, he clearly distinguishes the *hypothesis* (which he calls *causa* and considers as a *definite inquiry*), from the *thesis* (which he calls *propositum*, and considers as an *infinite inquiry*, i.e. a question of a general nature); then, the theoretical inquiries (these are the ones for which the proposed aim is science) and the practical inquiry.

Finally, some general questions arise at the philosophical level. For example: is the foundation of the law natural or contractual? (90)

On Duties

This work by Cicero is structured in three books: the first two completed in October of 44, and the third, finished in November/December of the same year. It is dedicated to his son Marcus. As witnessed in the correspondence, Cicero began the composition of this work after Caesar's death in Rome; once the first *Philippic* was pronounced, he retired to the villa in Puteoli (*Att.* 16.13.6 of 25 October) and there he resumed the composition. He completed it also using a summary of Posidonius' work *On duties according to the circumstances*, of which he had become aware just before starting (*Att.* 16.14.4).

Oratory and philosophy are closely intertwined in this work, and the dedication to his son Marcus, at that time in Athens at the school of the Peripatetic Crantor, also shows a pedagogical and social intention. This treatise constitutes the conclusion of the project started ten years before with *On the Republic*, when Cicero clarified his ideas concerning society and community, organized in the name of the law and on the basis of a natural tension.[44] However, while in *On the Republic* the perspective consisted, above all, in delineating the ideal of the excellent prince (see the V book), in *On Duties* the theory is anchored to praxis, according to a project calibrated around the institutional and juridical dimension. Therefore, here is the continuous series of examples – taken especially from Roman history[45] – which refer to the 'duty' of safeguarding the life and society of men, to the autonomy of decisions even with respect to the divine will. In this sense it is clear the reference to Stoicism mitigated in the direction of Panaetius and its ideal of an active life.

The concept of 'duty' is central to the first book,[46] and the problematic approach, characteristic of Academic probabilism, seems to give way to Stoic philosophy:[47] especially Panaetius represents the reference point for Cicero. First of all, non-absolute duties (τὰ καθήκοντα = *communia officia*) and absolute duties (τὰ κατορθώματα = *recta officia*) are distinguished (8); furthermore, as Panaetius pointed out, it is fundamental to know how to choose between what is morally right and what is advantageous, when a certain action can be qualified as right or wrong. Initially, for this purpose, justice, morality, liberality, courage and temperance are examined; then, with the utmost scrupulousness, Cicero devotes himself to addressing the question of 'nature' and how it should be followed, which passions should be controlled and if, and how, publicly adopted conventions should be followed (105–132). In any case, it remains confirmed that:

> If that virtue [Justice] which focuses in the safeguarding of human interests (*quae constat ex hominibus tuendis*), that is, in the maintenance of human society (*ex societate generis*

---

44 See *Rep.* 1.39, *infra*, pp. 112–113. See *Off.* 1.157: "As a swarms of bees do not gather for the sake of making honeycomb but make the honeycomb because they are gregarious by nature (*cum congregabilia natura sint*), so human beings – and to a much higher degree – exercise their skills together in action and thought because they are naturally gregarious (*natura congregati*)." Long 1995a, 213–240, considers Cicero's work important not so much for its practical relevance to political action, but rather for an attempt to diagnose what had gone wrong in Roman Republican ideology and what would be required to put it right.

45 On this strategy, see Blom 2010, 1–26. Blom examines Cicero's use of historical exempla (61–148), and Cicero's role models (149–286). This is interesting, because Cicero's public *persona* seems to have consisted of various roles.

46 See 1.5: "For who would presume to call himself a philosopher, if he did not inculcate any lessons of duty?", *Quis est enim, qui nullis officii praeceptis tradendis philosophum se audeat dicere?* In the third book (3.1) explicitly Cicero says to follow above all the work *On duties* by Panaetius, while introducing a series of corrections.

47 See also *Off.* 2.8.

humani), were not to accompany the pursuit of knowledge, that knowledge would seem isolated and barren of results (*solivaga cognitio et ieiuna videatur*).[48]

From the moment that wisdom is considered the first of virtues, justice can only be the first duty. In the second book, Cicero deals in detail with 'what is expedient': "The principle with which we are now dealing is what is called 'expediency' (*id ipsum est, quod utile appellatur*)."[49] First in reference to oneself (and here it is a question of *honor*, *decorum*), then with reference to society. The latter are defined as the characteristics and methods of behaviour and relationship; Cicero wonders what importance the glory[50] and the power to argue and defend justice have; what it means to 'serve the state' and avoid grabbing unjust benefits and rents. The conclusive part of the second book (52–75) is dedicated to the theme of *beneficium* as a value and an instrument of government. Cicero underlines how important and dignified it is for wise men to work hard on public affairs (65–66).

After an introductory reference to the forced (though put to good use) *otium* in which he also found himself (1–3), in the third book Cicero compares 'what must be done' and 'what is expedient to do'. Since only the wise man is perfect, only for him do duty and utility coincide perfectly. This is not the case for the common man, who must know how to relate himself with what nature and the law propose. In evidence is the conflict between justice and what, at first sight, appears advantageous (46). Cicero states:

> Let it be set down as an established principle, then, that what is morally wrong can never be expedient (*quod turpe sit, id numquam esse utile*) - not even when one secures by means of it that which one thinks expedient; for the mere act of thinking a course expedient, when it is morally wrong, is demoralizing (*calamitosum est*).[51]

Hence the problem of morality in business and politics. In conclusion, Cicero refers to the example of *maiores*, to trust and observance of oaths. He points out the importance of the laws, but is aware that:

> The law disposes of sharp practices (*astutias*) in one way, philosophers in another: the law deals with them as far as it can lay its strong arm upon them; philosophers, as far as they can be apprehended by reason and conscience. Now reason demands that nothing be done

---

48 *Off.* 1.157.
49 *Off.* 2.9.
50 See *Off.* 2.31. To the subject of 'glory' Cicero dedicates a homonymous treatise, unfortunately lost, always composed in 44. See *Att.* 16.2.6; 16.6.4.
51 *Off.* 3.49.

with unfairness, with false pretense, or with misrepresentation (*ratio ergo hoc postulat, ne quid insidiose, ne quid simulate, ne quid fallaciter*).[52]

In the concluding paragraphs Cicero returns to the topic of *decorum* and other socially relevant *virtues*: *moderatio* (reasonableness), *modestia* (sobriety), *continentia* (self-restraint), *temperantia* (self-control) (116). Finally, he wonders if it is the pleasure of having to guide the wise man in his choices (this was the thesis advocated by Epicurus) and whether having obtained it is really an advantage (117–120). According to Cicero, in fact, pleasure and morality cannot be reconciled.

---

52 *Off.* 3.68. Composed in the years of *On the Republic*, *On the Laws* is also part of the research that develops between *On the Republic* and *On Duties*. *On the Laws* is another treatise of clear ethical formulation, strongly related to the Stoic thought especially in the book I, in which the positive law is anchored in the natural law. Cicero thinks, therefore, that natural law is based on a set of moral values, which are assumed to be universal, see Harries 2013, 107–137.

3 Contemporary Research on Cicero as a Philosopher

3.1 Introduction

Contemporary research on Cicero's philosophy and on Cicero as a philosopher began its current stage with its concern to define more precisely the meaning of 'philosophia'. By ancient 'philosophia' we no longer mean exclusively the theoretical and scientific research which aims to become an organic system where the various aspects of knowledge and action find their balance and justification; nor do we mean the mere adoption of a certain morally committed life project as representative of a specific *Weltanschauung*. Today it is clear that, with respect to different historical, geographical and cultural contexts, the very idea of 'philosophy' takes on multiple and complex values and meanings, even if – at least in the context of the Western world – they can be traced back to a tradition that is in any case decipherable and justifiable. In this perspective, Cicero can no longer be considered as a rhetorician with a particular passion for the world of culture and the technique of argumentation. Nor can he be reduced to the image of the erudite (either lawyer or statesman), capable of reading and understanding the works of the Greek tradition, from which he is able to draw and then to derive a formidable wealth of ideas, writings and insights useful to the Roman cultural world.

We have recently begun to consider Cicero a philosopher, precisely in consideration of the meaning that the concept of 'philosophy' acquires in the first century BCE in Rome. There is no doubt that, at the end of the second century BCE in the context of the Roman cultural background, the reflection on Greek philosophy, linked to the Hellenistic schools, had begun its development. This particular situation allows him to formulate a very clear work project: on the one hand, he aims to render the doctrines of the Greeks – and their special way of relating to reality – understandable to the Romans (and therefore acceptable to their mentality); then to explain the apparently abstract problems that were debated in the various 'schools'. On the other hand, he promises to make philosophy the theoretical basis for political action, the most effective tool for framing the conscience and morality of the Romans in the best way: this is consistent with the tradition of the *maiores*.

Cicero reveals a thoughtful and constructive approach to 'philosophical knowledge'. He is committed to showing that any of his choices or strategies is not inconsistent, but rather reflects the suggestion of established philosophical

https://doi.org/10.1515/9783110661835-003

doctrines and originates his confrontation with the contemporary masters of philosophy. Cicero appears supported by a strong predisposition to confrontation, debate, and critical approach. That is, he is a new type of philosopher. He is not a theorist, detached and mostly disengaged from the world of concrete reality; rather, he is a man heavily engaged in the decisive issues of his own age, who has developed the need to find, in the theoretical and critical-philosophical knowledge, the necessary tools so as to overcome the difficulties connected with the events of political contingency.

Some works emerge today as fundamental along this path of research of modern historical-philosophical criticism.

A) In the broader perspective of the Roman cultural context, the following collections of essays have acquired more and more importance:

1) *Römische Wertbegriffe*, edited by H. Oppermann (1976); a general compilation dedicated to the Roman concept of 'value'. The papers of the best scholars of the German school of the early 1900s are assembled here: in particular H. Drexler (on *res publica* and *honos*); H. Roloff (on *maiores*); K. Meister (on *virtus* and *amicitia*); L. Curtius (on *virtus* and *constantia*); H. Haffter (on *humanitas*).

2) *Römische Philosophie*, edited by G. Maurach, *ibid.* (1976), in which Cicero is included among the protagonists. Among other things, the author of this collection raises the question whether those who have been considered eminent Roman philosophers were ever aware of the 'Roman' character of their thinking and how they were eventually independent from the context in which they lived. As for Cicero, U. Knoche's essay, *Cicero ein Mittler griechischer Geisteskultur*, focuses precisely on this.

3) *Das Staatsdenken der Römer*, edited by R. Klein, *ibid.* (1980), in which the topic is the theoretical-political thought in Rome and Cicero is in the foreground. In all the essays that deal with him, Cicero appears as a conscious protagonist of the moral role of the philosopher and of his political task. The papers by R. Heinze, F. Solmen and R. Stark focus on *On the Republic*.

These collections of essays, almost all originally printed around the mid-twentieth century, are now accompanied by:

4) the two-volumes *Philosophia Togata I. Essays on Philosophy and Roman Society*, edited by M. Griffin & J. Barns (1989), and *Philosophia Togata II. Plato and Aristotle at Rome*, edited by J. Barnes & M. Griffin (1997). These two collections of essays aim to focus on the way Plato, Aristotle and Hellenistic philosophy are present in Rome. As for Cicero, J. Annas, *Cicero on Stoic Moral Philosophy and Private Property* (1989, 151–173), addresses the problem of the centrality of ethics and of what is morally right, in reference to book III of *On Duties*. J. Barnes, *Roman Aristotle*, faces (1997, 1–69) the problem of Cicero's knowledge of Aristotle. He

does not exclude that Cicero knew and used Andronicus' edition, but he prefers to think that Cicero's knowledge of Aristotle was not dependent on Andronicus and hence that any evidence Cicero offers us is evidence of a pre-Andronican state of affairs. A. Lintott, *The Theory of the Mixed Constitution at Rom* (1997, 70–85), compares the different approach of Polybius and Cicero. In particular he points out that Cicero does not believe in an automatic natural decline of every *res publica*; he rather believes that society is not founded on natural weakness, but on natural social instinct, based on the consensual acceptance of law and the pursuit of common interest. M. Griffin, *From Aristotle to Atticus: Cicero and Matius on Friendship* (1997, 86–109), studies the debt of Cicero's conception of friendship to Aristotle and Theophrastus; she compares Cicero's relationship with Atticus and Matius, both linked, albeit in different ways, to Epicureanism.

More recently, a new collection of essays has been published:

5) *Roman Reflections. Studies in Latin Philosophy*, ed. by G.D. Williams and K. Volk (2016). In this work Cicero the philosopher is at the centre of the technical-philosophical debate of the republican period. T. Reinhardt, *To See and to Be See: On Vision and Perception in Lucretius and Cicero* (63–90), addresses the question of the objectivity of vision, with particular attention to the meaning and function of *videre / videri* (to see / to appear). G. Reydams-Schils, *Cicero on the Study of Nature* (91–107), examines how physics fits into the histories of philosophy that Cicero includes in his works on oratory, and argues that physics is still unmistakable foundational for ethics both in Cicero's works and in the Stoicism he presents.

B) The fundamental research on the Academic school developed by C. Lévy in his work: *Cicero Academicus. Recherches sur les 'Academiques' et sur la philosophie cicéronienne* (1992). Lévy proposes a rereading of Ciceronian works of ethics and physics in the light of the problems formulated in the Academics through the intermediary of doxography. In *Dictionnaire des philosophes antiques* (1994, 1, 373–382, and 2003, Supplément, 666–675), Lévy briefly reconstructs the frame of the approaches of Cicero's scholars until the end of the last century, underlining the progressive detachment from the simple *Quellenforschung*, the search for sources. An update can be obtained from the introduction of Cappello (2019), 1–10.

Lévy's work is followed by the collection of essays of which B. Inwood and J. Mansfeld are the editors: *Assent & Argument. Studies in Cicero's 'Academic Books'* (1997). In the ten essays assembled in this book, both the presence of the masters of the Academy,[1] and the problems related to the philosophical stance of Cicero[2] are addressed.

C) The collection of 12 essays published by J.G.F. Powell: *Cicero the Philosopher* (1995); this fundamental collection is the first to deal, point by point, with different aspects of Cicero's philosophical thought. In his introduction, J.K.F. Powell (1–36) studies the background of Cicero's works and the Ciceronian translations from Greek; A.A. Long (37–62) introduces us the Cicero's Plato and Aristotle; M. Schofield (63–84) faces the definition of *Res publica* and W. Görler (85–114) the continuity of Cicero's scepticism in *On the Laws*. In a comprehensive essay, J. Glucker (115–144) studies the concepts of *probabile, veri simile* and the related terms; M.C. Stokes (145–170) faces Cicero's interpretation of Epicurean pleasure, M.R. Wright (171–196) self-love and love of humanity as they occur in *On the Ends of Good and Evil* 3rd book, and P.R. Smith the question of leisure. A.E Douglas (197–218) studies *Tusculan Disputations* and R.W. Sharples (247–272) *Topica* and *On Fate*. S.A. White (219–246) offers us an analysis of Stoic suffering according to Cicero and of the different rival therapies. Finally, M.T. Griffin (325–346) focuses on a more historical than philosophical problem: she aims to gauge the extent, the depth, and the nature of philosophical knowledge and interest in Rome, by studying Cicero's letters.

D) Two monographs explicitly dedicated to Cicero's philosophical thought:

1) K. Bringmann, *Untersuchungen zum späten Cicero* (1971). This work aims to highlight Cicero's specific motivations in planning and organizing his philosophical work.

2) W. Görler, *Untersuchungen zur Cicero's Philosophie* (1974). Görler tried to show that in Cicero's philosophical writings there are no contradictions in the common sense of the term, nor even significant indecisions. We must be able to identify the different analytical levels he places himself at: that of 'rational certainty' (*rationale Gewißheit*) which satisfies the needs of the mind, that of 'desired belief' (*erwünschten Glauben*), which pertains to common experience. There is also a median level where the figure of insecurity with respect to scientific demonstration remains. The philosopher Cicero is constantly subjected to a double attraction. The mind wants to believe that thought cannot by its nature leave the level of the demonstrable. But human being, as a being constituted not only

---

1 See the papers by M. Griffin, 1–35, J. Glucker, 58–88, T. Dorandi, 89–106, K.A. Algra, 107–139, R.J. Hankinson, 161–216, G. Striker, 257–277.
2 See the papers by W. Görler, 36–57, J. Barnes, 140–160, J. Allen, 217–256, M.F. Burnyeat, 277–310.

of mind and thought, necessarily holds judgment in abeyance. According to Görler (206–207), however, it remains difficult to conceive that Cicero could never have presented, in a theoretical essay, 'his system', his individual form of Sceptical thought.

E) Some studies (or collections of essays) dedicated to specific aspects of Cicero's philosophical thought:

– W.W. Fortenbaugh and P. Steinmetz (eds.), *Cicero's Knowledge of the Peripatos* (1989);
– I. Gildenhard, *Paideia romana. Cicero's 'Tusculan Disputations'* (2007);
– W. Nicgorski (ed.), *Cicero's Practical Philosophy* (2012);
– J.W. Atkins, *Cicero on Politics and the Limits of Reason. The Republic and Laws* (2013);
– J. Zarecki, *Cicero's Ideal Statesman in Theory and Practice* (2014);
– R. Woolf, *Cicero: the Philosophy of a Roman Sceptic* (2015);
– S. Maso, *Grasp and Dissent. Cicero and Epicurean Philosophy* (2015);
– W.H.F. Altman, *The revival of Platonism in Cicero's late philosophy: Platonis aemulus and the invention of Cicero* (2016);
– J. Annas and G. Betegh (eds.), *Cicero' De finibus. Philosophical Approaches* (2016);
– W. Nicgorski, *Cicero's Skepticism and His Recovery of Political Philosophy* (2016);
– O. Cappello, *The School of Doubt: Skepticism, History and Politics in Cicero's 'Academia'* (2019);
– M. Schofield, *Cicero: Political Philosophy* (2021).

All these works are significant because of the original points of view adopted; they bring new ideas for further study and undoubtedly confirm the fertility of the modern exegetical approach, aimed at highlighting the different aspects of Cicero as a philosopher.

F) Finally, G. Gawlick and W. Görler's work on Cicero is important, since it constitutes one of the sections of the fourth volume of the great *Die Philosophie der Antike*, and it is organized in the traditional way: a careful development of the editions of the texts of Cicero (§ 54), an essential but reliable biographical profile (§ 55), the presentation of Cicero's writings (§ 56), his philosophy (§ 57), his legacy (§ 58). Section 57, in particular, aims to highlight some aspects of Cicero's thought and action by noting the importance but also the problematic nature of his purpose.

3.2 Cicero Academicus and Epistemology

The monograph of Carlos Lévy and the collection of essays published by Brad Inwood and Jaap Mansfeld represented, in the final part of the twentieth century, an important turning point on studies on the Academic school and on Cicero's philosophy. The *Academica* are, in fact, not only an irreplaceable source for the knowledge of the philosophical tradition of the first century BCE: they constitute the main reference text for the reconstruction of the theoretical debate about the powers, limits and claims of reason: in practice, they concern gnosiology and epistemology. These are some of the issues that interest Cicero and it is in reference to them that he elaborates his own method of work. Cicero develops a personal strategy in arguing and in gradually making his personal interpretative line: beyond the purely linguistic/stylistic aspects, he shows to prefer direct reference to the ancient thinkers who preceded him. In this way, however, he seemed to transform himself into a real doxographer, and for this reason he was often not considered to be an original thinker, but rather a scholar who, superficially and at times clumsily, re-proposed the thoughts of others. Today no one doubts the usefulness of Cicero's work (and the *Academica* in particular) as a means to learn about the cultural background and the tradition of the Hellenistic schools; moreover, the thesis that he gained his own autonomy in theoretical reflection is also confirmed: therefore, we must look at him as a thinker, though in some aspects certainly "unsystematic", nevertheless capable of validly and acutely addressing and arguing on the issues of epistemology, method and ethics.

Cicero is not satisfied with facing reality, while remaining anchored to habit and 'common sense'; he has a plan and, based on it, he prefers to take a position or, better, to compare the different theses, so that everyone (and himself) can feel more secure with respect to the choices he makes and the strategies he adopts. It is not surprising that, in the *Academica*, he acts as a supporter of the New Academy. The Academic school went back, in theory, to Plato's teaching. The so-called Second Academy had its founder in Arcesilaus (around 315–240 BCE). It was characterized by the reference to the Platonic/Socratic practice of interrogation and examination through the discussion of what is in favour and what is contrary. By opposing Zeno of Citium, Arcesilaus confirmed – according to Cicero – that it is not possible to know anything, that it is not possible to perceive anything and that even what Socrates had granted (namely "knowing not to know": *ut nihil scire se sciret*) was not reliable (*Varr.* 45).[3] We can never assure someone about

---

3 The rise of Stoicism, assumed as a positive development of Socratic philosophy, has probably led Arcesilaus to highlight Socrates' critical or Sceptical elements; see Thorsrud 2009, 56–58.

the validity of somethings, nor can we affirm or approve it. We must curb our innate tension to accept as true some things that are actually unknowable or false. And there is nothing more shameful than, with your consent (*assensionem approbationemque*), going beyond (*praecurrere*) what you have just perceived (*perceptioni*) or would like to know (*cognitioni*). At this point Cicero clearly summarizes what Arcesilaus did in practice:

> His practice was consistent with this theory – he, arguing against the opinions of all men, diverted most of his listeners from their opinion, so that when equally weighty reasons were found on opposite sides on the same topic, it was easier to withhold assent from either side.[4]

Note that this is also what Cicero finds particularly suitable for his rhetorical vocation, for his method of approaching reality. To withhold assent (*sustinere assensionem*) corresponds to the ἐποχή and this is what opens the door to Scepticism; but it is also what allows Cicero to find an authoritative foundation for his dialectical strategy and to free himself from the Stoic (and also the Aristotelian) approach to reality.

Carneades of Cyrene (around 214–129 BCE) was the founder of the so-called Third Academy (according to Sextus Empiricus); he continued to develop a sceptical/probabilistic approach to the world. Precisely the concept of πιθανότης, which Cicero translated with *probabilitas*, became the means to question the Stoic doctrine of the *kataleptic representation* (the καταληπτικὴ φαντασία, that is, the 'comprehensive representation' of all possible physical aspects). Since Carneades deliberately left nothing in writing, his doctrine – collected by his pupil Clithomacus in an unfortunately lost work – is difficult for us to reconstruct. As for the concept of πιθανώτης, see S. Obdrzalek, 'Living in Doubt: Carneades' *Pithanon* Reconsidered' (2006), 243–279. Certainly, through it Carneades intended, on the one hand, to demolish the Stoics' ἀπραξία charge, while, on the other hand, peacefully coexisting with the Academics' commitment to ἐποχή (withholding assent). Cicero had great respect for Carneades, as shown by the role he lets him play in *On Fate*, a dialogue dedicated to determinism and to the problem of man's will to decide. Carneades' Academy was followed by the Academy of Philo of Larissa and finally by that of Antiochus of Ascalon. Whereas Sextus Empiricus[5] distinguished these five 'phases' of the Academy, Cicero, instead,

---

4 *Varr.* 45.
5 Sext. Emp., *PH* 1.220, writes: "There have been three Academies, as most scholars say: the first and oldest was Plato's; the second, or middle, was that of Arcesilaus, hearer of Polemon; the third, and new, was that of Carneades and Clitomachus. Some add a fourth, that of Philo and Carmis, and others count a fifth, that of Antiochus". Partially different is the reconstruction of

distinguished only the Ancient Academy (of Plato and Arcesilaus) from the New Academy (of Carneades). Sextus Empiricus' narrative is probably more reliable; Ch. Brittain, in his monograph dedicated to *Philo of Larissa* (2001), 173–191, claims that Cicero has interpreted the events of the Academy in an artificial way, in order to confirm the unity of the school.

The exciting events relating to the confrontation between Philo and Antiochus (in which he felt personally involved) were, according to Cicero, nothing more than an internal development in Carneades' *change of course*. It is precisely of those ones that he informs us, and with respect to those ones he strengthens his position. Carlos Lévy believes that, in the presentation of the conflict between his two teachers, Cicero tries to show himself as 'neutral'. Indeed, by asking himself about the problems and motivations inherent in this *dissensus*, Cicero would have tried to formulate his own solution proposal. According to Lévy, this constitutes the starting point of a systematic philosophical research by Cicero. It is no coincidence that attention is paid to *Sosus* (which has not come down to us), a pamphlet with which Antiochus, in 87, distanced himself clearly and in a detailed manner from Philo: in particular from the so-called two Roman books, which contained the lectures that Philo had pronounced after his arrival in Rome. What was the reason for this dissent?

Cicero assures us that, for his part, Antiochus was very perplexed by the thesis supported in the *Roman Books* and did not want to believe (see *Luc.* 11–12) that their content really corresponded to the thought of Philo, with whom Antiochus, instead, had been in consonance for a long time when both were in Athens. From the way Cicero presents the question, we can assume that Philo: (a) claimed to support the continuity of his thought with that of the Platonic tradition; (b) rejected the Stoic thesis that κατάληψις (*comprehensio*, 'perception') is a real φαντασία καταληπτική, i.e. an 'apprehensive impression', ultimately a true impression (and therefore an 'evidence') caused by a real object.[6]

As for point (a), it is clear that Cicero would like to read the history of the Academy and Platonic doctrine in a unified way, so that the sceptical/doubtful approach adopted by Philo would be a coherent evolution of the Socratic attitude.[7]

Diog. Laert. 1.19: "Plato was the founder of the Ancient Academy; Arcesilaus of the media Academy, Lacydes of the new Academy". Lacydes was a pupil of Arcesilaus, see Dorandi 2008, 32.

6 *Luc.* 1.18: "When he attacks and rejects this sort of impression (see the Stoic thesis), Philo rejects the criterion of the known and unknown, from which it follows that nothing can be known".

7 On this line is also the thesis of Brittain 2001. It is not clear, however, if Philo went so far as to claim that the nature of things is understandable, as Sext. Emp., *PH* 1.235, would suggest.

As for point (b), it is clear that, if the problem was posed in this way, Antiochus would have good reasons to be perplexed: how was it possible to reject both Scepticism and the Stoic definition of κατάληψις (i.e. an anti-sceptic alternative)?

Probably, in *Sosus*, Antiochus proposed his reference to the authentic orthodoxy of the Academy as the most *consistent* and secure solution; in §§ 40–60 of *Lucullus*, the ἔλεγχος is highlighted and its manifestation is determined in the following manner : (a) someone claims to have a rule of conduct that allows him to act in one way rather than another, and which allows him to research what it's true; (b) this same man maintains that we have no way of distinguishing true from false.

It is evident that, if we eliminate the instrument of knowledge (which allows us to distinguish true from false) we cannot then think that we have preserved, in this way, the possibility of knowing reality.

Through Lucullus, Antiochus, using an example, specifies:

> Just as if anybody were to say that when he has deprived a man of his eyes, he has not taken away from that man the possible object of sight.[8]

In short, following Philo's thesis, the criterion of true and false would be at risk and the attempt to introduce the criterion to rely on what is most likely would also lose any meaning:

> But the height of absurdity is your assertion that you follow probabilities if nothing hampers you. In the first place, how can you be unhampered, when there is no difference between true representations and false? [9]

On the other hand, following the thesis of Antiochus, the reference to the presumed orthodoxy could imply a strong rapprochement between Stoicism and Plato. For this reason, Cicero summed up as follows:

> He was called an Academic, but was in fact, had he made very few changes, the purest Stoic.[10]

As for the text that Cicero proposes in the *Academica*, the debate is still open and can hardly be closed. A useful focus on it can be found in DPHA s.v. *Philon*, R.

---

8 *Luc.* 33.
9 *Luc.* 59.
10 *Luc.* 132. The research path that studies the convergence of Stoicism and Platonism is now being investigated by Bonazzi 2017, 120–141.

Goulet (2012, V 412–432). T. Reinhardt is currently editing a new commented edition of the *Academica*, at Oxford University Press, which will be very helpful in this regard. J. Glucker holds that *Varr.* 15–42 and *Luc.* 13–39 derive from *Sosus*, and that *Luc.* 40–60 derives from a later work of Antiochus. He holds that, instead, *Luc.* 64–146 come from Philo's lost reply to *Sosus*,[11] and that Cicero's lost *Catulus* derives in part from *Sosus* and in part from Philo's *Roman Books*.[12] This scholar, therefore, imagines that Cicero limited himself to juxtaposing the perspectives of his two masters. On the contrary, Barnes not only believes that the text of *Sosus* is not necessarily behind Lucullus' speeches, but that there are probably more sources to it, and, indeed, Cicero's memory of his lecture in Athens.[13] Cicero could very well have proposed an interpretative path to overcome the *dissensus* which had caused a real clash between his two teachers. In this direction see now O. Cappello, *The School of Doubt* (2019), 228–260; Cappello claims that Cicero was personally committed to demythologizing the break between Antiochus and Philo. In particular Cicero would exclude the fact that this break had been sudden and clear; rather it should be interpreted as the inevitable evolution of the Academy in the transition from Athens to Alexandria and Rome: "Cicero's philosophy is inclusive of a variety of phases ... It purports to present a comprehensive and far-reaching picture of the philosophical tradition", 259–260.

According to Lévy, in Cicero we are witnessing the progressive questioning of dogmatism and, therefore, also of the dogmatism of the Academy and the Stoa: the dogmatism which, especially on the ethical level, ensured a perspective and an aim to action; in his eyes, the exercise of doubt and the acceptance of a probabilistic strategy, which makes him embrace what was for him the New Academy (that is, the one that started with Carneades), becomes increasingly interesting and constructive. This allows him to proceed in his search for truth.[14] It is, therefore, a question of opportunity, favoured by a carefully adopted method, that can produce a series of important results, especially in the field of epistemology.

---

11 We don't have Philo's reply to Antiochus. Only a text of Augustinus has come down to us, from which, moreover, it appears that Cicero had placed himself on the side of Philo and his Sceptical attitude: "But the old arms were taken up again: Philo resisted him (*scil.* Antiochus) until he died, and our Tully destroyed all that remained of him (*omnes eius reliquias Tullius noster oppressit*), unwilling that anything he had loved should in his lifetime fall or be corrupted", Aug., *Acad.* 3.41.

12 See Glucker 1978, 406–420. *Contra* Giusta 1964, I, 101–112, who denied that Cicero used the work of Antiochus. On Philo, see the work of Görler 1994, 915–937; Brittain 2001, 129–168.

13 According to Barnes 1989, 64–68, Cicero was familiar with Antiochus' thought and was capable of producing an Antiochian argument without copying it from a written text.

14 Lévy 1992, 175–180.

In his important reconstruction of the Academic tradition in Rome, in particular of the Academy of Philo, H. Tarrant, *Scepticism or Platonism? The Philosophy of the Fourth Academy* (1985), focused on the very definition of the historiographical category of Medioplatonism. The research in this direction has continued, among others, with Bonazzi (2012a), 313–333: a study dedicated to the Fifth Academy of Antiochus. In addition, we can appreciate both the reprint of most of the writings published by Tarrant (2011) on this topic, and the work of W.H.F. Altman, *The Revival of Platonism in Cicero's Late Philosophy: Platonis aemulus and the Invention of Cicero* (2016). Altman proposes the study of three steps: the foundations of Cicero's Platonic revival; the literary fruits of Cicero's Platonism; Cicero's Platonism in action.

In the collection of essays edited by Brad Inwood and Jaap Mansfeld, the contribution of R.J. Hankinson (161–216) focuses on an eminently epistemological question: the foundation of transparency of judgment. He examines Antiochus and Philo. As the author of 'comparison' Hankinson chose Galen, the doctor known to be linked to the Stoic school. Actually, according to Galen, there seem to be no big differences, on matters pertaining to epistemology, between the Stoics and the New Academy: the discrimination between true and false is reduced to impression (φαντασία) and, perhaps even more, to differences in terminology. The Academics' convincing impressions and the Stoics' cognitive impression are really close. This opinion of Galen is probably exaggerated. However, it is precisely with Antiochus that a form of syncretism is affirmed, according to which what is reasonable in doctrines of different schools also deserves to be accepted. Along this path, his anti-sceptical inclination also ends up perfectly meeting with Galen's 'methodica' address, which considers experience as a sure datum.

A key point, therefore, remains the question of 'evidence', ἐνάργεια. Yet, the real problem is the following: what lies behind 'perception'? Is there a natural reality or is it the subject who knows and how he organizes himself to know?

According to Cicero, Antiochus (and certainly also the Stoics with him) comes to the conclusion that the properly 'kataleptic impression' does involve 'internal markers' (*propria percipiendi nota*),[15] which are such as to distinguish it from any

---

15 *Luc.* 34; 36; 101. According to Sext. Emp., *Adv. Math.* 7.252, the Stoics argue that a kataleptic representation (καταληπτικὴ φαντασία) has its own peculiar characteristic (τι τοιοῦτον ἰδίωμα) which allows one to grasp what is at the bottom of things; the Academics, on the contrary, argue that it is impossible for a representation to be completely similar to the object, and, at the same time, that it is possible to find a false representation which is, however, completely similar to the kataleptic one. See Hankinson 1997, 180–183.

non-kataleptic congeners; these internal markers characterize the kataleptic impression as evident. They are the link with the natural world. If so, it is difficult not to come to the conclusion that Antiochus' epistemology is profoundly Stoic.[16]

Cicero, however, is not satisfied with what Antiochus concludes, nor with what he refers without caution to Philo's Scepticism. First of all, he would like to clarify that he does not intend to abolish the truth. In fact, just because something appears anyhow, we have the possibility to proceed to establish whether something can be considered true or false (*Luc.* 111: *probandi species est*). Secondly, he disputes Antiochus' claim that there can be no false representation of the same sort as a true representation (*Luc.* 113: *tale verum quale falsum non possit*).

Finally, Cicero declares himself in agreement with two statements:

a) "The only thing that can be perceived is what is true and of such a sort that there could not be a false one of the same sort (*id solum percipi posse quod esset verum tale quale falsum esse non posset*)";

b) "The wise man never holds an opinion (*sapientem nihil opinari*)", *Luc.* 113.

From these passages we deduce that Cicero keeps the distinction between 'representation' and 'perception' clear. With respect to the former, the problem remains of establishing a criterion of truth purely based on the mechanisms of logic and language; with respect to the last, the evidence of sensitive experience is in the foreground.

On the basis of this, we can understand that Cicero, although presenting himself as the heir of the Academic school, is actually gaining a particular position which, recently, Thorsrud (2009), 87–91, has defined as 'mitigated Scepticism'.[17] Neither does the Stoic epistemology of the Fifth Academy of Antiochus, nor does the relative demanding approach to the problem of knowledge by the Fourth Academy of Philo, nor does the suspension of judgment (ἐποχή), which Arcesilaus reached, completely satisfy Cicero.

This course of study has been recently taken up and developed in order to better grasp the implications that follow, both in terms of the reconstruction and understanding of Cicero's psychology and on that of the political perspective. This is the case with the volume by Cappello (2019). Cappello combines the analysis of the *Academica* with the investigation of the Ciceronian correspondence, and comes to read the *Academica* in a perspective that can be defined as 'holistic'. This allows him to grasp the functional aspect of the epistles with respect to the philosophical project and the political context, and to highlight a truly problematic question: is Cicero a man who, in his letters, reveals traces of his character

---

16 See Brittain 2012, 113–123.
17 On the difference between Academics and Pyrrhonists see Bonazzi 2012b, 271–298.

and, in particular, an evident form of anxiety, or is his philosophical approach – which favours doubt – that pushes him to portray himself as doubtful, in a complementary way to the attitude we find in the *Academica*?[18] According to Cappello, the Sceptical philosophy of the Academy constitutes the overcoming of the security represented by Stoic philosophy, especially in the political sphere. Carneades' Scepticism becomes, in Cicero, the tool to rethink the paradigms of Roman political and intellectual life at the moment of the impending affirmation of Caesar's power. In this direction we can see also W. Nicgorski, *Cicero's Skepticism and His Recovery of Political Philosophy* (2016), 155–243, which aims to highlight how, in Cicero, political action retains some of the instances of the Socratic/Platonic project.

3.3 Rhetoric and Philosophy

The cultural tradition of classical and medieval Latinity and the *paideia* of modern and contemporary Europe, at least as regards the linguistic-argumentative side, have an extraordinary debt to Cicero's use of the Latin language. See, for example, *Brill's Companion to the Reception of Cicero*, edited by W.H.F. Altman (2015), or the more generalist *The Cambridge Companion to Cicero*, edited by C. Steel (2013), or, finally, the most focused on this issue: *Brill's Companion to Cicero: Oratory and Rhetoric*, edited by J.M. May (2002a). The greatest importance has been paid to the precise connection Cicero advocates between rhetoric and philosophy: the acknowledgment that this was a conscious and premeditated operation constitutes one of the assets that characterize him as a philosopher and rhetorician.

At the opening of *Tusculan Disputations*, the annotation with which he complains of how few scholars and philosophers are capable of writing a philosophical text in a Latin language that is both effective and pleasant to read, can prove it; there are very few men who do not waste the *otium* they can profit from. He considers the need to transmit the contents of philosophy as fundamental (to whatever school he refers to): obviously it is important to take into account the problems related to the form of the text and the receivers of the 'message':

> It is incumbent on me to be more elaborate, because there are said to be many books in Latin now, written carelessly by men of the finest character, but not sufficiently learned.

---

18 See in particular ch. 3, 36–81. Cappello summarizes, 80: "Doubt and hesitation, so far simply evaluated as marks of vulnerability, assume strategic importance when considered in relation to the letters and the *Academica* as key to philosophical discourse".

For it can happen that a man has right ideas and yet cannot put what he thinks into words in an elegant fashion. To commit one's thoughts to writing, however, without being able to give them a proper arrangement or exposition or to attract readers by anything that can give them delight (*qui eas nec disponere nec inlustrare possit nec delectatione aliqua allicere lectorem*) is the behaviour of someone who outrageously abuses both leisure and letters (*hominis est intemperanter abutentis et otio et litteris*).[19]

Cicero appears aware of the delay that, with regard to philosophy, the Roman people have towards the Greek people; he intends to fill it and be valuable in this way to his fellow citizens. In this operation, however, he identifies what strategy should be privileged, in order to overcome the boundaries of the schools within which the various doctrines remained closed. What is needed is a new language for philosophy, to open up to a wider audience than pure scholarship. Cicero proposes himself as the most suitable person: after having gained fame as an orator and rhetorician, now is the time "to try and make accessible, with even greater zeal, the sources of philosophy (*fons philosophiae*), from which the same eloquence derives", *ibid*.

Cicero is aware of his qualities as an orator; we receive *direct* evidence of this from the impressive series of orations received, and *indirectly* from the writings on rhetorical art. Among the most interesting theoretical improvements that Cicero reached is the definition of the ideal Orator, proposed in *On the Orator* and in *Orator*:[20] first of all, the ideal Orator must be nourished by a vast culture, capable of embracing literature, history, philosophy, jurisprudence and also, as far as possible, the specific *artes*. But then he must have the ability to direct the will of the audience, he must therefore not only be competent, but master the techniques of persuasion. In this regard, wonderful is the series of analysis on Cicero's argumentative technique, inaugurated by the theoretical study on rhetoric and argumentation by Perelman–Olbrechts-Tyteca (1958), in particular the chapters dedicated to the adaptation of the orator to the audience, to the choice of data and their adjustment in view of the argumentation, the order of the speech for persuasion, the importance of the *exordium*. For a comparison with modern oratory art techniques and the audience expectations, see May (2002b), 49–70.

---

19 *Tusc.* 1.6. Smith 1995, 301–323, in one of the essays included in the important collection of Powell 1995, delves into this aspect by emphasizing that Cicero evokes not only clarity, but also polish and an attractive charm.
20 See Wisse 2002, 375–400; Narducci 2002, 427–444; Dugan 2005, 81–104; Zarecki 2014, 45–76. On the failure of the *Rector*-ideal in Cicero's post-Caesarian philosophy, see Zarecki 2014, 132–159.

To master the techniques of persuasion, the mere preparation of the schools of oratory cannot be sufficient; in fact, Cicero – in addition to the more generic erudition – relies on philosophy, on that specific type of philosophy that lends itself to highlighting the strategies and dynamics of thought and eloquent dialectics. This ideal Orator cannot be limited to the simple private dimension or, in any case, formally limited to the professional sphere; necessarily, he must open up to the political perspective. In an explicit way *otium* must become the starting point for public action, so as to translate the cultural tradition and wisdom of the *maiores* and Greeks into practice in a reasoned and motivated way.

In the third book of *On the Orator*, Cicero makes L. Licinius Crassus, one of the great lawyers of his time, the protagonist. He witnesses how important, though limited, are the technical skills, the theory of language and communication; in novice young people, they contribute to creating the illusion of power and superiority, which easily translates into impudence and cheekiness. It is necessary to look further, so that the eloquent style constitutes the noblest tool for the presentation and reflection concerning the most serious and valid arguments, not only on the juridical level, but also for the reflections they entail on the moral one. It is undoubtedly a big goal, but Crassus is confident:

> I do not, however, determine and decree on the point, as if I despaired that the subjects which we are discussing can be delivered, and treated with elegance, in Latin; for both our language and the nature of things allow the ancient and excellent science of Greece to be adapted to our customs and manners; but for this work such men of learning are required, as none of our countrymen have been in this department; but if ever such arise, they will be preferable to the Greeks themselves.[21]

The Romans can surpass the Greeks, therefore. An orator will be born in Rome who will interpret these expectations; obviously, it is clear that Cicero is, with his agreeable game, thinking of himself: Cicero himself is the ideal Orator, the one who aspires to rival in eloquence even with the Greeks themselves. Cicero gives a specimen of the perspective within which he wants to move both by building the *On the Orator* as a real Platonic dialogue and by setting it in the Tuscan villa of Crassus, in which there seems to relive the ambience of ancient Athens, and imagining, in imitation of Socrates and his friends as described in *Phaedrus*, Crassus and his interlocutors resting under a plane tree to converse placidly:

---

21 *De Or.* 3.95.

But on the next day, when the older part of the group had taken sufficient rest, and had come to have their walk, he (i.e. Cotta, a friend of Cicero's) told me that Scaevola (i.e. Cicero's old teacher in Roman Law), after taking two or three turns, said, 'Why should not we, Crassus, imitate Socrates in Plato's *Phaedrus*? For this plane-tree of yours has reminded me of it, propagating its spreading boughs to overshadow this place, not less widely than that one, whose cover Socrates sought, and which seems to me to have grown not so far from the rivulet as described in the language of Plato: and what Socrates, with the sorest of feet, used to do, that is, to throw himself on the grass, while he delivered those sentiments which philosophers say were uttered divinely, may surely, with more justice, be allowed to my feet.' Then Crassus replied, 'Nay, we will yet further consult your convenience,' and called for cushions; then they all, said Cotta, sat down on the seats that were under the plane-tree.[22]

Evoking the cultural world of Greece and introducing *exempla* from Roman history or from eminent men of the contemporary world is the typical seal of Cicero's eloquence.[23] All his treatises – presented in the form of a dialogue – show acculturated Roman men who can rise to the role of *exempla*. It is important to note that Cicero, using this strategy, aimed to 'build' an ideal world to refer to, so as to legitimize his aspiration to integrate into it: obviously, to the extent that this aristocratic/oligarchic environment found it convenient to provide that opportunity to a *novus homo*, who, after all, Cicero continued to be. In this regard, H. van der Blom, *Cicero's Role Models: the Political Strategy of a Newcomer* (2010), 293–315, faces, among other things, the problem of Cicero's self-awareness in setting himself as an example both for society – in the different roles he played – and for the young generation. As for the rhetorical figure of *novus homo*, and self-fashioning, see J. Dugan, *Making a New Man. Ciceronian Self-fashioning in the Rhetorical Works* (2005), 1–15. The key historical moment in which the Ciceronian project of eloquence, aimed at political purposes, began to translate into reality is 65/64, when Cicero competed for the consulate. *Oratio in toga candida* (of which only fragments have survived) and *Commentariolum petitionis* (written, almost in counterpoint, by his brother Quintus) belong to 64.

Cicero never failed in his strategy. In the choice of the protagonists of the various dialogues, the laborious drafting of the *Academica* testifies to Cicero's attention to the political, cultural and philosophical profile of each character.[24] We can check all the philosophical works: for example, we will grasp the paradigmatic function constituted, in *Laelius On Friendship*, by the protagonist, Gaius

---

22 *De Or.* 1.28–29. Cf. Plat., *Phaedr.* 229A–230B.
23 Apart from *Tusculan Disputations*, Cicero usually likes to build a screenplay for his dialogues in which he evokes the Platonic setting adapting it to the model of the Roman villa.
24 Cf. *supra*, pp. 24–26.

Laelius, a true model (*sapiens ... et amicitiae gloria excellens, Lael.* 5) in his relationship with Scipio Aemilianus, as that of his father with Scipio Africanus had been.[25] Or we can think of the figure of Cato the Elder, in *On Old Age*. On this occasion, Cicero not only greatly sweetens the character of the old censor (an illustrious authentic *novus homo*), transforming it into a companion of Scipio Africanus, but also idealizes him. Cicero makes Scipio the authoritative and prestigious spokesman for his personal meditation on old age and, together, the ancestor of Cato the Younger (the Uticensis), the Stoic politician whom Cicero had admired, since the time of the conspiracy of Catiline.

Of course, Cicero does not need to indicate only positive models: the opportunity of representing negative *exempla* also appears fundamental, naturally with an apotropaic intention. On the strategy adopted by Cicero and on the defamatory technique implemented against his opponents or the models to be opposed to, we can refer to A. Thurn's work, *Rufmord in der späten römischen Republik: Charakterbezogene Diffamierungsstrategien in Ciceros Reden und Briefen* (2018).[26] We have the impression that Cicero engaged in this matter with extreme skill and rhetorical strategy: it is enough here to mention the cases of Verres, Catiline and Marcus Antonius in the latest *Philippics*. The series of speeches prepared against these characters works as long as each of them is elevated to the rank of negative *exemplum* for citizens: any citizen must immediately recognize, on the basis of their intentions and actions, what honest behaviour towards Rome and its values should have been. In this direction it is very important to note that Cicero often relies on more recent examples than those historically established; what is essential, however, is the perception of closeness between the historical *exemplum* and the individual or event to which it is applied.[27] In addition, some exemplary characters refer to each other. In the case of M. Antonius, it is interesting to note how – in the *Philippics* – Cicero instructs a parallel with Hannibal to negatively characterize his exemplary role.[28] We observe this also on the occasion of

---

25 Gaius Laelius is also one of the main interlocutors in *On the Republic*. For both these texts, the critical edition is edited by Powell 2006.

26 The *Introduction* to Powell–Paterson 2004, 1–57, is a study of forensic discourse as defence; the editors collect 15 contributions on the role, meaning and modalities in Rome of the legal procedure and on a series of Ciceronian case studies.

27 Blom 2010, 103–128, who studies the nature and functions of historical *exempla* in Cicero, underlines the decisive importance of their plausibility, in view of their rhetorical and moral effectiveness.

28 *Phil.* 5.25–27, 6.4–6.

the parallel between M. Antonius and Catiline[29] and between Verres and Mithridates.[30]

Studying the way in which Cicero uses exemplary characters is not only useful for reconstructing which ideal world of values he intended to refer to and what his social-political project was;[31] it is also necessary to cast a correct light on his philosophical mission and on the ethical foundation that supports it. Cicero's eloquence is thus transformed into a real 'philosophical eloquence', where the use of language becomes an instrument of the message and of the content the message refers to. In the third book of *On the Orator*, Cicero lets us understand, through the words of Crassus, that the authentic philosopher and, similarly, the serious orator end up coinciding. It is essential to be provided with both wisdom and eloquence. The philosopher who expresses himself in a broken way is not appreciable, as it is not to be praised someone who, though provided with effective talk, shows to be devoid of ideas.[32] Obviously, then, the problem will arise of seeing to what extent the orator and the philosopher will agree on the problem of which truth to relate to: that is, to what extent the technical instrument of rhetoric can move away from the immediacy of truth, perhaps with the pretext to 'strengthen' it. Is the performance of the speaker comparable to the performance of the actor?[33] Can the *veritas* of emotions coincide with the *veritas* of philosophical tension?

This is a path still to be investigated. We can also see in the background the thesis which Cicero proposes: rather than with truth, we are dealing with likelihood, with the 'probable';[34] this means that what we are referring to must be strengthened to be accepted as persuasive. Eloquence lends itself to this. *Ethos* and *pathos* must find ways to combine in order to achieve it.

---

29 *Phil.* 2.1, 2.118, 4.15, 13.22. Cicero significantly imagines that M. Antonius loves to identify himself with Catiline: *se similem esse Catilinae gloriari solet* (*Phil.* 4.15).

30 *Verr.* 2.2.51, 2.2.159.

31 On the artificial 'construction' of reality in order to support his theoretical assumptions, see Gildenhard 2011.

32 *De Or.* 3.142–143.

33 See *De Or.* 2.194: *neque ego actor sum alienae personae, sed auctor meae?* Remer 2017, 34–62, focuses on the relationship between speaking and ethical strategy; he underlines the relationship between manipulation of emotions and morality, and the implications that derive from it on the political level.

34 While in Cicero's philosophical works *probabile* and *veri simile* are often interchangeable, in rhetorical context it seems rather reliable to translate πιθανόν as *probabile* and εἰκός as *veri simile*. See Glucker 1995, 115–133. See *infra*, pp. 139–142.

3.4 Ethics and Philosophy

What is philosophy for? Its usefulness is measured in reference to knowing and acting. In the first case, we have already seen how – strengthened, in its presentation, by an adequate linguistic and rhetorical set – it can be linked to a particular tradition of the Academic school and continue, on the track of Socratic teaching, along the process of approximation to the truth, both in the field of epistemology and in those of physics and theology. In the second case, philosophy can offer itself as the main way to face the problems of ethics and answer the questions and ἀπορίαι that dominate it; it can also be employed as a guide for man, both as a human being and as an individual belonging to a society. Also, in this second case, some scholars, especially in recent times, have attempted to make explicit the peculiar features of Cicero's ethics, trying to abandon the usual attitude that for a long time has aimed only to reveal, behind Cicero, his Greek sources.

In a passage from *On the Nature of the Gods* Cicero assures us that:

> If all philosophical precepts are relevant for life, then, I think, both in my public and my private affairs I have fulfilled the prescriptions of reason and philosophical teaching.[35]

This is an important statement, because it immediately offers the key to find out where, according to Cicero, the interrelation between theory and practice rests. The rationality of the philosophical investigation has a precise confirmation in the coherence and rationality of the precepts referred to acting, in a world where the private and public dimensions intertwine. Reydams-Schils (2016), 91–107,[36] recently stressed that the ethics Cicero refers to is not independent of the physics he refers to by relying on Greek thinkers. In particular in *On the Nature of the Gods* and *On the Ends of Good and Evil* the reconstructions that the Arpinas presents are functional to clarify the possible consequential outcomes in the ethical context, on the basis of which we must then take sides.

Leaving in the background the simple exploration of the philosophical tradition on which *On the Nature of the Gods* rests and which philology has mostly

---

35 *ND* 1.7.
36 The scholar stresses that Cicero's approach to the study of nature finds a parallel in the relationship that Pericles has with Anaxagoras and the study of physics that he has carried out. The positive enhancement of physics involves the consideration of values related to life and death, pleasure and pain and the implication (as in *On Duties*) between the community of gods and men and the concept of justice. What needs to be done is related to the way the universe is made up.

taken on, it is important to underline both the methodology implemented by Cicero and the theoretical project that he pursues. It is also crucial to emphasise the audience for whom this methodology is functional. In short: Epicurean and Stoic theology are compared. Cicero does not take sides either way and, in the first book, he leaves the Epicurean Velleius to argue for an Epicurean theology, and Gaius Cotta, an Academic Sceptic, to reply to him. Then, in the second book, Quintus Lucilius Balbus argues for Stoic theology. Finally, in the third book, Cicero lays out Cotta's criticism of Balbus' claims.

Cicero organizes the treatment of the two theologies in opposition to each other: compared to the Roman religious tradition and to the traditional conception of divinity, the Epicurean one presents itself as a 'weak' model of theology, in which the usual characteristics of the divinity are reduced to the essential, to the point that the Epicurean god seems represented as non-existent. Epicurus, despite having written a book on 'holiness' (*De sanctitate*), seems to be making fun of believers and, rather:

> He does not really believe that gods exist, and what he said about immortal gods, he said for the sake of deprecating popular odium.[37]

Cicero opposes this theology with the severe Stoic model: a model in which divinity becomes all-encompassing, assuming and taking to the extreme limit the features that actually qualify mankind. Hence, Stoic theology becomes theology of nature: it becomes the place where rationality is translated, where celestial and terrestrial realities are admired and the providential character of the divine is manifested:

> I therefore declare that the world and all its parts were set in order at the beginning and have been governed for all time by divine providence (*et initio constitutas esse et omni tempore administrari*).[38]

In both theologies the contrast between divinity and world is treated in opposite ways: in Epicureanism everything is reduced to atoms (so the supernatural is excluded); in Stoicism, everything is reduced to nature (so, even in this case, the supernatural is excluded).

On this path Cicero takes full advantage of his strategy of arguing for opposing parties (*in utramque partem disserere*) and concludes by 'suspending' judgment, even if he suggests some predilection for the Stoic perspective as presented

---

[37] *ND* 1.123. On Epicurean theology revisited by Cicero, see Maso 2015, 81–101.
[38] *ND* 2.75.

by Balbo. When the fictitious interlocutors of *On the Nature of the Gods* leave, Cicero concludes:

> We parted, Velleius thinking Cotta's discourse to be the truer (*verior*), while I felt that Balbus' approximated more nearly to a semblance of the truth (*ad veritatis similitudinem videretur esse propensior*).[39]

The starting point for the study of Cicero's theology can only be the detailed commentary in the critical edition of A.S. Pease (1955). In this work the attention is first of all devoted to analytically grasp the structure and language of the Ciceronian text and to verify his strategy in the use of sources, in particular Epicurean and Stoic ones and, above all, Posidonius. More generally, however, Pease supports his research with a formidable collection of critical annotations to Cicero's text that allow contemporary scholars to gain a complete overview against which to decide their own interpretation.

Taking advantage of new materials from the Herculaneum papyri, Holger Essler[40] was recently able to compare the Epicurean Philodemus of Gadara's *De pietate*[41] with the work of Cicero, obtaining fruitful results in reference to the use of sources from the Epicurean school and to the method of Ciceronian work.

Previously, however, M. van den Bruwaene, *La théologie de Cicéron* (1937), had tried to grasp the philosophical thought of Cicero himself, which somehow emerged in the theological works. Today it seems increasingly necessary to connect *On the Nature of the Gods* at least to the first book of *Tusculan Disputations*, where the problem of soul survival and its divine character is addressed; then to the second book, in which Cicero addresses the problem of existence, of nature, of the organization of the world and of providence. Along this path it will then be necessary to focus attention on the research carried out by Cicero in *On Fate* and, therefore, in *On Divination*. It is precisely on these topics that, more recently, scholars have focused: in both these two works by Cicero, scholars have tried to see not only the physical and logical problem together (on which see below in § 4.3), but also the ethical implications.

In principle we note that Cicero is facing a dead-end street. The theoretical research concerning the problem of causality (αἰτία) and the principle (ἀρχή) seems to bring him closer to the proposal of Stoicism than to that of the Academy or the Peripatos (obviously according to what appears to be the Ciceronian

---

39 *ND* 3.95.
40 Essler 2011, 129–151.
41 For the text of Philodemus, see the 1996 Obbink edition, together with what has been collected by H. Diels in *Doxographi Graeci*.

knowledge of these doctrines, on which cf. *infra* § 4.1). However, the simplistic way in which the mechanism of the cause/effect relationship is placed and addressed, especially by the ancient Stoa, implies an inevitable series of consequences with respect to the logical and temporal dimension. If we find that a certain event B is the effect of a previous cause A and if we find that always, in the cosmos, it is possible to recognize the causes of the events for which we deduce a physical and logical order from them, then we will have to recognize that this order is pervasive to the point of being valid not only for the past (and being recognizable *a posteriori*), but also for the future. Hence the problem of fate, of foresight and of providence.

This opens up the important problem that currently involves research concerning the foundations of determinism in Cicero and the inevitable consequences on his conception of human action and, more generally, of ethics. In which terms can Cicero accept to reconcile determinism with the decision-making autonomy of what is today the so-called 'subject'? Does it make sense, in this perspective, to introduce modern concepts of will and responsibility into action?

Is the reference to man's *virtus* inserted in a certain historical, social and political context sufficient?

With respect to this last question, one of the main reference works is *On the Ends of Good and Evil*. In this work Cicero – in a completely different way from modern philosophical treatises – does not deduce ethics from physical and theoretical investigation or from the questions that refer to determinism: in particular he will deal with this aspect in *On Divination* and *On Fate*. In *On the Ends of Good and Evil* (as well as in *Tusculan Disputations*) he questions himself directly about the possible ways of leading his life. He wonders what is the greatest good (*summum bonum*) for man and how the rules of behaviour can be determined: how man can experience an 'art of life' and apply it in an effective *paideia*.[42] Cicero asks the same question that Aristotle had asked himself about the virtuous life and the happy life; however, he responds in a different way, referring to social customs and reviewing the doctrines proposed in this regard by the various philosophical schools (cf. *supra* at § 2.2).

The investigation of nineteenth-twentieth-century scholars has especially focused on the different protagonists and their different proposals (Epicurean, Stoic, Academic/Peripatetic), aiming to read the Ciceronian work in an instrumental way, almost always for the purposes of the *Quellenforschung*. While Nicolaus Madvig in 1839 was the pioneer and theorist of this line of research, Rudolf

---

42 See Gildenhard 2007, 207–275. Here the scholar examines the techniques used by Cicero in his attempt of implementing the project to educate the Roman élite.

Hirzel was the most systematic interpreter of it in the nineteenth century, creating the impressive and still valid series of *Untersuchungen* concerning the philosophical writings of Cicero in 1871, 1872, 1883. On the limits of the *Quellenforschung* referred to Cicero, we can see the paper of P. Boyancé, 'Les Mèthodes de l'histoire litteraire. Cicéron et son oeuvre philosophique' (1936b), 288–309. Clearly, the attempt to find the sources of Cicero's work in the Hellenistic philosophical literature, which had been completely lost, is unrealistic. The various hypotheses cannot be definitively controlled and remain only conjectural. The outcome is a progressive departure from the sources received, and an exponential and vacuous increase in secondary literature.

Nevertheless, for a long time in the twentieth century this type of research was pursued. In some cases, excess was reached. I propose an exemplary case, testifying to the way in which Cicero's works have been used. In 1934, starting from the certain hypothesis that the Stoic Panaetius[43] was behind the Ciceronian *On Duties*, the great philologist Max Pohlenz attempted to reconstruct the contents of the books of the περὶ τοῦ καθήκοντος, proposing, en passant, also the retroversion from Latin to Greek of Panaetius. To do this he used a quote from *On Duties* and a quote from Aulus Gellius.[44]

Still referring to Cicero's ethical work, an important but problematic outcome was the research completed by Michelangelo Giusta, with his two volumes dedicated to ethical doxographers (1964/1967). This scholar focused on an original theory[45] according to which, upstream of Cicero, there would be a single source for moral philosophy: the collection created by Arius Didymus, a doxographer probably of Stoic training, but open to the teaching of *Academia*,[46] who had lived in the 1st century BCE.

Cicero himself invites this type of operation (i.e. *Quellenforschung*), when, with regard to his writings, he specifies to his friend Atticus that:

> These are copies: they don't require much effort; I only put the words, which I have in abundance (ἀπόγραφα sunt, minore labore fiunt; verba tantum adfero, quibus abundo).[47]

---

43 Cicero himself assures it in a letter: "In two books I concentrated the discussion on the 'convenient' (i.e. *de officiis* = περὶ τοῦ καθήκοντος), which Panaetius deals with", *Att.* 16.11.4.
44 See Cic., *Off.* 1.80–81; Gell., *N.A.* 13.28. See Pohlenz 1934, §§ 61–92, 40–55; in particular 50 n. 1.
45 On the limits, but also on the importance of Giusta's work, see Lévy 2012a, 1–12.
46 Giusta 1964, I, 189–205, believes Arius Didymus to be the author of the so-called *Vetusta Placita*. On the texts attributable to Arius Didymus transmitted by Iohannes Stobaeus cf. Fortenbaugh 2018.
47 *Att.* 12.52.3.

However, in *On the Ends of Good and Evil*, Cicero is keen to clarify:

> For our part we do not fill the office of a mere translator (*nos non interpretum fungimur munere*), but, while preserving the doctrines of our chosen authorities, add thereto our own criticism and our arrangement (*eisque nostrum iudicium et nostrum scribendi ordinem adiungimus*).[48]

In any case, today the question of Ciceronian ethics must certainly be addressed again. On the one hand, we must take into account the historical context in which the Arpinas lived and his family history, the reference to the traditional values constituting the *mos maiorum*, the meaning and importance that natural law assumes, and the political importance that ethics acquires. On the other hand, it is not possible to overlook the implications in the practical development of civil life: in particular, the sense of duty appears to be central, as it is theorized – always in comparison with the Greek tradition – in *On Duties*.

While in *On the Ends of Good and Evil* the focus is on *telos*, in *On Duties* there dominates the comparison (A) between the *officium* (what must be done: duty), and the *honestum* (what it is nice to do); (B) between the 'profit', common to all people, and the 'maximum profit', that is obtained by serving civil society. Although Cicero has tried to address the various issues by trying to keep the theoretical aspects separate from the operational ones, it is nevertheless evident that he leaves great room to verify, in practice, what are the best operations to give meaning to active life.

There are not many general studies on this issue, above all because most scholars have once again read Cicero's work as the most clever and effective way to reconstruct the ethical doctrine of Stoicism and the Academy.[49] Recently, however, J. Annas and G. Betegh have published a collection of essays, focusing on *On the Ends of Good and Evil*, which opens new avenues for exploring the ethical theories presented there: *Cicero's De finibus. Philosophical Approaches* (2016). Among the essays included in the Powell (1995) collection, the study by M.R. Wright (171–195) deals with the theme of the relationship between subject, family and society, by an analysis concerning the need for self-preservation of oneself and also of life. Crucial is the third book of *On the Ends of Good and Evil* where the reference to the Stoic theme of οἰκείωσις is evident.[50] This is a delicate ques-

---

48 *Fin.* 1.6.
49 See for example Brennan 2005, 119–230.
50 The secondary literature on οἰκείωσις is today very thorough. After Pembroke 1971, see Striker 1983, Lee 2002, Bees 2004. See *infra*, pp. 133–134.

tion, because it is not clear if Cicero is exposing the Stoic doctrine or if he is following the interpretation that Antiochus has given of it.[51] In opposition to what Cato affirms (the interlocutor who illustrates Stoic ethics in the dialogue), Cicero maintains that only a formal difference exists between Stoic and Peripatetic ethics.[52] Indeed, Stoicism would have no reason to exist as an independent philosophy from the Peripatetic one. Therefore, the theme of οἰκείωσις should also be traced back to the Peripatetic school. In this regard, however, Pohlenz (1940), 1–47, argued that, contrary to what M. Pupius Piso (the orator and Peripatetic philosopher, one of the interlocutors of the Ciceronian dialogue) affirms in the fifth book of *On the Ends of Good and Evil*, the notion of οἰκείωσις was not present, neither in the ancient Academy nor in the Peripatos, so we would be faced with an artificial reconstruction due to Cicero.[53]

More generally, the question remains as to what the conclusions of *On the Ends of Good and Evil* are or whether it can be considered as an aporetic dialogue. Lévy[54] points out the limits of the Ciceronian dialogue, generally inspired by Hellenistic naturalism, but indicates, as a decisive point, the position sustained in *Tusculan Disputations*, in which the reference to Plato allows to overcome the ἀπορίαι found in *On the Ends of Good and Evil*.

Stokes' study (1995), 145–170, focuses on another of the central topics for Hellenistic ethics: the question of pleasure.[55] Crucial is the question concerning the Ciceronian interpretation of the Epicurean texts. In particular, according to the scholar, it is clear that Cicero was a great deal less casual and less radically against Epicurus than many other ancient sources.[56] Among the key points on

---

51 Gill 2016 explores the question of the distinctive features of the two οἰκείωσις presentations offered in 3.16–22 and 62–68 on the one hand, and in 5.24–74 on the other. The scholar thinks that both Stoic and Antiochean accounts of the social sides of the development have certain elements in common: but Cicero's assessment of the two presentations aims to offer the opportunity for dialectical comparison between the different positions.
52 On this topic, Ioppolo 2016, 167–175.
53 *Contra* Dirlmeier 1937 and, recently, Georgia Tsouni (see Gill 2016, 227–229).
54 DPHA 2003, supplément, 670.
55 In the Annas–Betegh collection see now Warren 2016, 41–76.
56 See now Maso 2015, 147–214. Cicero is an excellent authority on Epicurus's proposed philosophy. In addition to the certified knowledge of the *Kyriai doxai*, it is possible to find in Cicero evidence of the use of *tetrapharmakon* as the interpretative scheme of Epicurean ethics. Warren 2016, 71–76, thinks that, according to Cicero, the Epicurean attempt "to combine the ideas that pleasure is the good and that painlessness is the ideal state", is simply impossible. Therefore, any interpretation, which tries to make coherent sense of Epicurus' hedonism, will collapse into one or other side of Cicerionian dilemma on pleasure presented in the first book of *On the Ends of Good and Evil*.

which modern comments focus on the centrality of Cicero's testimony is the distinction between *katastēmatic* and *kinetic* pleasures. In this regard, Lucretius sometimes appears less effective and useful than Cicero.[57] However, it remains clear that Cicero – in the field of ethics – exaggerated in an important point: in his criticizing Epicurus as a supporter of unbridled sensuality. Certainly, this criticism does not invalidate the whole series of reliable Epicurean testimonies that he transmits to us.

Beyond all this we must ask ourselves: how did Cicero conceive of his 'activity' as a citizen and intellectual in the years of his 'withdrawal' from public life? How did he shape the organization of his day and what kind of *bios* did he draw inspiration from?

In this regard, the curvature he gradually gave to his interpretation of *otium* appears instructive. It was this, as is well known, one of the traits characterizing the ethical proposal of Epicureanism: the withdrawal from public activity and the fall back on the private dimension of study and social relationships. But, from a premise for the achievement of 'pleasure', Cicero rather transforms the *otium* into the instrument and the opportunity to find himself and reorganize his own philosophical and political thought. It was necessary to elaborate an interpretation of *otium* that was not in contradiction with *honestas* and *dignitas*: that is, with the reference values which he had always supported. An *otium* not in contradiction with what constitutes, first of all etymologically, its negation: the *negotium* (*nec-otium*), i.e. public 'activity', business. Cicero already in a letter to Atticus (dated December 61) had shown himself able to grasp the positive aspects of *otium*, and thus confessed to his friend:

> What may be called ambition has led me to seek political advancement (*me ambitio quaedam ad honorum studium*), while another and entirely justifiable way of thinking (*alia minime reprehendenda ratio*) has led you to an honourable *otium*.[58]

Cicero was most likely trying to focus on a new conception of civil commitment from which a choice between the 'contemplative' life (the Aristotelian βίος θεωρητικός) and the life dedicated to political activity (βίος πολιτικός) did not neces-

---

57 See the case of the mechanism of taste in the experience of pleasure, in Lucr. 4.622–632. The presentation of the kinetic pleasure and the concept of *varietas* in Cic., *Fin.* 2.10 is here much clearer and more reliable.

58 *Att.* 1.17.5. On the progressive reworking of the *otium* from the civil to the philosophical dimension, see Lintott 2008, 215–252; Maso 2009, 85–94.

sarily derive: a project that provided for the alternation between public and private not in an occasional or idealized form (as at the time of *De re publica*),[59] but balanced and definitive. In this regard, some scholars have spoken of βίος σύνθετος:[60] an ideal of life that would allow the 'virtuous man' – and therefore 'honesty' itself – to manifest itself in reference to philosophical truth (i.e. in 'aiming for the truth', *prospicentia veri*) and to the public good (i.e. taking care of men's society, *in hominum societate tuenda*).[61] Certainly, in Scipio Aemilianus, one of the fathers of the homeland, Cicero believed he found the model for this life project, the valid example to be proposed in general to the wise *vir Romanus*.

---

59 In *Rep.* 3.5, written between 54 and 51 BCE, Cicero wrote: "What could be more splendid than when the management and practice of great political affairs is combined with the study and knowledge of the related sciences?".

60 Grilli 1971, 89–118 and 201–223.

61 Concerning this βίος σύνθετος (the genre of life 'synthesis' of the other two) there is a precise trace in *Off.* 1.15–19. Augustinus, *Civ.* 19.3, confirms the Academic ancestry of this project. See Maso 2015, 211–214.

4 Problems in Cicero's Philosophy

4.1 Foundations: Is it an unsolvable question?

Cicero professes his ideal affiliation to the Academic school and informs us that he first followed the teaching of Philo (known in Rome in 88) and then of Antiochus (whose pupil he had been in Athens in 79). However, Cicero, as we know, was also a young pupil, in Rome, of Phaedrus (Epicurean) and then of Diodotus, who brought him closer to the contents of the Stoic school. There is no doubt that he had an extremely varied, stimulating and complex education. Also, it is evident that his Sceptical attitude depends not only on the difficulty of reaching a certain and definitive knowledge of reality, but that it also concerns the efficiency of a criterion of truth with respect to the content of knowledge. Perhaps for this reason we observe that a particular form of eclecticism has been attributed to Cicero: thanks to it, he was able to move in an unorthodox way between the various schools and doctrines. From all this, however, there arises a difficulty that contemporary scholars have faced, but have not been able to solve in a shared way; a difficulty, moreover, independent of Cicero's will and his approach to philosophy: much of what we know about and on the philosophical schools of the II and I century BCE *only relies* on Cicero.

Consequently, two problems arise:
1. the problem of the originality of Cicero's philosophical works;
2. the problem of the reliability of the evidence we get from these works.

With respect to the first point, it is not easy to reach a definitive conclusion, because the criteria available to decide are different and not very objective. Lockwood's (2020), 46–57, reasonable proposal may be helpful. Lockwood classifies the works according to the method adopted in the use of sources: a) works drawn upon historical sources primarily to orient and provide conceptual resources to philosophers analysing complex problems; b) works in which Cicero depicts the historical opinions of the Hellenistic schools in a polemical or partisan fashion; c) works in which Cicero uses the historical views of the Hellenistic schools, philosophizing 'in the spirit' of one of the schools without being beholden to all its dogmas.

However, we must remember that on several occasions Cicero himself ensures us that he is actually an 'adapter' of the ancient text: that is, not a simple translator. Take for example *On Duties*: we know that Cicero – with this work – intends to let the Romans know about Panaetius' books on 'duty' (περὶ τοῦ καθή-κοντος). In the *Letter to Atticus*, dated 5th November 44, he says he reduced to

https://doi.org/10.1515/9783110661835-004

two books what Panaetius had developed in three books (*quatenus Panaetius, absolvi duobus. Illius tres sunt*).[1] The Latin verb 'absolvere' literally means 'to complete a task' or 'to reduce in a few words': two meanings that cannot be immediately traced back to unity. Not necessarily, in the passage in question, we must interpret as 'concentrate' / 'summarize', as translators usually do. In fact, Cicero writes in the same letter that Panaetius organized the matter into three parts: 1) on the honesty or dishonesty of an action; 2) on the usefulness or damage that follows; 3) on the criterion of discernment to choose when utility and damage are in conflict with each other. But then he specifies that Panaetius wrote nothing (*nihil scripsit*) of the third part. Therefore, we are not faced with the reduction of three books to two, but most likely Cicero only completed the available part of the work. In confirmation of this, Cicero also writes in the same letter that Panaetius' pupil, Posidonius, has undertaken the development of the third part (*Posidonius persecutus est*). Precisely for this reason Cicero first tries to get the book written by Posidonius and then asks Athenodorus Calvus (his correspondent and, like Posidonius, a pupil of Panaetius) to get him at least the summary (τὰ κεφάλαια) of that work. Finally, in a subsequent letter,[2] Cicero tells us that he has received a *compendium* (ὑπόμνημα)[3] of Posidonius' work and that he has, therefore, been able to begin composing the third book of *On Duties*. It is not clear whether Cicero could later read Posidonius' book directly: certainly, for the third book of *On Duties* he made use of only a *compendium*, which he assures us to be *bellum*, that is 'well done', 'accurate'.

At this point we could conclude in two more or less alternative ways:

a) the first two books of *On Duties* are an 'adaptation' by Cicero of Panaetius' incomplete work, made up of three books up to that point; the third book of *On Duties* is a reconstruction from a 'summary' or a *compendium*;

---

1 *Att.* 16.11.4. In *Off.* 1.6 Cicero specifies his intent: he does not propose to follow the Greek thinkers "as a translator (*non ut interpretes*), but, as we usually do, we will draw from their sources, based on our judgment and our will (*iudicio arbitrioque nostro*), how much and in any way it will seem appropriate to do so". See *Fin.* 1.6: "For our part we do not fill the office of a mere translator (*non interpretum fungimur*), but, while preserving the doctrines of our chosen authorities, add there to our own criticism and our arrangement (*nostrum iudicium et nostrum scribendi ordinem adiungimus*)".

2 *Att.* 16.14.4. This letter, from Arpinum, dates mid-November 44.

3 Not only, therefore, of Athenodorus' *kephalaia*, which he says he no longer needs, *Att.* 16.14.4.

b) the first two books are not an adaptation, but the 'reproduction' in Latin of the only books that Panaetius wrote; the third volume is written by Cicero keeping in mind the first two parts completed by Panaetius and having the notes (or the work) of Posidonius available.[4]

In either case, however, Cicero's intervention cannot be considered negligible. From a structural point of view, he followed the system conceived by Panaetius; from an operational point of view, he deliberately brought together the contributions of at least two different philosophers. With respect to interpretation, Cicero intervened in order to adapt the theses and conclusions of the Stoic philosophers to the theoretical project that he himself had in mind. Precisely for this reason he long reflects, in both letters, and then asks Atticus for an opinion on how to translate καθῆκον:

> I don't feel any doubt that what the Greeks call καθῆκον is our *officium*. Why do you doubt that it would apply perfectly well to public, as well as private, life? … It fits perfectly – or give me something better (*aut da melius*).[5]

This last ironic request suggests that Atticus was not entirely convinced of this translation, but that Cicero instead intended, on this path, to innovate.[6] Probably he wanted to transfer an ethical project, concentrated on the primarily individual dimension, to a more politically engaged landing, focused on the duty of the consuls, on the duty of the senate, on the duty of the commander (*consulum officium, senatus officium, imperatoris officium*).

Finally, as for the content of his *On Duties*, Cicero expressly declares to have followed Panaetius with particular attention, while making some corrections (*nos correctione quadam adhibita potissimum secuti sumus*).[7] He then confirms that Panaetius did not complete what he had intended, but he is convinced that he did this deliberately for a precise theoretical reason: because, according to

---

4 Pohlenz 1934, 6–7 and 85–90, believes that Cicero finally had the work of Posidonius in his hand, but that what was expected was not discussed in it. What Athenodorus Calvus possessed would have been a kind of *commentarius*, not Posidonius' published work. Athenodorus – remembered as the Stoic master of Augustus – may have used the work of another disciple of Panaetius: Hecaton of Rhodes. Hirzel 1882, II, 722–736, supposes that, on the basis of this *commentarius*, Cicero would have composed, with a certain autonomy, the third book of *On Duties*.
5 *Att.* 16.14.3.
6 Brunt 2013, 188–189, believes that 'duty' is inadequate translation for both καθῆκον and *officium*.
7 *Off.* 3.2.7.

Panaetius, "it would never happen that profit (*utilitas*) is in contrast with virtue (*cum honestate pugnare*)".[8]

Regarding this last point, which would correspond to the third part (*Att.* 16.11.4), Cicero adds another detail: even Posidonius, in some of his commentaries, would have addressed it only in passing, even though he considered it to be among the most philosophically important topics (*a Posidonio breviter esse tactum in quibusdam commentariis, praesertim cum scribat nullum esse locum in tota philosophia tam necessarium, Off.* 3.2.8).[9]

Therefore, we have confirmation that neither Panaetius nor Posidonius were direct sources for the third part of the treaty: particularly in his third book Cicero elaborates materials of various origins in a particularly free way, highlighting his ethical-political convictions. In his recent book Brunt, *Studies in Stoicism* (2013), 180–240, opposes this thesis, which, however, almost everyone today agrees. He assumes Cicero concerned himself with transmitting the views of Panaetius with historical accuracy. Anyway, the *officium* is always in evidence: a duty, however, in which the original universalism of the Stoic doctrine translates into the philosophical justification of the Roman right to dominate the 'inferior peoples'.

Complementing this, it is interesting to consider the different methodological choices adopted by the various editors regarding Ciceronian records that can be attributed to Panaetius and Posidonius. For example, with regard to Panaetius, we have on one hand the extremely strict criterion of Van Straaten (1946), who only accepted the records where the name of Panaetius was mentioned and who, from *On Duties*, selected the materials with caution (though without specifying a definite criterion). On the other, that of Alesse (1997), who draws to a greater extent and in a non-episodic way, on the Ciceronian treatise. Alesse uses Cicero to try to reconstruct Panaetius' personality, beyond the Περὶ τοῦ καθήκοντος (= *On Duties*), and his relations with other intellectuals, highlighting the controversy between the Stoa and the Academia and Panaetius' reaction to Carneades' Scepticism. In her collection, a lot of evidences from Cicero's *On Duties* are traced back to *Ethics* (*test.* 53–91), from the themes and structure of Περὶ τοῦ καθήκοντος (*test.* 92–103) to the controversy against Carneades (*test.* 104–117).

In his edition of Panaetius, Vimercati (2002) selects Ciceronian evidences in a partially different way; but above all, he considers it necessary to distinguish more clearly (among the different fragments in which Panaetius' name is present)

---

8 *Off.* 3.2.9.

9 Cicero, *Off.* 3.2.10, explains that Posidonius agreed with P. Rutilius Rufus, another Panaetius' pupil, according to whom it would have been impossible finding someone capable of completing, in a worthy way, the parts of the work left incomplete by Panaetius.

between the fragments that can be certainly attributed and the fragments of controversial or uncertain attribution. He aims to gain a more complete view of Panaetius' personality, where the aspects relating to physics and politics are also highlighted. Both Italian scholars are convinced, however, that Cicero – while treasuring the original – certainly included his own ideas and considerations.

The most recent studies aim to better define the traits of Panaetian Stoicism (Alesse 1994; Tieleman 2007), in particular his psychology (Prost 2001) and the concept of duty (Lefèvre 2001), always in reference to Cicero.

As for Posidonius, Cicero is seldom referred to, in the editions of Edelstein-Kidd (1972) and Theiler (1982). However, also in this case we are faced with two opposite tendencies: Edelstein-Kidd, like Van Straaten, are severe and cautious; Theiler is quite 'generous'.

Vimercati (2004) once again aims at mediation, but finally he proposes only a passage from the third book of *On Duties*, a passage, moreover, which is usually classified under distinct aspects by previous editors: 3.2.7–10 (= T9; T13; 41c Edelstein–Kidd = T7; 432 Theiler).[10]

As for *On Duties*, so also for *Laelius On Friendship* and for the second book of *On the Nature of the Gods* there are scholars who thought that the source was Panaetius, although in these cases Cicero's compositional autonomy appeared in such a clear way as to hinder almost all attempts to use his work as a means to reconstruct the original texts of the lost sources. F.A. Steinmetz, *Die Freundschaftslehre des Panaitios, nach einer Analyse von Cicero* (1967), remained one of the most convinced scholars in the practice of 'disassembly', the technique he applies to Cicero's *On Friendship*: in almost every passage Steinmetz believed he could distinguish Stoic from Peripatetic elements and managed to give 'editorial existence' to the work of a philosopher – Panaetius – by whom, in fact, not a single line has come down to us. According to Steinmetz, once again Περὶ τοῦ καθήκοντος, in particular the second book, would be behind the *Laelius*. Actually, behind the *Laelius* there is something more complex: on the one hand, there is Aristotle and above all the Περὶ φιλίας of Theophrastus;[11] on the other, Epicurus. Only in this complex context, which Cicero elaborates is it possible to trace, in a central position, the Stoa and therefore Panaetius. Hence the Ciceronian concept of 'friendship', its value as an expression of the natural *infinita societas generis humani* (*Lael.* 19–20) and the ethical-political aspect it assumes. In her important work, *Struttura e pensiero del 'Laelius' ciceroniano* (1970), M. Bellincioni,

---

10 As an evidence of Cicero's work of source contamination, note that Posidonius is also mentioned in the conclusion of the first book: see *Off.* 1.45.159 (= 177 Edelstein-Kidd).

11 We even owe Aulus Gellius, *N.A.* 1.3.11, the reference to Theophrastus.

enhances the original Ciceronian attempt to lower, in the Roman mentality, the philosophical concept of friendship developed in the Greek world. T.N. Habinek (1990), 165–186, underlines the political tension present in Cicero's ethical elaboration of the *amicitia* relationship, according to new values and, therefore, not in a merely patronizing and practical key.

As for *On the Nature of the Gods* – and, in particular, the second book in which Lucilius Balbus presents the Stoic doctrine, then criticized in the third book by C. Cotta –, some scholars have referred to Posidonius's Περὶ θεῶν (quoted in conclusion of the first book, *ND* 123, and then occasionally at 2.88), and to Panaetius' Περὶ προνοίας: Cicero shows he has knowledge of the latter work, since he asks for a copy of Atticus in a letter dated 8 June 45 (*Att*. 13.8), shortly before that of dedicating himself to writing the treatise. Even in this case, however, it is not possible to gain any certainty about the sources that Cicero uses.[12] However, his intention remains clear and evident – not only in *On the Nature of the Gods*, but also in the whole trilogy dedicated to divinity, prediction of the future, and destiny[13] – to bend the sources to an autonomous theoretical project. Overall, this is a project that turns out to be a serious analysis of Epicureanism and Stoicism, starting from the sources, although not common, in any case attributable to the circle of philosophers and cultured men that Cicero had attended in his life and, in particular, in his training period. However, the result of this analysis not only depends on the usual methodological and strategic Academic approach, but rests precisely on the theoretical results that Cicero attributes to the Academy: to the new Academia, whose school head had been Carneades. In confirmation of this we find, in the proem to the second book of *On Divination* (§§ 1–4), the overall plan of this trilogy, which Cicero, also from a chronological point of view, completed in a brisk manner without interruption. Thus, if in the third book of *On the Nature of the Gods* we find the Academician Cotta replying to the Stoic conception of divinity (and if in the background of it we can suppose Carneades),[14] in *On Divination* the approach is replicated, always in reference to Stoicism and the Academy. In this case Cicero's plan is even more

---

12 Here too, the *Quellenforschung* was not lacking. See the setup in Pease 1955, 36–50, comment.
13 Cicero himself considers *On the Nature of the Gods*, *On divination*, *On Fate* a trilogy built in such a way as to satisfy even the most demanding about the theological question: *erit abunde satisfactum toti huic questioni* (*Div*. 2.3). From his note we deduce then that the *On the Nature of the Gods*, in three books, has already been concluded, that he is writing the *On Divination*, and that *On Fate* is in planning.
14 Since Carneades has not left any written work, Cicero may have consulted the work of Clitomachus – a pupil of the school led by Carneades – or, more simply, that of Philo of Larissa, in his turn a pupil of Clitomachus. Cf. Brittain 2001, 207–219.

explicit: in the *first book* Quintus, Cicero's brother, defends divination; in the *second book*, Cicero himself refutes divination.

On this issue, we can see, first of all, Narducci (2009), 389–416. Recently Wynne (2019), 50–82, through a comparative analysis of *On the Nature of the Gods* and *On Divination*, has confirmed the literary unity of these two dialogues, guaranteed by the authorial prefaces, by the common theoretical tension, by the dramatic characterization, by the use of the philosophical sources. However, beyond the important convergence, with respect to *On the Nature of the Gods* (a very committed work on the theoretical level),[15] the reference to Roman religion and tradition in *On Divination* is much more documented. We observe Cicero distinguishing here between natural divination and artificial divination.[16] The first refers to direct intervention by the divinity, who reveals the future to man through dreams or through the mediation of the seer; in the second one, the *signum* is central: to decode it, we need the contribution of the interpreter, a real official art specialist who is able to decrypt the anticipatory signs of the future that can be found in the bowels of animals, in the flight of birds, or in other wonders. In particular, artificial divination found fertile ground in Rome (and previously among the Etruscans) and received strong institutional recognition.[17] Hence Cicero's attention to providing a documented and valuable discussion of the arguments for and against it.

But how does Cicero define divination?

In Div. 1.9 he writes that it is *earum rerum quae fortuitae putantur praedictio atque praesensio*. In Div. 2.13 he confirms that: *divinationem esse earum rerum praedictionem et praesensionem quae essent fortuitae*.[18]

The question of whether or not to believe in divination underlies all the work and derives from the logical and physical conception of Stoicism; according to it,

---

15 In the third book of *On the Nature of the Gods*, Cicero refers to the great masters of Stoicism and ennobles the argument with extensive and committed quotes from the Roman classics: Ennius' *Medea*, Accius' *Medea* and *Atreus*, Terentius' *Eunucus* and *Phormio*, Caecilius Statius' *Synephebi*.

16 For the distinction between *divinatio naturalis* and *divinatio artificiosa* see 1.11, 1.34, 1.72, 1.109–110, 2.16–27, 2.100.

17 For example, think of the religious-political role that the members of the College of Pontiffs or of the Collegium Augurum played. In *ND* 3.5 Cicero recalls that: "The religion of the Roman people comprises ritual, auspices (*in sacra et in auspicia*), and the third additional division consisting of all such prophetic warnings as the interpreters of the Sybil or the soothsayers have derived from portents and prodigies (*praedictionis causa ex portentis et monstris Sibyllae interpretes haruspicesve monuerunt*)".

18 The two definitions are similar. They should be understood as follows: "Divination is the foreseeing and foretelling of events considered as happening by chance".

the cause/effect relationship, in the dynamics of natural reality and human action, is inserted in the perspective of the cosmic order, i.e. of the *logos*. Consequently, just as it is possible to see the natural law in the development of the 'past', it must likewise be possible to see the same natural law in the development of the future. Therefore, it does not appear to be meaningless: on the contrary, questioning about the possibility of predicting the future, of knowing in advance what will happen or, even, what will be done, becomes crucial.

In *On Divination* the approach is not naive. In fact, the attention does not focus on the events that will happen in the future, but on those that *seem to have to happen* in the future without any motivation: by chance (*fortuita*). Consequently – as Quintus does, and Cicero correctly recognizes – it is necessary to distinguish among those who are concerned with predicting the future. On the one hand, there are experts who adopt a 'scientific' approach: they predict the future thanks to practice (*arte*), reasoning (*ratione*), experience (*usu*), conjecture (*coniectura*). On the other hand, there are the soothsayers: that is, those to whom "nothing remains but the prophecy of those fortuitous events that cannot be predicted with any practice or with any science (*quae nulla nec arte nec sapientia provideri possunt*)".[19] Clearly, behind this approach there is not simply the doctrine of Chrysippus or his successors[20] accompanied by a hasty contestation of its foundation: above all we find Carneades. Thanks to his 'probabilistic' approach he could recognize different degrees of approximation to the truth, avoiding falling into a radical form of Scepticism; consequently, he could seriously question the dogmatic approach of the Stoics and, specifically, their belief in divination, and thus open the way to the autonomy of man's decision and action. The latter topic is carefully addressed in one of the most remarkable works by Cicero as a philosopher: *On Fate*.

These are but a few examples concerning the problems that Cicero's reader and scholar faces today when approaching his philosophical works.[21] One thing, however, seems to me fairly well-established: Cicero is not a naive interpreter of the Hellenistic philosophical tradition, but a committed reader who tries to clarify some of the pre-eminent theoretical connections. Though we might never definitively solve the questions relating to the *Quellenforschung* (given the total loss of

---

19 *Div.* 2.14.

20 Scholars cite Zeno of Tarsus, Diogenes of Babylon, Antipater of Tarsus, Boethus of Sidon (cf. Timpanaro 1988, lxii–lxxiv).

21 Beard 1986, 33–46, and Timpanaro 1988, vii–ci, in their studies dedicated to the *On Divination*, confirm Cicero's commitment in terms of historical documentation; on book II, see Dyck 2020. Schofield 1986, 47–65, focuses on the use of language and exhibition strategy, making it an example of the so-called philosophical rhetoric.

the works of the Academicians), there is still room to better ascertain what we have to attribute directly to Cicero.

4.2 Natural order or free will?

As we saw,[22] *On Fate* has come to us mutilated in the first part and above all in the final part. Cicero and Hirtius, the former lieutenant of Caesar, face the problem of destiny. In this case too, as for all Ciceronian work, the problem of the sources, of Cicero's technical competence, of his theoretical, didactic and disseminating intention can be posed; we must identify with his argumentative strategy to grasp the efficacy of his use of the Latin language and understand the difficulties and linguistic choices he adopted. In this regard, questions arise with respect to the word *fatum*, which literally refers to the verb *fari* (φημί, 'say') and therefore to what has been said or decreed. By it, however, Cicero intends to translate the Greek word εἱμαρμένη: we deduce it from *On Divination* (1.125), where it was interpreted as "An orderly succession of causes wherein cause is linked to cause and each cause produces an effect out of itself".[23] On this path we see in the background the role of ἀνάγκη, i.e. the 'need' that connects everything together; but we cannot fail to perceive also what, in the mythical and religious perspective of Homer and Hesiod, is called μοῖρα or αἶσα: that is, the fate which is distributed to mortals and which, as decreed to every human being and every living being, chains them to a condition and to a role that cannot be avoided. Fate and destiny, therefore, seem synonymous. Yet, in *fatum* it would be necessary also to grasp another nuance, absent in the modern meaning of the word 'destiny': the unknown face of destiny that mortals interpret as 'randomness' and 'chance' (τύχη), which even seems to govern the moment when the Μοῖραι fix what will come true. That is, the *fatum* would refer to whatever is logically and consequentially determined, but which also retains the 'unpredictable' element lying at the basis of the same necessitating logical-causal determination called 'destiny' (from which it proceeds).

On Fate has greatly interested scholars especially for the contribution it offers on at least six issues.

---

22 See *supra*, pp. 40–42.
23 *Fatum autem id appello quod Graeci* εἱμαρμένην, *id est, ordinem seriemque causarum, cum causae causa nexa rem ex se gignat.*

1. The 'principle of bivalence' and its validity with respect to future events (it is the so-called problem of 'future contingents'). This is the recovery of what Aristotle had focused on in ch. 9 of *De interpretatione*: there he questioned the truth or falsity of the assertion "There will necessarily be a naval battle tomorrow" (or "Necessarily there will be no naval battle tomorrow"). In this regard, a reliable introduction is the research of R. Gaskin, *The Sea Battle and the Master Argument: Aristotle and Diodorus Cronus on the Metaphysics of the Future*, (1995).

2. Diodorus Cronus' 'master argument'. Through it the Megaric philosopher Diodorus addressed the problem of 'future contingents' purely logically, introducing an accurate distinction between what is necessary and what is possible.

3. The 'lazy argument'. In this sophism the usefulness / uselessness of deciding something, if everything is already fixed by destiny, arises as a theme. A first starting point is provided by the documented discussion in S. Bobzien's volume, *Determinism and Freedom in Stoic Philosophy*, (1998).

4. The Stoic doctrine of causality. §§ 41–45 of *On Fate* provide one of the main sources for its reconstruction. Obviously, we must then confront the later sources, in Greek, of Plutarch, of Alexander of Aphrodisias, and of Sextus Empiricus; and, finally, with the materials obtained from Joannes Stobaeus and Clement of Alexandria. For the most reliable interpretations it is necessary to turn first to the works of Michael Frede (1980), Anna Maria Ioppolo (1994), Robert W. Sharples (1995), and Susanne Bobzien (1999).

5. The Stoic doctrine of assent. Through the Ciceronian text we can focus on one of the most interesting proposals related to the theory of decision and action by Stoicism ever formulated; as a consequence, the question of 'compatibilism' between autonomy of decision and Stoic determinism arises. On all this, in addition to the recent collection of essays edited by Marie-Odile Goulet-Cazé (2011), the collection accomplished by Anthony A. Long (1971) and the work of Ricardo Salles (2005), expressly dedicated to the compatibilist hypothesis, deserve to be studied.

6. The Epicurean doctrine of the *Clinamen*. In §§ 18–26 and §§ 46–48 of *On Fate* Cicero attacks the Atomistic doctrine of Epicurus. It is one of the oldest testimonies in which the doctrine of the *clinamen*, intended as 'minimum deviation' (ἐλάχιστον), is offered. In addition to the more general works, such as those of David Sedley (1983), Walter G. Englert (1987) and Timothy O'Keefe (2005), it is important to clearly grasp, behind the controversial tension, the value of the Ciceronian interpretation of the *clinamen* and the way in which it should allow to

resolve the fracture between the material structure of the universe and the ethical-libertarian dimension of human action.[24] Clearly this implies a reflection on the more technical concept of 'what depends on us', as discussed by Erik Eliasson (2008) and Maso (2014a).[25]

If, in addition, we want to consider the studies that, with greater breadth, have focused on *On Fate*, in the first place, there are the commentaries: starting with the historical one, edited by Adrianus Turnebus in 1552, which, alongside the text of the main printed editions of *On Fate*, has been for centuries the most useful tool for understanding this most difficult work of Cicero's. Extracts of Turnebus's work have been reproduced in the critical edition of *On Fate* edited by Karl Bayer (1963).

Octave Hamelin's commentary, printed for the first time only in 1978 by Michel Conche, should instead be placed in the first decade of the twentieth century. Today, however, the two contributions of Robert W. Sharples (1991) and Magnus Schallenberg (2008) are fundamental: the first, which also provides the critically revised text of *On Fate*, is noted for the extreme accuracy with which it sought to address the philosophical *côté* of the Ciceronian work; the second – which presents an in-depth and reliable examination of all the most important critical and exegetical materials available today – focuses particularly successfully on the logical-philosophical aspects.[26]

Bobzien's 1998 book, dedicated to freedom and determinism in Stoic philosophy, is not a true commentary, even if organized around the structure and themes of *On Fate*. Bobzien (a) dealt with the central topics of physics, logic, epistemology and Stoic ethics, researching the premises that lie at the base of the problems that were later discussed also in *On Fate*; (b) she reconstructed the different attitudes and developments or solutions that followed within the Hellenistic and Roman philosophical tradition. In all this, the study of the notion of cause is decisive. And it is no coincidence that Bobzien takes up the same issue again in another essay the following year, with the aim of explaining the meaning of the complicated system in which Chrysippus' conception of cause is resolved.[27] The important paragraphs 41–42 of the Ciceronian *On Fate*, in which the cryptic

---

24 See in particular Asmis 1990, and Purinton 1999.

25 Eliasson's book deals with the historical evolution of the concept; my essay is focused on Cicero's *On Fate*.

26 Two critical editions with translation and commentary have recently been published: in Italian, Maso 2014b; in German, Weidemann 2019.

27 According to Bobzien 1999, 197–217, the taxonomy of causes, as presented in *On Fate*, does not belong to Chrysippus, who would have limited himself to making only a series of basic distinctions.

doctrine of the cause is addressed, are particularly delicate to analyse. According to Bobzien, the Ciceronian passages show that it is true that the *causae adiuvantes et proximae* (auxiliary and proximate) and the *causae perfectae et principales* (perfect and primary) are implicated in the cause/effect relationship; however, they are so in an alternative, non-cooperative way. Both types of cause, in this way, can be considered *causae antecedentes* (antecedent causes). For this reason, it seems arbitrary to draw the conclusion that Chrysippus theorized a complex and hierarchical structure of causality.

As a consequence of this, we must think that Cicero did not limit himself to translating expressions or texts of Stoic origin, but that he proposed an exegesis of technical terminology, adapting it to express the overall interpretation of the Chrysippean thesis which he himself was gradually focusing on. It is probably no coincidence that, more than once, a pair of Latin words is combined with a single Greek term: this is also the case with the *causa perfecta et principalis*,[28] or with the *causa adiuvans et proxima*.[29] In short, we are faced with a refinement strategy, whereby the choice of one or the other technical term reflects an increasingly explicit interpretative project.

It is important to note the coherence with which Cicero moves. He cannot accept the radical conception of Stoic determinism, nor the opposite and equally radical conception of Epicurean anti-determinism. A soft interpretation that contemplates fatalism, which perhaps can be attributed to Chrysippus, could probably work; but the latter's position does not appear sufficiently firm and indeed, according to Cicero, Chrysippus ends up flattening himself on the radical interpretation of determinism. Carneades' arguments seem more congenial to Cicero: at least, according to the way they are presented to us. In this sense we could speak of a Cicero/Carneades, who opposes Epicurus' *mechanistic* indeterminism but who, on the other hand, would never renounce his belief that *non omnia fato fiunt* (§ 31), sure that, at any rate, there is always something in our power (§ 42). These are the foundations on which a 'libertarian' concept of life may be based and from which man's autonomy descends: a man who sometimes decides which action to perform or not to perform.

----

28 The *causa perfecta et principalis*, according to the Christian theologian Clement of Alexandria, *Strom.* 8.9 [= *SVF* 2.351], could correspond to the αἴτιον συνεκτικόν (the overall cause that in itself contains everything); unfortunately, however, Clement himself also makes it correspond to αἴτιον αὐτοτελές (the completed cause, *SVF* 2.346).

29 This cause could be the correspondent of προκαταρκτικὸν αἴτιον (the previous cause, *SVF* 2.346).

However, Cicero does elaborate and propose a definitive solution to the problem of man's decision-making autonomy, an individual inserted in a structure of events that appears to have its own order. What can be considered as clear are, after all, only three essential items: (a) there is no denying the existence of apparently 'uncaused' events, whose cause is not connected to something 'external' to the event itself; (b) Chrysippus' solution (a soft form of determinism) is interesting but not sufficient; (c) a serious problem remains to be solved: how to combine logical and causal determinism with each other.

Chrysippus is reliable – according to Cicero – especially for the results achieved in defining the different types of cause. Furthermore, the defence of the 'principle of bivalence' (against the Epicureans) and the non-negation of the 'possibility' (against Diodorus) are also undeniably elements in favour of Chrysippus. On the other hand, he does not appear up to the point when it is a question of demonstrating, and not only of recognizing *a posteriori*, that the truth, in order to be truly such, must *in any case* characterize the cause/effect relationship: not only in relation to what has happened in the past, but also to what will happen in the future. In fact, Chrysippus remains bound to a rigid conception of causality, according to which motion without cause does not exist – and conversely the fate and eternal causality of future events exist – only if the 'principle of bivalence' is confirmed *in absolute terms* (to achieve which, as is known, it must always be possible to establish that a sentence is either true or false).

The ultimate consequence is that the conclusions, reached by following Chrysippus, end up not only being similar to those of the scholars who *simpliciter* deny the possibility of separating destiny from the previous and necessary causes of a given event, but also to oppose *de facto* those who admit the possibility of *causae fortuitae*, that is, of causes manifesting themselves as being freed from an immediately detectable cause/effect relationship.

Going back to Cicero's conclusions: Cicero cannot allow himself to deny the existence of the *causae fortuitae*, because this would constitute the first and most serious obstacle to the recognition of the existence of an 'internal' causality on the basis of which personal decisions can be defined as independent of fate and all *in nostra potestate*. Only by admitting that not everything can always be foreordained and predictable (and therefore a *weak* conception of destiny, not a *strong* one as that which is attributable to Carneades) does he leave room for what happens by chance and that could have happened or not happened; and already the mere admission that something can happen or not happen in turn opens the space to the thesis that the individual man can, *motu proprio*, decide to make something happen or not happen.

That this compromises a fatalistic conception of destiny, but does not, for this reason, prevent us from seeing a logical sense in the happening of historical and human events, is what Cicero would like to be able to support.

4.3 Academy and Scepticism: only a method or a serious belief?

As we saw in chapter 3.2, the Academic school was the main reference point for Cicero. We verified how well his method of research and study was in harmony with the Academic project. The choices in the stylistic and technical-exhibition field were consequently derived, and we highlighted the approach for which it becomes fundamental, according to Cicero, *in utramque partem disserere*, when we want to try to reach an acceptable level of probability in the knowledge of truth. In *Academica* he confronted both Philo and Antiochus; there has been much discussion about his philosophical stance. But now it is important to ascertain whether, in addition to being a method or a type of strategic approach in an epistemological perspective, 'Scepticism' can be considered as the philosophical doctrine in which Cicero really believes.

However, it is necessary to distinguish the *sceptical attitude* from 'Scepticism' as an autonomous school or philosophical current. As far as the latter is concerned, reference should be made to Aenesidemus, twenty years younger than Cicero. Aenesidemus resumed Pyrrho's teaching, further distancing himself from the Academy; Cicero, however, does not seem to have known Aenesidemus: therefore, some caution is needed in defining Cicero *tout court* a 'Sceptic'. Woolf (2015), 10–33, aims to define Cicero undoubtedly 'a Roman Sceptic'. If the attribute is intended in a broad sense, we can agree. However, Lévy (2017), 9–24, correctly points out what complex meaning the Academy had for Cicero, in reference to Plato and Peripatetics; Cicero considered the *disputatio in utramque partem* the meeting point between the practice of the forum, the teaching of Philo, and the work of Aristotle (according to the presentation that Antiochus had made to him). Recently Aubert-Baillot (2019), 271–282, has analysed the influence of the *disputatio in utramque partes* on Cicero's letters, at the microtextual and macrotextual level: in her opinion, this confirms, in addition to the undoubted technical-rhetorical value, Cicero's political and philosophical scepticism, especially at the time of the civil war.

In any case, according to *Luc.* 65–66, Cicero seems really to have embraced – at the time of his last writings – the Academic school. In fact, in replying to Catulus, about Lucullus' criticisms of the Academy, Cicero declares that he wants to be coherent with his ideas and confident that he can defend them. This is not a pure dialectical question:

> For if my own motive in choosing to adhere to this particular philosophy (*ad hanc potissimum philosophiam me adplicavi*) was some sort of ostentation or combativeness, I would consider that not only as a folly on my part but also that my moral character deserves condemnation.

Cicero swears he wants to come to the truth:

> I am full with zeal for the discovery of the truth (*studio veri reperiendi*), and I really hold the opinions that I am stating (*et ea sentire quae dicerem*). For how can I fail to be eager for the discovery of truth, if I rejoice whenever I discover something that resembles truth (*si simile veri quid invenerim*)?

Cicero alludes to the truth which only the wise by definition can reach (otherwise he would not be wise, as the Stoics in particular claim). He adds, however, that he knows he is not wise: therefore, he is aware of giving assent – in many cases – to what is false (something that should not happen to the Stoic wise man, but that could happen in the perspective of sceptical fallibilism). Rather:

> For my own part I am a great opinion-holder (*magnus quidem sum opinator*): for I am not a wise man (*non enim sum sapiens*).

As Görler (1997), 36–40, points out, this last statement by Cicero is surprising and, therefore, interesting. According to Arcesilaus' doctrine and Academic Scepticism, it is not possible to have reliable perceptions of reality. Cicero considers himself a great opinion-holder; therefore, from this point of view, he seems to be in tune with the dogma of the sceptical scholar, who claims the impossibility of going beyond opinions and reaching the truth: nonetheless, he defines himself as 'not wise', thus distancing himself from the teachers of the Academy. Thorsrud (2012), 138–142, analyses this point in reference to the positions firstly of Carneades and then of Clitomachus and Philo. Thorsrud believes that, despite being opposed to the Stoic thesis, Cicero does not reach a point of radical Scepticism, but falls back on a mitigated version of it.[30]

---

30 Unlike Thorsrud, Brittain 2016, 12–28, following his analysis of the Ciceronian sceptical method employed in *On the Ends of Good and Evil*, argues that Cicero is not a mitigated sceptic, but rather a radical or a Carneadean sceptic.

It is important to note how far this statement goes beyond the claims of Arcesilaus and other orthodox members of the school, and evokes the *Socratic assumption*,[31] beyond a more or less convinced approval of the *Socratic method*.[32] Cicero, namely, believes in the depth of the philosophical choice; he intends to move beyond the *destruens* side of Scepticism (anchored primarily to dialectics) and to achieve not really the dogmatism of the Stoics, but rather the *constructive* probabilistic dimension.

In this way, Cicero seems to stand in an original position, beyond what we believe today to be Carneades' philosophical stance, founded on the acceptance of the plausible or convincing impression (πιθανὴ φαντασία). Unfortunately, our only reference for the reconstruction of Carneades' position with reference to the doctrine of probable and plausible remains *Luc.* 98–100, and there is the danger of falling into a sort of 'circularity' in the investigation. As for Carneades, see Ioppolo (1986), 193–216, who considers Carneades to be a simple continuator of Arcesilaus; more recently Ioppolo (2009), 131–189, has re-evaluated his role and pointed up a particular aspect: Carneades would have placed the 'probable' (τὸ πιθανόν) as a criterion of conduct, once its inconsistency had been demonstrated as a criterion of truth. This leads Thorsrud (2010), 75–80, to consider Carneades a fallibilist, at least with regard to practical matters. Allen (1997), 223–228, believes it is important to distinguish, in Carneades, between *peirastic* (i.e. refutative) and *dialectic* approach.

In his examination of Cicero's position as an Academicus, Thorsrud emphasizes: "The problem is that Cicero's mitigated Scepticism is a significant departure from his Academic predecessors. He accepts neither the Stoic epistemology of Antiochus' Fifth Academy nor the less demanding account of knowledge that characterizes Philo's Roman books. Nor does he accept the severe view of ἐποχή (the suspension of judgment) championed by Arcesilaus and Carneades".[33]

Precisely the ἐποχή, with its radical Scepticism, on one side, and Carneades' fallibilism on the other, seems to constitute what Cicero the philosopher intends

---

31 Nicgorski 2016, 59–96, defines Cicero's approach to philosophical research as 'Socratic Scepticism', combining the seeking of truth with the task of guiding and comforting in the conduct of life.

32 Although Cicero repeatedly declares that he is an heir of the Socratic method, in fact on several occasions he considers it inadequate to guarantee philosophically solid results. See Gorman 2005, 179–191.

33 Thorsrud 2009, 88. For a comparison between Arcesilaus and Carneades, see Lévy 1992, 14–46; Thorsrud 2010, 58–80. Recently Cappello 2019, 167–176, analysed in detail how the arguments of Arcesilaus and Carneades are segmented and presented in the final section of *Lucullus*: the status of probable and its interpretation in anti-stoic function appears fundamental.

to move away from. In this perspective, Cicero's first step is certainly significant, when he shows himself in agreement with Carneades and defends the thesis that the fact that everything is probable (*probabile*) does not imply that everything is uncertain (*incertum*):

> He (*i.e.* the wise man) is not afraid lest he may appear to throw everything into confusion and make everything uncertain (*non metuit ne confundere omnia videatur et incerta reddere*). For if a question be put to him about duty (*de officio*) or about a number of other matters in which practice has made him an expert (*in quibus versatus exercitatusque sit*), he would not replay in the same way as he would if questioned as to whether the number of the stars is even or odd, and say that he did not know; for in things uncertain there is nothing probable (*in incertis enim nihil est probabile*), but in things where there is probability the wise man will not be at a loss to know either what to do or what to answer (*non deerit sapienti nec quid faciat nec quid respondeat*).[34]

The distinction between what is *uncertain* and what is *probable* allows Cicero to propose the problem of truth in updated terms; Cicero does not intend to abolish it and therefore does not intend, conversely, to abolish even falsehood. Indeed:

> We observe some things that are true just as we observe some that are false. But there is 'appearance' as a basis of approval (*probandi species est*), whereas we have no mark as a basis of perception (*percipiendi nullum signum*).[35]

Cicero is aware that in this way the distinction between true and false is no longer located in the thing as perceived, but in the judgment expressed on it; this certainly brings him closer to Peripatetics (*Luc.* 111–112). For this reason, Cicero takes a second step: what leads him to overcome the separation between theory and practice, and to go beyond the ἀπραξία, of which Arcesilaus was accused, as he preached the ἐποχὴ περὶ πάντων, i.e. the suspension of judgment in any case.[36] For Cicero will not limit his reflection to the theoretical level, but will see the implications in the field of active life, as will emerge in *On the Ends of Good and Evil* and in *Tusculan Disputations*.[37]

In *Luc.* 129, meanwhile, Cicero directs the search for a criterion of truth in the direction of ethics and asks:

---

34 *Luc.* 110.
35 *Luc.* 111.
36 See Ioppolo 2009, 202–208.
37 See Brittain 2012, 123–130, who rightly, in this regard, evokes the presence of Antiochus.

> In the matter of good and evil what certain knowledge have we got? Clearly the task is to determine the Ends which are the standards of both the supreme good and the supreme evil (*fines ... bonorum et malorum summa referatur*).

From these short notes it seems clear that Cicero clearly confirmed his philosophical stance; above all, he seems not to have limited himself to following the doctrines of the Academy, but he has *both* interpreted some theoretical proposals in an original way, showing particular attention to assessing their practicability,[38] *and* recognized the limits where we constrain ourselves to exploiting only their rhetorical-dialectical potential.[39] However, it seems interesting to ask why Cicero, the *novus homo* who rose to the highest levels of social visibility and political success, did not find advantageous to valorise the theoretical result he had reached; he minimized its importance by modestly limiting himself to remarking only his own contribution as an accurate interpreter of the Academic philosophy.

Certainly, the particular historical moment and the psychological condition of Cicero in the years of forced retreat from politics influenced his attitude and choices; perhaps we can agree with Harald Thorsrud that Cicero "was confronting the problem of convincing the ruling class of the value of romanizing Greek philosophy", but that, for reasons of political opportunity, "it would have been particularly unsuitable for a statesman of Cicero's standing to put himself forward as an innovator".[40] But maybe, more modestly, Cicero considered himself more a politician and a jurist than a philosopher; so he never felt the urgency of identifying and officially qualifying himself within a school, nor of showing himself as the protagonist of the process of renewal of a doctrine: a school, the Academy, whose affairs, however, officially ended with the death of Philo, the head of the School (84/83), and which actually died out with the death of Antiochus, the 'renovator' (68).[41] This happened at least twenty years before Cicero concentrated on writing his philosophical works.

---

38 In this sense, we must interpret the convinced combination between εὔλογον (what is reasonable) and πιθανόν (what is persuasive because it is likely) that Cicero makes when, to translate the second, he uses both *veri simile* and *probabile*. See Lévy 1992, 276–290.

39 A few years later, in *Leg.* 1.39, Cicero denounces the limits of the Academic school, at least in the legal field: "And let us also pray that this new Academia of Arcesilaus and Carneades, disturbing all these matters, be silent (*exoremus ut sileat*); because if they broke into these matters, which seem to us to have been wisely prepared and ordered by us, it would lead to a great ruin (*nimias edet ruinas*)".

40 Thorsrud 2009, 89.

41 Since Antiochus of Ascalon founded his own school (which scholars today call Fifth Academy), Philo of Larissa is to be considered the last head of the *official* Academy. See Dorandi 2008, in *CHHP* 31–35.

4.4 Stoicism and Epicureanism: does Cicero grasp and dissent?

Stoicism and Epicureanism constitute the two great schools with which Cicero engages to better define the reasons for his propensity for the Academic school, that is, the characteristics of his philosophical stance. As already noted, Cicero has long been considered not only a 'ferryman' of Greek philosophical doctrines, but also a 'simplifier' who was not always able acutely to understand the tenets of philosophical thought. Today, as we are seeing, we are moving in the opposite direction: Cicero was not only able to document himself directly and to study with competence the doctrines supported in the various Hellenistic schools, but also capable of orienting himself independently, supporting or criticizing some tenets or doctrinal aspects. Today we consider him capable of expressing his own interpretative line and reaching his own autonomy of judgment.

We can see this mostly in reference to (A) Stoicism and (B) Epicureanism.

(A) Let's take a look at the *Paradoxa Stoicorum*: first of all, Cicero presents two concepts, which, placed side by side, are particularly difficult to reconcile:

1. "Only what is honourable is good", *quod honestum sit id solum bonum esse*;
2. "Virtuous is someone who lacks nothing to live happily", *in quo virtus sit, ei nihil desse ad beate vivendum.*[42]

In the first paradox the Stoics use the word καλόν for indicating virtue:[43] they believe that only what is fine or morally good is good at all, and since it is the highest good, it corresponds to virtue. In the second paradox the Stoics believe that virtue is enough for happiness, under all possible circumstances. If ἀγαθόν corresponds to καλόν, εὐδαιμονία corresponds to ἀρετή. Virtue (i.e. moral good) is given a unique and absolute value; consequently, all that is not moral good or, on the contrary, moral evil is removed from every value. The existence of an intermediate territory between virtue and vice is therefore denied; there are no gradations. What is neither good nor bad is indifferent. So, all good deeds are equal to one another, just as all evil deeds are equal to one another.

---

42 As for the first paradox, ὅτι μόνον τὸ καλὸν ἀγαθόν, see 3.31–32; about it: Bett 2010b, 139–152. As for the second one, see 1.187; 3.49–67; about it: Annas 1993, 162–166, 388–411; Vogt 2017, 183–199. Galli 2019, 67–162, presents a useful linguistic commentary.

43 Here is the Greek text of the two paradoxes: 1) ὅτι μόνον τὸ καλὸν ἀγαθόν; 2) ὅτι αὐτάρκης ἡ ἀρετὴ πρὸς εὐδαιμονίαν. Cicero slightly arranges the Latin translation of the second one; literally Greek means: "That virtue is sufficient for happiness". On other occasions he is more adherent to the original: e.g. *Deiot.* 37; *Div.* 2.2; *Fin.* 1.18; *Tusc.* 2.29.

Yet, without denying this thesis, the Stoics also argue that what is neither good nor bad – and therefore is indifferent – can have its intrinsic value, positive or negative: practically, the area of non-virtue, which in itself should coincide with vice, can lead to behaviour that can also be morally appreciable. Reading this from an evolutionary perspective, we will see that it is a prelude to the gradual transition from foolishness to wisdom. We are thus faced with a dual doctrine of the highest good, and therefore with a form of serious inconsistency in Stoic ethics, unless we proceed to distinguish between an 'ideal doctrine' to which the *sapiens* belongs and a 'practical doctrine' to which the *proficiens* belongs.[44] Or, we can see that we are faced with a development of the doctrine, which involves the mitigation of the original rigour.

In *On the Ends of Good and Evil* Cicero reconstructs with great clarity the general position of the Stoics; he imagines Cato the Younger presenting and defending it, touching on issues related to οἰκείωσις, to καθῆκον (i.e. the duty to keep in the state of nature), to the ὁρμή (i.e. the appetitive faculty of the soul), to the τέλος (i.e. to the 'end' in reference to which everyone must organize his own life), to the κατόρθωσις (i.e. to the 'righteousness' of our actions). Cicero also proposes the question of the ἀδιάφορα: the *indifferentia* which – although they have no value to give happiness or unhappiness and are, therefore, from this point of view, 'indifferent' – nonetheless have variants among them and can be considered 'indifferent' in a more favourable (προηγμένον) or more unfavourable way (ἀποπροηγμένον).[45] However, the objection that Cicero ultimately moves, translates into proposing a single alternative: either the Stoics hold firm that the only good is the moral good, or they admit different types of good. By accepting the first, however, we fall into the 'indifferentism' of Pyrrho and Ariston of Chios;[46] accepting the second, the position of the Stoics is confused with the Peripatetic

---

44 In particular, Seneca studied this latter aspect thoroughly. See *Epp.* 94 e 95.

45 Cf. *Fin.* 3.50–54. Cicero tries, for προηγμένα, the translation *producta* ('what is elevated'), then *promota* ('promoted'), *praeposita* ('preferred'), *praecipua* ('primary'); for ἀποπροηγμένα: *remota* ('removed'), *reiecta* ('rejected'). The definition he gives of what we call advantageous or superior is as follows: it is indifferent but with a moderate value (*indifferens cum aestimatione mediocri*): see *infra*, pp. 118–119. For the reference to Panaetius about this thesis, see Kidd 1971, 150–172. The contradiction in Stoic ethics, after having been detected by Cicero, is taken up by Plutarch, criticizing the Stoic 'indifferents' throughout two essays: *De Stoicorum repugnantiis* and *De communibus notitiis*.

46 In the first paragraphs of the third book of *On the Ends of Good and Evil* Cicero replies to Cato, and says, § 11: "Splendid words, Cato, but are you aware that you share your glory with Pyrrho and Ariston, who declare all things to be equal (*qui omnia exaequant*)?" Cicero repeats this concept shortly afterwards, in § 12.

one, from which it differs – Cicero maintains – only for the terminology used. Keeping the two alternatives together would be contradictory, as Cato evidently intends to do.

This objection, which Cicero moves to Cato at the opening of *On the Ends of Good and Evil* book III and which remains in the background of the whole presentation of Cato, is taken up again by Cicero in the conclusion of book IV, § 78:

> Hence (and here I conclude my discourse) your Stoic school seems weighed down above all by one particular flaw, namely that of believing that they can uphold two opposing views (*putant duas contrarias sententias obtinere*). Nothing could be more contradictory than claiming that what is moral is the only good (*quod honestum sit solum id bonum esse*), and at the same time that we have a desire, which springs from nature, for the things that are conducive to life (*appetitionem rerum ad vivendum accommodatarum a natura profectam*). When they want to maintain views that are consistent with the first principle they turn out like Ariston. When they seek to avoid this position, they are actually defending the same thesis as the Peripatetics (*re eadem defendunt quae Peripatetici*), while clinging doggedly to their own terminology (*verba tenent mordicus*).

The meticulous analysis of the Greek language and the effort to achieve a correct interpretation show – without a shadow of a doubt – how Cicero aimed to present the Stoic thesis objectively, so to speak. Only from this awareness does the space open to criticism, approval or rejection. But it is important to underline again that Cicero goes further: once a thesis has been presented and discussed, he draws a series of consequences and ends up proposing his 'way' as well.

In the discussion about *indifferentia*, one of the key problems is where to place duty:[47] if only what is 'honest' is 'good', honest actions (i.e. the fulfilment of one's duty) should be the logical consequence, even though it cannot be possible to place one's duty – according to the rigid Stoic doctrine – neither within good nor within evil. Cicero makes Cato speak, reporting a Stoic definition[48] of 'duty':

> Duty is any such action that a reasonable explanation could be given of its performance.[49]

At this point Cato argues that:
1. there may be something useful about what is neither a virtue nor a vice (*quiddam quod usui possit esse*);
2. it should not be rejected (*tollendum id non potest*);

---

47 *On Duties* is the direct confirmation of the importance that Cicero attaches to 'duty'.
48 See Diog. Laert. 7.107. Cf. *SVF* 1.230; 3.494.
49 *Fin.* 3.58.

3. a certain type of action, too, is included in this category: one that is such, that reason demands that it be realized (*talis ut ratio postulet agere*): that is, reason requires that something intermediate be done;
4. whatever is done with reason (*ratione actum est*) is called duty (*officium*);
5. conclusion: duty (*officium*) falls under the category of what is neither good nor the opposite (*nec in bonis ponatur nec in contrariis*).

As is evident, Cato abandoned the rigid position of the Stoic school and opened up space for intermediates. Cato then insisted, and it is inevitable to think that Cicero intended to insist through him (*Fin.* 3.59), that:

1. even the wise man sometimes acts by performing median actions (intermediates);
2. when he does so, he judges that such action is an appropriate action, i.e. a duty (*officium illud esse*);
3. since the wise man judgement is flawless (*numquam fallitur in iudicando*),
4. duty will belong to the sphere of the intermediates (*in mediis rebus officium*).

At this point it is not just a matter of recognizing the characteristics of what is good and what is bad, but one wonders about the 'practical' value of all this; according to Cato (and according to Cicero), 'duty' constitutes the moral implication of the definition of what is good. Therefore, if 'duty' does *not immediately* coincide with good (with the *honestum*), it must in any case be traced back *de facto* to the *honestum*. It is not possible to deny this conclusion and neither does the wise man do so, as he, *de facto*, deems it essential that what 'must be done' should be done and, precisely for this reason, he himself (who, by definition, cannot be mistaken) does it.

This sensitivity to the 'practical value' of theoretical reflection certainly belongs to Cicero. And it is precisely Cicero who, in replying to Cato, stresses that the abstract principles on which the Stoic doctrine is based are inadequate. According to them, even those who have made great progress towards virtue, but have not been able to fully achieve it, find themselves *de facto* at the height of unhappiness (*summe esse miserum*, 4.21), to the point that between their lives and that of wicked men there is no difference (*neque ... quicquam omnino interesse*).

Cicero reiterates that the true Stoic, supporter of an austere life without compromise, cannot think of solving the problem by changing the name of things (*nomina rerum commutantem*): he cannot believe that changing the name of things does not change thinking at all (*verba modo mutantem, de opinionibus nihil detrahentem*, 4.21).

We must abandon the rigid stoic theory. Moving towards a realistic conception of man and of the goal he attains to, Cicero then takes one last step: man by nature perceives who he is, and perceives to be formed of soul and body (*ex animo constamus st corpore*, 4.25). Only on such basis it is possible to proceed to formulate what is the extreme term of the supreme and only good for which 'by nature' we must strive (*ut prima appetitio naturalis postulat*). We cannot misunderstand this. Therefore, Cicero wonders why these serious recommendations, which come directly from nature, have been neglected by the wisdom (*a sapientia relictae sint*, 4.26) that the first Stoic masters preached. An animated being made up only of the mind, and not also of the body, makes no sense (*si quod esse animal quod totum ex mente constaret*, 4.28).

Cicero's conclusion is as follows:

> Virtue cannot be achieved at all, unless it takes on the primary objects of nature, i.e. to pertain to the supreme good. We are seeking a virtue that does not abandon our nature but protects it. Yet virtue, as you (i.e. Cato, as a stoic philosopher) advocate it, protects one part but abandons the rest.[50]

For Cicero the Stoic doctrine is clear; as such, however, it is unsustainable.

As in *On the Ends of Good and Evil*, also in *On Fate* Cicero shows his remarkable ability to read and understand the texts of the Greek philosophers and to manifest his autonomy of judgment. In this case Cicero criticizes both the Stoic and the Epicurean doctrine. It is clear what accurate knowledge he has of both. Take for example the problem of *adsensio* (*On Fate* 39–40), central to the discussion between those who believe that everything takes place at the behest of fate and those who admit that the motions of the soul are free from the necessity of fate. Either assent is produced out of necessity, given that the presence of fate is confirmed, in any case and everywhere, or it must be released from the fatalistic conception according to which assent would be produced only by necessity. Those who oppose the omnipresence of fate show that, if we consider the tendency (*adpetitio*) to be a cause – and if it is agreed that it is not in our power – then neither consent nor actions will be in our power: which is why neither reward nor punishment would make sense. Since, however, according to Cicero, this deduction is not correct, then it is probable that not everything that happens, happens by fate: *non omnia fato fieri quaecumque fiant* (40).

At this point Cicero reports a taxonomy of causes; Chrysippus would have proposed it to try to safeguard, through this path, the concept of fate and, at the same time, to escape the necessity. Cicero does not seem convinced of this and

---

50 *Fin.* 4.41.

summarizes the overall panel of the hypotheses that can be envisaged, hinging his argument on the relationship between the 'mental representation' (*visum*) of something and the eventual 'assent' (*adsensio*) to this 'representation'. He presents a series of distinct theses. The first one (a) is set out by those who deny that the assent takes place by fate (¬F) and are convinced that it can take place even in the absence of preceding causes (¬PC). From this thesis, however, if you grant (PC), the second one (b) derives: i.e. the thesis of those who deny that assent takes place by fate (¬F), but admit that it cannot take place in the absence of previous causes ¬ (¬PC). The third one (c) is set out by those who admit that it occurs in the presence of previous causes (PC), even if this does not imply that the consent takes place by fate, since it would not constitute an immediate and contiguous cause. Obviously in the background there lies, though not mentioned by Cicero, the absolutely deterministic thesis (d), supported by those who believe that the assent takes place in the presence of previous causes (PC), and that this is due to fate (F).

Summing up:

- (a) = (¬F) ∧ (¬PC);
- allowing (PC) → (b) = (¬F) ∧ ¬ (¬PC);
- (c) = (PC) ∧ (¬F);
- (d) = (F) ∧ (PC).

Thesis (d) is clearly the typical one of rigid determinism, while the other theses refer to compatibilist interpretations (b) and (c), or libertarian (a). Cicero is convinced of this and in practice makes it clear that this happens because what in (b) *has been granted* (i.e. PC) allows to reach the same result of the thesis (c), according to which only fate appears *not to be granted* (¬F) and we simply deny that fate, if the assent is caused by previous causes, is implicit *in itself*.

Cicero then undertakes to show how the position of Chrysippus is that of those who refuse (d) by pointing to (c); in order to do this, he takes advantage of the distinction, just gained earlier, between generic 'previous causes' and specific 'previous necessary causes'. In fact, Chrysippus on the one hand confirms that everything happens for previous causes, on the other denies that everything happens for previous and necessary causes (*omnia causis fiant antecedentibus et necessariis*) and, together, by destiny (*omnia fato fiunt*).

As for assent, we know[51] that Chrysippus distinguishes between the 'immediate and contiguous cause' (*proxima et continens causa*) of assent – that is, the

---

51 See *supra*, pp. 85–87.

cause of assent that is placed in the representation – and the 'preceding and nec-essary cause' (*antecedentes et necessariae causae*) of assent;[52] this is consistent with the statement that everything happens for previous causes, without this im-plying that these are always necessary causes. Those who dissent from Chrysip-pus – that is, those who accept the thesis (d) – can do so because they consider representation as a 'previous and necessary cause', inserting it in the causal chain, so that nothing that happens can happen, except as a result of a previous cause (*nihil fieret nisi praegressione causae*), and they can thus conclude that eve-rything happens by fate (*fato fieri omnia*).

We can ask ourselves: but are Chrysippus and his objectors really contradic-tory?

Despite everything, in the eyes of Cicero the conclusion reached by Chrysip-pus (*soft determinism*) differs only in words from those who dissent from him (*hard determinism*): both ultimately accept the thesis (d). According to Chrysip-pus, since everything happens for 'previous causes' (and among these, in reality, the 'previous and necessary causes' cannot be excluded), everything ends up happening by destiny; according to those who disagree, since everything hap-pens by fate, in each event 'previous [and therefore 'necessary'] causes' can be detectable.[53]

(B) In *On Fate* Cicero (as already in *On the Ends of Good and Evil*, in *On the Nature of the Gods* and in *Tusculan Disputations*) does not deal only with the Stoic school: one of his main opponents is undoubtedly the Epicurean doctrine. How-ever, we must be very careful: Cicero shows he is a fine connoisseur of Physics and Epicurean Ethics. Above all, he shows that he has perfectly grasped the ar-gument that allows Epicurus to avoid Stoic determinism: a determinism which he, on the contrary, could not accept.

It is important that we know how to look beyond certain Ciceronian rhetorical modalities that may be useful to put the opponent in difficulty and guarantee the reader's consent.[54] Epicurus despises and laughs at the whole dialectic (*Luc.* 97);

---

52 Cicero is attempting to clarify the most evident characteristics of the preceding cause, which is, therefore, neither primary nor perfect. In *proxima* we can also grasp the temporal aspect; in *continens* the spatial one. In addition to Cicero, the Stoic distinction between the causes is testi-fied by Alexander of Aphrodisias, *De fato* 22.192.17–19; moreover, he speaks of 'swarm' of causes. On this topic see: Frede 1980, 245; Ioppolo 1994, 4491–4545; Hankinson 1999, 488; Bobzien 1999, 215–217; Schallenberg 2008, 265–269; Maso 2014b, 169–175.

53 On the compatibilist perspective that Chrysippus would embrace, see Salles 2005, 69–89.

54 In the invective *in Pisonem* Cicero sarcastically defines his opponent *barbatus Epicurus* (20); *Epicure noster ex hara producte non ex schola* (37); *ex argilla et luto fictus Epicurus* (59). That is:

he is the one who places the standard of judgment entirely in the senses and in the notions of objects and pleasure (*Luc.* 142); "as for your master Epicurus ... which one of his utterances is, I do not say worthy of philosophy, but compatible with ordinary common sense?" (*ND* 1.61). Epicurus is a man who admits that he cannot resist fate in any other way than "by recourse to these fictitious atomic swerves" (*Fat.* 48).[55]

However, Epicurus, as a person, is judged positively: "Epicurus himself was a good man, and many Epicureans were and are faithful friends, who live their whole life through with integrity and dignity, letting duty rather than pleasure guide their decisions", *Fin.* 2.81; "You may well remind us once more of those admirable words that Epicurus spoke in praise of friendship", *Fin.* 2.84; "Epicurus, not at all an evil man, indeed an excellent man", *Tusc.* 2.44; "Epicurus says that it is not possible to live pleasantly, except by the exercise of virtue", *Tusc.* 3.49.[56]

As for the general knowledge of the Epicurean doctrine, it is worth remembering that, in addition to having studied with Phaedrus and Zeno of Sidon, Cicero probably knows the work of Lucretius and certainly had in his hands some Epicurean works.[57]

Cicero, however, is in a very difficult situation; on the one hand, he does not intend to accept Epicurus' ethical proposal, focused on the theory of *katastēmatic pleasure* as an end; and since Epicurean Ethics is based on the materialistic foundations of Atomism, Cicero knows that, in order to show its inconsistency, Epicurean Physics will have to be demolished first. On the other hand, Cicero realizes

---

a bearded old man; a man who comes from a pigsty, not a school; one that is made of clay and mud.

55 Luc. 97: *totam dialecticam et contemnit et inridet*; Luc. 142: *omne iudicium in sensibus et in rerum notitiis et in voluptate constituit*; ND 1.61: *Epicurus vero tuus (nam cum illo malo disserere quam tecum) quid dicit quod non modo philosophia dignum esset sed mediocri prudentia?*; Fat. 48: *aliter obsistere fato fatetur se non potuisse nisi ad has commenticias declinationes confugisse.*

56 Fin. 2.18: *ipse bonus vir fuit et multi Epicurei et fuerunt et hodie sunt et in amicitiis fideles et in omni vita constantes et graves nec voluptate, sed officio consilia moderantes*; Fin. 2.84: *licet hic rursus ea commemores, quae optimis verbis ab Epicuro de laude amicitiae dicta sunt*; Tusc. 2.44: *Epicurus, homo minime malus vel potius vir optimus*; Tusc. 3.49; *negat Epicurus iucunde posse vivi, nisi cum virtute vivatur.*

57 Regarding extant Epicurean texts that circulated at the time, Cicero cites a number of these works accurately. First of all, the *Ratae sententiae* (Κύριαι δόξαι), in *Fin.* 1.16; 2.20; *ND* 1.45; 1.85; 1.113; *Off.* 3.116; *Fam.* 15.19.2. Then the *Ep. ad Idomeneum*, in *Fin.* 2.99; the *Testamentum*, in *Fin.* 2.103; *De fine* (Περὶ τέλους), in *Tusc.* 3.41 and 44; *De voluptate* (Περὶ ἡδονῆς), in *Div.* 2.59; *De pietate* (Περὶ εὐσεβείας), in *ND* 1.115; *De sanctitate* (Περὶ ὁσιότητος), in *ND* 1.115 and 122; *De regula et iudicio* (that probably corresponds to Περὶ κριτηρίου ἢ Κανών), in *ND* 1.43–44.

that the Atomistic conception of Epicurus is at the basis of a functional anti-deterministic interpretation of reality: an interpretation that would justify man's free ability to act much better than the Stoic one. As we know, Cicero proceeds to the radical critique of Atomism and thus precludes the possibility of overcoming the *aporia* that prevents him, the Stoics and even Carneades from convincingly explaining free will.

It is particularly instructive to check the way in which Cicero deals with the theory of atomic motion and *clinamen*. Obviously, Cicero believes that Epicurus elaborated the *clinamen* theory to explain becoming and change without getting stuck in an absolutely deterministic conception of the world. But the result would not live up to what was expected: according to Cicero, the mechanism inherent in the Atomistic doctrine cannot leave room for solutions that consider autonomous (not initiated) movements and subjective (not predetermined) choices. In this context, the *clinamen* theory seems wholly inadequate and even contradictory to him.

Looking closely at the Ciceronian interpretation, we find that, according to Cicero, Epicurus's atom is not a *quid materiale* that 'falls', because of its two properties:
1. the weight that continuously makes it fall in a straight line;
2. the *clinamen* that *occasionally* occurs, eventually interfering with the 'linear falling'.[58]

Cicero, instead, imagines the atom as a particle (*corpusculum*) that exhibits a state of *constant deviation* (*declinare paululum*), however small. Epicurus's seems to Cicero an explicitly contradictory and unsound assumption, since undisturbed rectilinear motion (*directo deorsus*) matched with non-rectilinear motion (*declinare paululum*) should always result in a *permanently deflected line*, i.e. a curve. It is clear, in fact, that a body swerved by a series of thrusts of perfectly equal intensity, angle of deflection, and frequency of succession can only draw a curved line in a space (provided that this space has no effect whatsoever on the body and its motion). If the swerve is thought in its absoluteness, free of all possible space-time variables and relationships, it can only show its perennial and constant change in direction.

In fact, only by introducing these variables (in particular, the temporal 'randomness' that Cicero leaves out in this context) will it be possible to give life to

---

58 This is the standard interpretation of the *clinamen*, see Aëtius 1.23.4, 319 D. = [157] Arr.: "Epicurus identified two types of motion: one that can be applied to weight (τὸ κατὰ στάθμην) and another that can be applied to deviation (τὸ κατὰ παρέγκλισιν)".

an endless series of clashes between particles and, therefore, to the very frequent (but not continuous) series of changes in the direction of each atom's fall. If we do not determine the strength, the angle, or the moment in time when the 'swerve' could happen, and then a real 'swerve' occurs, a continuous, curved movement will result, as when the sequence of thrusts is smoothed into a single event: such a 'curved' movement is by definition the exact opposite of a rectilinear one.

Cicero states this point as follows:

> (Epicurus) says that the atom, while being dragged down in a straight line because of gravity and its weight, makes a very slight swerve. To affirm something like this is worse than not being able to defend one's position.[59]

Note that Cicero has Lucretius' version in mind:[60]

> When bodies are borne by their own weight
> on a downward path straight through an empty space,
> at absolutely undetermined times and random places,
> they swerve a little – not much, just enough
> so, you can say they have changed direction.[61]

Lucretius' text identifies:
1. the free fall (*cum deorsum rectum ... feruntur*);
2. the swerve (*depellere paulum*);
3. the univocally identifiable, though absolutely unknown time at and space in which (2) the swerve intervenes.

Incerto tempore ferme incertisque locis describes the inability to identify the precise moment or moments when the swerve occurs – not the negation of the moment or moments when it happens unexpectedly. In other words, Lucretius stresses the *unpredictability* of the swerve – an *unpredictability* that, in itself, can also *not* imply absolute randomness, though it involves the absence of any predetermined space-time.

---

59 ND 1.69. *Ait atomum, cum pondere et gravitate directo deorsus feratur, declinare paululum. Hoc dicere turpius est quam illud quod vult non posse defendere.*
60 In 54 Cicero, *Q. fr.* 2.9.3, writes to his brother Quintus: "Just as you write, Lucretius' poems are of brilliant talent and high art".
61 Rer. nat. 2.217–220: *Corpora cum deorsum rectum per inane feruntur / ponderibus propriis, incerto tempore ferme / incertisque locis spatio depellere paulum, / tantum quod momen mutatum dicere possis.* See 2.243–244; 2.259–260; 2.292–293.

The explanatory power of the Epicurean/Lucretian model primarily emerges through the manner in which the swerve's *randomness* is safeguarded: it is still *randomness* both as in (A) 'a non-predetermined time or space,' and (B) 'spatio-temporal randomness'. One way or another – but in (A) it only refers *in infinitum* to (B) – two otherwise incompatible motions can be taken together: a rectilinear one and a deviation.

Yet, there is no trace of any of this in Cicero. He resumes Lucretius' thought *lexically*, but in his words, the (1) fall (*cum pondere et gravitate directo deorsus feratur*, 1.69) seems to *always have been* accompanied by a (2) swerve (*declinare paululum*). There is no trace of (3) 'randomness' for indefinite but completely and individually discernible moments. Thus, there is no trace of what would have allowed this contradiction to be *circumvented*, a contradiction of which Epicurus seems to have been aware of. Cicero appears subtle – in my opinion beyond the limits of interpretative accuracy, since the 'moment' and 'place' of the swerve are intentionally omitted – when countering, in *On the Nature of the Gods*, the Epicurean thesis through Cotta as a spokesperson.

On Fate (written some months after *On the Nature of the Gods*) raises the problem of motion once more: Cicero resorts to a more complicated reconstruction of Epicureanism to demonstrate its inconsistency. According to him, Epicurus would introduce *a third type of motion* distinct from the 'weight' and the 'received push' (i.e. the 'rectilinear' and 'diverted' motions): 'the deviation by very little' from its own axis: *tertius quidam motus oritur extra pondus et plagam, cum declinat atomus intervallo minimo – id appellat ἐλάχιστον* (22).[62]

We must consider the procedure followed by Cicero in challenging the Atomistic solution of Epicurus particularly refined. The precise knowledge of the theory and the masterly elaborated reinterpretation (with the intentional misunderstanding that we have found within it) allow Cicero to demolish Epicurean materialism at its foundations.

As for the doctrine of pleasure: it constitutes the real critical point of Epicureanism, the very one for which young Ciceronian interest gradually changed into conflict and then into opposition. The entire *On the Ends of Good and Evil* – whose first books are set in Cicero's Cumaean villa in roughly 50 – is dedicated to the problem of the *ultimate end* of man's actions; Cicero begins this immense effort, which includes Carneades' ethical doxography,[63] by exploring Epicurean and

---

62 Concerning the problems related to the Lucretian explanation and this third motion, see Maso 2015, 63–74.

63 See *supra*, pp. 27–28. Cicero considers this Carneadean *division* as fundamental both in *Fin.* 2.34–35 and in *Tusc.* 5.84–85. As we saw, according to this division, the 'ultimate end or supreme

then Stoic morality. Epicurean morality made 'pleasure' its *telos* and, at a first glance, Cicero does not seem interested in clarifying how pleasure should be interpreted so as not to be misconstrued: whether *katastēmatic* or *kinetic*, an exclusively physical experience or the condition of rationally explained 'well-being', the conclusion is that 'pleasure' is the Epicurean's *telos*, and that from his point of view, action and reason must be secondary.

For Stoicism, the situation is completely opposite: 'pleasure' does play a role in its ethics, but it is a 'strict pleasure' entirely secondary to its *telos* and consists exclusively of 'virtue'. The pleasant satisfaction of being virtuous even appears in more general Stoicism as a corollary of moral perfection.[64] This is a pleasure defined as 'feeling good', an εὐπάθεια.[65] But if joy directly depends on *rationality* (which is the source of its existence), we should also note that pleasure is usually understood by the Stoics as pure passion – an ἄλογος ἔπαρσις, as Arius Didymus said[66] – a purely physical expansion of the spirit, typical of the instance when we obtain something we wanted or escape what we fear. Obviously, Arius Didymus here does not refer to anything 'against nature', but rather to something that is perpetually natural and so human, that it implies a rebellion against rationality.[67] However, Cicero, when referring to Stoicism and to the idea of the Stoic wise man, has only one form of pleasure in mind – cleansed of all unnatural aspects – that refers to εὐπάθεια, or the positive emotion of joy that seems to emerge whenever we satisfy a reasonable desire. In *Tusculan Disputations*, to indicate this kind of

---

good' can be pursued 'regardless' of moral worth (and here, although distinct from each other, Aristippus and Epicurus, Hieronymus, and Carneades are included); in conjunction with moral worth (in the case of the Peripatetics and the ancient Academy, of Polemon, Calliphon, Diodorus, and Dinomachus); and directly accompanying moral worth (in the case of Stoicism). Each part of this threefold division plays a fundamental role in the manner in which we refer to nature and its principles. See Lévy 1992, 353–376; Algra 1997, 107–139; Ioppolo 2016, 173–175.

64 This happens when a 'decision' is made and its outcomes are recognized. Brennan 2005, 182–202, confronts this problem by comparing the different attitudes of Stoicism and Epicureanism. More generally, however, Stoicism still allows a glimpse of its active tension, 'the active exercise of virtue', which is identified as 'happiness', as Annas 1993, 388–411, points out, with a reference (388–389) to Arius Didymus in Stob., *Ecl.* 2.7.6e,1–4, pp. 77 W.: "One's aim, [the Stoics] say, is being happy, for the sake of which everything is done, while it is not done for the sake of anything further; and this consists in living according to virtue, in living in agreement and further (it is the same thing) in living according to nature".

65 See Graver 2017, 207–211, on εὐπάθεια and the emotional response such as caution and wishes.

66 Arius Didymus in Stob., *Ecl.* 2.7.10b.10–12, p. 90 W., makes the point: "Pleasure is a rising spirit rebellious to reason (ἄλογος ἔπαρσις), and it causes one to think that there is an actual good for which it should rise".

67 ἀπειθὲς τῷ λόγῳ: see Ar. Did., in Stob., *Ecl.* 2.7.10a.1–2, p. 89 W.

desire, Cicero curiously applies the term *voluntas*;[68] he then meaningfully uses the term *gaudium* to denote one's being in possession of good: "When the mind is moved quietly and consistently, in accordance with reason, this is termed 'joy'".[69] When properly understood, the theoretical plan of Stoic orthodoxy suggests the manifestation of a *perfectly natural 'virtus'* that, in and of itself, implies success. 'Feeling good' is precisely this εὐπάθεια: the experience of *gaudium*.

Stoic action reveals its own purpose, and Cato the Younger confirms this point in his presentation of Stoic Ethics in the third book of *On the Ends of Good and Evil*:

> Here (in wisdom) the end, namely the performance of the art, is contained within the art itself, not sought outside it.[70]

Epicurean action, by contrast, aims at 'pleasure'. Furthermore, in the first book of *On the Ends of Good and Evil* the Epicurean L. Manlius Torquatus wonders why Cicero so strongly opposes Epicureanism. Glad to find the always 'dynamic' Cicero as *otiosus* for once, Torquatus takes the opportunity to make a request:

> I am determined to hear what it is about my master Epicurus which I shall not say you hate, as those who disagree with him generally do, but which at any rate you do not approve of (*non tu quidem oderis, ut fere faciunt qui ab eo dissentiunt, sed certe non probes*).[71]

Essentially, Torquatus posits that the contrast could perhaps simply be reduced to an issue of language, and that Cicero's true contention with Epicureanism

---

68 *Tusc.* 4.12 [= *SVF* 3.438]; see *infra*, p. 124. Brennan 1998, 36 and 55–57, interprets the 'will/good desire' as a genuine emotion, in particular emphasizing that "the εὐπάθειαι are thus all directed at genuine goods and evils", 57.

69 Tusc. 4.13: *nam cum ratione animus movetur placide atque constanter, tum illud gaudium dicitur.*

70 *Fin.* 3.24: *In ipsa insit, non foris petatur extremum, id est artis effectio.* And since "only wisdom is entirely self-contained" (*sola enim sapientia in se tota conversa est*), it follows necessarily that all those who possess it – the wise men – "always enjoy a life that is happy, perfect, fortunate, and free from obstacles, prohibitions, or deprivations", § 26. Here Cato is explaining Stoic ethical thought in its most official form. But Cicero will distance himself from this position, arguing that within the definition of the sole good, 'preferred things' (*res appetendae*) cannot be irrelevant to a life consistent with nature. This stance, of course, promotes the Academic/Peripatetic view as represented by Antiochus, according to which, since an individual's perfection consists of spirit and body, the body's 'well being' contributes to happiness. Otherwise, Cicero concludes ironically: "To live in armony with nature would mean distancing oneself from it! (*id est convenienter naturae vivere: a natura discedere*)", *Fin.* 4.41.

71 *Fin.* 1.14.

could be more a matter of formality than one of any real content: this point granted, Torquatus would certainly have no problem admitting (as he would, in fact, end up doing) that Epicurus's expository style was less *ornate* than Plato, or Aristotle, or Theophrastus. But even if one would bracket the stylistic issue for the time being, Torquatus still cannot believe that Epicurus's authentic thought would be something Cicero would not share.[72]

Cicero counters with a strong reply:

> 'You are quite mistaken, Torquatus'... 'It is not the style of that philosopher which offends: his words express his meaning, and he writes in a direct way that I can comprehend' (*nam et complectitur verbis quod vult et dicit plane quod intellegam*).[73]

It is precisely the contents that do not satisfy Cicero, *re mihi non satisfacit*, (*ibid.*); Cicero explains, as we already know, that he perfectly understands the Epicurean doctrine, having studied it himself with Phaedrus and Zeno. Assuming they have not misled him:

> Hopefully you do not believe Phaedrus and Zeno have lied to me. I have heard both of them lecture, though, to be sure, they convinced me of nothing but their own devotion [to the teacher], and thus I know the whole of Epicurus's opinions well enough (*omnes mihi Epicuri sententiae satis notae sunt*).[74]

In his comprehensive response, presented in the second book of *On the Ends of Good and Evil*, Cicero will indeed be able to reverse his interlocutor's perspective, by expressing his surprise over such a point of view: as his friend Torquatus had shown disbelief for Cicero's radical aversion to Epicureanism and its form of expression, here Cicero will assert his own incredulity over the fact that Torquatus 'seriously' accepts this philosophy and accuses him of inconsistency:

> Believe me, Torquatus, you cannot take these doctrines seriously if you truly take into account your person, your ideas, and your interests (*si te ipse et tuas cogitationes et studia perspexeris*).[75]

The play of characters is cleverly constructed: there is a Cicero who, through Torquatus the Epicurean, supports overcoming a linguistic hurdle and posits a min-

---

72 *Fin.* 1.14: "For I can hardly believe that his views (*quae senserit ille*) do not seem to you to be true (*tibi non vera videantur*)".
73 *Fin.* 1.15.
74 *Fin.* 1.16.
75 *Fin.* 2.69.

imal distance between the two philosophical positions. As antagonist there is another Cicero who, always invoking the true meaning of concepts and expressions, invites Torquatus to abandon the Epicurean faith and to embrace the Academic or Stoic positions. It is as if Cicero, wishing to reach a conclusion, believed to have clearly identified and understood some points of the Epicurean doctrine only to declare these views incompatible not only with his own ethical-philosophic prospective, but also with the natural reality in which every human being lives and which cannot be interpreted in any other way.

4.5 Eclecticism: is it a valid label?

Stoicism, Epicureanism and the Academy (especially in its sceptical version), were the most active philosophical movements during the first century BCE. In the first one, a succession of protagonists deepened the various aspects of the doctrine, brought innovations and, often confronting or sometimes diverging, kept the cultural climate lively, giving an equally very important contribution to the elaboration of the political projects of Rome. The second one maintained a precise continuity in passing on the founder's doctrine, contributing, nonetheless, to a form of renewal, especially in the ethical-moral sphere.[76] As for Platonism (i.e. the Academic school), the question is more complex, because the succession of teachers and schools testified from time to time to the different role played by Plato's writings or the reference to Socrates and his alleged approach to the world of knowledge, or the influence of the Peripatetic environment or, again, the explicit sceptical attitude towards reality. Most of all, the Academy still appears to be a real philosophical laboratory that thrives in comparison with other schools and which stands out above all for its particularly flexible and effective critical method.

Cicero declares himself belonging to the Academy: therefore, his references should be his direct masters, Philo and Antiochus. This is true only in part: it was precisely the way in which these two philosophers clashed that allowed him to remain open to the voices and issues discussed in the Stoic and Epicurean schools.[77] Is this enough to define Cicero as an eclectic?

---

76 On the 'Ipse dixit' approach, see Sedley 1995, 97–103.
77 As for Cicero's philosophical affiliations, Glucker 1988, 34–69, proposes the following thesis: from a first adhesion to the moderate Scepticism of Philo's Fourth Academy, Cicero would have passed to an affiliation lasting over thirty years (79–46), to the doctrinaire Platonism of Antiochus. In Cicero's final years – his most fertile period of philosophical composition – we observe a return to the position of the Philonian New Academy.

What does 'eclecticism' mean?

The label that defines a certain approach as 'eclectic' is modern and conceals a sort of negative connotation, as if it necessarily characterized a phase of mere intellectual reworking following a period of great theoretical development. In applying it to the ancient world, we must, therefore, be cautious,[78] since the Hellenistic period was not at all a phase of decline for philosophy: the opposite would be said for the Roman world. Furthermore, as for the term itself, before Potamon – philosopher of the Augustan era – nobody was defined as such by the ancients.[79]

Certainly, more interesting is the position of Antiochus, the noble and wise philosopher with whom Cicero spent six months:[80] from what we can derive above all from the Ciceronian *Academica*, Antiochus tried to prove the basic agreement between Platonism, Aristotelianism, and Stoicism and tended to make these three schools coincide and form a single common doctrine.[81] It is probably correct to define this approach to philosophy as syncretic.[82] In fact, Antiochus does not select the parts of the three rival doctrines, which interest him, to assemble them in some new doctrinaire system. This is the typical way in which an authentic 'eclectic' would proceed. According to Antiochus, Stoics, Peripatetics, and Academics are partners rather than competitors. But the difficulty in understanding how Cicero relates to the doctrine of other schools is evident in the disagreement that has prevailed among scholars until today.[83]

As for Cicero: the situation is still different. We are faced with neither an 'assembler' of materials from other schools, nor a developer of a syncretic project. Certainly, Cicero believes that he follows the Academic 'method', and on this we can easily agree. But the operation he does is in many respects original: he faces

---

78 Donini 1988, 31–32, distinguishes six possible meanings in reference to the concept of eclecticism.

79 Potamon of Alexandria is the only one described as representing an *eclectic vocation* (Suda s.v. Potamon, 2126 Adler; Diog. Laert. 1.21).

80 *Brut.* 315.

81 See Barnes 1989, 78–81; Lévy 1992, 51–57.

82 According to Sext. Emp., *PH* 1.235, "Antiochus brought the Stoa into the Academy, so that they actually said of him that 'he does Stoic philosophy in the Academy'". This is because he found the basics of Stoicism in Plato (*ibid.*).

83 In Sedley 2012 we can see the disagreement of some scholars with reference to Antiochus' relationship with Peripatetics and Platonism (Irwin, 151–172; Bonazzi, 307–333), and above all with the Stoics (Brittain, 104–130, Schofield, 173–187).

Stoicism, often declares himself in agreement[84] with it, although he does not hesitate to contest some of its aspects; he faces Epicureanism and condemns it, even if on many occasions he shows he understands its reasons; he interprets Aristotle and the Peripatetics,[85] as well as he refers to Socrates and Plato, showing above all their convergences and willingly adopting their mediation strategy. We can say that Cicero's approach is very similar to what a modern scholar of ancient philosophy would do today: he tries to obtain the documentary sources and then study them; he compares the positions, he attempts to elaborate a more or less original interpretation with reference to perspective angles that he has selected and decided at the start; secondary literature is taken into account; he willingly attends to some of the authors examined, but without exempting himself from criticism and discussion; finally, he produces a work that tries to be documented and objective, possibly useful to other scholars. The originality lies in the step forward that he presumes to have taken, within the cultural environment in which he lives and has been trained. Obviously on many occasions it seems that we repeat ourselves, even if we are only trying to better elucidate and verify hypotheses and theses; in fact, it is inevitable that a series of previous conclusions are 'incorporated' into the set of elements that constitute the outcome of research. However, the step forward is there, and research gains meaning, if the conclusion illuminates the theses previously developed and assumed in a new, sensible way, arguing perhaps unexpected suggestions and spaces for further study.

When Cicero plans *On the Ends of Good and Evil* or *Tusculan Disputations*, or *On Fate*, or *On Duties* and, in short, all his philosophical works, he does not present himself as a theorist, as a thinker capable of building a system; he proposes himself as an interpreter of Greek thought who intends to offer the Romans the fruit of his studies, focusing and problematizing in an original way what he considers immediately useful for the training of a cultured and socially engaged Roman. Cicero had Antiochus among his teachers. Antiochus, in its later period, was

---

84 In this sense, the declaration of following the Stoics regarding 'duty' is explicit, *Off.* 1.6: *Sequimur igitur hoc quidem tempore et hac in quaestione potissimum Stoicos.*

85 On Cicero's knowledge of the Peripatos, see the collection edited by Fortenbaugh–Steinmetz 1989; in particular the essays of Runia, 23–38, where we find a study on the conjoined references to Aristotle and Theophrastus; and the three essays where the Aristotelian material is addressed, specifically in *On the Ends of Good and Evil* (Gigon, 133–158), in *Tusculan Disputations* (Classen, 186–200); in *On the Nature of the Gods* (Furley, 201–219). Wisse 1988 examines the evolution of some central aspects of ethics in the transition from Aristotle to Cicero. Long 1995, 52–61, highlights the key aspects, which, especially from a methodological and ethical point of view, affected Cicero.

a Stoic in his epistemology and a Peripatetic of sorts in his ethics. As we know,[86] Cicero wrote that: "He was called an Academic, but was in fact, if he had made very few changes, the purest Stoic" (*Luc.* 132). As for Panaetius: he was a lover of Plato and Aristotle, and Cicero writes: "He was always ready with a quote from Plato, Aristotle, Xenocrates, Theophrastus or Dicaearchus" (*Fin.* 4.79). There is no doubt that Cicero on them – and on philosophers who showed a similar approach to philosophy, often by modern scholars defined as 'eclectic' – modelled his own philosophical research. With at least two specific characters: the sceptical methodological predisposition, as inculcated by Philo, the last teacher of the Academy, who always pushed him to compare and examine the different positions (*in utramque partem disserere*);[87] and the use of a new philosophical language, sensitive to the value of rhetoric.

Explicitly Cicero stated that it is not so important to declare one's affiliation with regard to the conclusions reached, because in a discussion one should not look for the authorities' weight as much as the arguments' weight.[88] Indeed, the teacher's authority properly ends up very often harming those who want to learn, because they cease to use their own judgment and definitively report the opinion of his leader.[89]

It is much easier to declare one's affiliation to such schools as Stoicism and Epicureanism and to commit to supporting already well-reinforced and tested theses and arguments, than to rely on a school that seems to overshadow[90] everything and that requires to study and understand each philosophical system. Cicero confesses:

> In an undertaking so extensive and so arduous, I do not profess to have attained success, though I do claim to have attempted it.[91]

However, Cicero is sure that he has made some progress: he claims not to be among those who, because of their *disserere in utramque partem*, believe that

---

86 See *supra*, p. 57.

87 On Cicero's relationship with the Academy of Philo and then with Antiochus, see Glucker 1988, 37–42.

88 ND 1.10: *Non enim auctoritatis in disputando quam rationis momenta quaerenda sunt.*

89 ND 1.10: *Desinunt enim suum iudicium adhibere, id habent ratum quod ab eo quem probant iudicatum vident.*

90 *ND* 1.6: "Many people are surprised at my choosing to embrace a philosophy that in their view robs the world of daylight and floods it with a darkness as of night (*quae lucem eriperet et quasi noctem quandam rebus offunderet*)".

91 *ND* 1.12.

nothing is true. So, he is not willing to embrace Scepticism in its absoluteness. Cicero coherently states that:

> All true things are associated with false ones so closely resembling them that they contain non-infallible marks to guide our judgment (*iudicandi*) and assent (*adsentiendi*). From this followed the corollary, that many things are probable (*ex quo exsistit et illud, multa esse probabilia*).[92]

The Academy's unpretentiousness and the fertility of its method of approach open the way for Cicero's research, a research that excludes the negative connotation often implicit in the label: 'eclecticism'.[93] Probably the suggestion recently proposed by Skvirsky (2019), 2–12, goes in the right direction. The scholar defines Cicero's methodological approach as 'eclectic probabilism': Cicero does not practice ἐποχή (the suspension of judgment) but rather insists on an anti-dogmatic approach that safeguards him from the dangers inherent in supporting an exclusive philosophical doctrine.

4.6 Philosophical experience and political life: is there a coherence problem?

It is very important to try to understand how much political faith influenced the organization of Cicero's philosophical thought and how, conversely, the philosophical research he undertook had repercussions for his choices and the political project he developed.

First of all, we should keep in mind that the *cursus honorum* constituted, for a Roman, the fundamental way of accessing a political career: that is, belonging to the ruling class and *tout court* to power. Cicero finalized his studies and his commitment as a lawyer to this.[94]

Moreover, it is very important to choose well who to be with, and, consequently, to decide one's political party. Distantly related to Gaius Marius, the leader of the *populares*, Cicero grew up in the period of the great civil struggle between *populares* and *optimates*. The end of the dictatorship of L. Cornelius Sulla (79) constituted a fundamental moment of renewal for the Republic. At that

---

92 *ND* 1.12.
93 A bibliography of scholars who have accredited Cicero's qualification as eclectic is in Glucker 1988, 38–39. On Cicero's particular eclecticism, see Zyl 1990, 118–122.
94 On the way Cicero understood the law and exercised it, see Powell–Paterson 2004, 19–60.

time, Cicero's approach to the *optimates* was crucial.[95] Already in 75, Cicero had obtained the quaestorship (the first magistracy of the *cursus honorum*) for western Sicily; his career culminated twelve years later with the consulship of 63. He was able to adapt to the dynamic political situation, but was determined to defend the *status quo* of the Republic in the name of the values of the *maiores*, ending up in the group of the *optimates* who gathered around Pompey. He, thus, became a declared opponent of Caesar and the political project that he embodied. In the name of the Republic and the Senate Cicero worked and also committed himself from a theoretical point of view. Two works are decisive in this context: *On the Republic* and *On the Laws*. The first was written between 54 and 51 BCE, when Cicero had already experienced exile, as a result of his opposition to the triumvirate. A strong appeal is addressed to the characters who make up the myth of Rome: above all Scipio Aemilianus, C. Laelius, Q. Mucius Scaevola, and Q. Aelius Tubero. In this work Cicero analyses the different forms of government and the possible degenerations. On the so-called political dialogues we can consult Narducci (2009), 328–356. Particular importance is given to the Ciceronian recovery, in a conservative key, of the Greek doctrine of the 'mixed constitution'. Zarecki (2014), 16–44, instead emphasizes how the theoretical approach, underlying Cicero's political philosophy, reflects the position of the Academic scepticism.

In *On the Republic*, with all evidence, Cicero takes his cue from the Platonic dialogue of the same name, and then proceeds according to the great Stoic thesis that favours the moral tension and the connection between public-political ethics and the moral virtue of private action. The theory of natural impulse to social life appears more decisive than the reference to a formal social pact, established to guarantee mankind's survival. Cicero eloquently summarizes it thus, giving the word to Scipio:

> Well, then, a commonwealth (*res publica*) is the property of a people (*res populi*). But a people is not any collection (*coetus*) of human beings brought together in any sort of way (*quoquo modo congregatus*), but an assemblage (*coetus*) of people in large numbers associated in an agreement with respect to justice (*iuris consensu*) and a partnership for the common good (*utilitatis communione sociatus*). The first cause of such an association is not so much

---

95 Cicero appeared as a *novus homo* in the Roman political environment, but it was his intention to gain credit and consensus among the *nobiles* and *optimates* rather than with the *populares*. See Blom 2010, 18–59.

the weakness (*imbecillitas*), as I would say, a natural propensity of men to aggregation (*naturalis quaedam hominum quasi congregatio*). For man is not a solitary or unsocial creature.[96]

In the third book the theme of justice is addressed. Very few fragments of the fourth and fifth books remain and the figure of the ideal citizen they outlined. Finally, in the sixth book, the figure of the statesman is emphasized[97] and, in an eschatological perspective, the eternal glory that belongs to him where he has pursued love for the homeland and justice. *Somnium Scipionis* belongs to this book,[98] in which the Platonic doctrine of the immortality of the soul and the prize it constitutes is flanked by the theme of values and political virtue.

On the Laws was probably composed in 52 BCE and should be considered complementary to *On the Republic*. It is a complex work of which we have the first three books; in it the philosophical commitment is accompanied by the technical-legal one. Cicero wonders about the existence of an eternal and universal law; on what is the relationship with existing laws; on how the comparison and debate between the different social partners should and can develop; he analyses the nature and organization of power; he wonders what the value of *libertas* is, what the role of the people in the republic may be. As for this crucial theme in Cicero, Ferrary (1995), 48–73, addresses the issue of the relationship between statesmen and the law in Cicero political works. Powell (2001), 17–39, explores the relationship between *On the Republic* and *On the Laws* and wonders if the laws in Cicero's *On the Laws* are the same as in Cicero's *On the Republic*. Harries (2004), 147–163, addresses the theoretical foundations of the law and explores Cicero's relationship, as a lawyer, with the law.

As Plato, who made *Politeia* succeed *Nomoi*, Cicero also established a close link between *On the Republic* and *On the Laws*. On the one hand, his research is not only an analysis of the theoretical forms of state organization and a diagnosis of the real situation of justice: it also becomes a project and a hope for the future, in a sort of utopian tension. On the other hand, Cicero recognizes the limits of

---

96 *Rep.* 1.39. Stark 1954, 332–347, provides a valid investigation of this passage and the Greek theoretical-philosophical context that is at its foundation.

97 On the virtues of the statesman see Powell 2012, 14–42. In particular: *sapientia, iustitia, temperantia, fortitudo*.

98 See Büchner 1976, 435–508, for a linguistic and philological commentary; the so-called *Somnium Scipionis* did not come to us from the famous seventh-century palimpsest discovered in 1819 by Cardinal A. Mai, but from a commentary by Macrobius dedicated to *De re publica*.

human rationality in applying himself to political affairs.[99] In general, it is clear today that Cicero's political thought is affected by his philosophical training and his political commitment; for this reason, it is not negligible, like the political reflection of philosophers such as Plato, Aristotle, Machiavelli, Hobbes, Rousseau, or Nietzsche. Correctly Nicgorsky (2012), 242–282, recently proposed a serious attempt to rehabilitate Cicero as a political thinker. Among other things, the scholar reports that mindless eclecticism is, perhaps, the most damaging charge to Cicero's possible stature as a political philosopher. Consequently, he thinks that Cicero could be considered at best as a source through which one can understand the course of philosophy and political philosophy from Plato and Aristotle to Christian times. Zetzel (2013), 181–195, provides an agile but committed study of Cicero's political philosophy. Recently Schofield (2021, 1–26) rightly places Cicero among the founders of modern political and social thought.

But what does Cicero actually believe in? Cicero believes in the values of the state and, in particular, of that state which lays its foundation in traditional moral virtue. He imagines a state where practical political life is accompanied by theoretical awareness, almost in a kind of interaction between the philosophical dimension and political responsibility. According to Cicero, this is a real 'service', in which the possible conflict between 'philosophical life' and 'political life' must be resolved.[100]

Even after retiring from public life, following Caesar's victory at Pharsalus in 48, Cicero feels the call for public commitment become more and more alive. The excited phase following the Ides of March 44 sees him at the centre of a feverish series of correspondence, especially with his friend Atticus. Cicero fears that the whole operation of the tyrannicides is being reduced to a simple change of chief.[101] Brutus and Cassius remain the political protagonists to which to refer, but in the background lurks the risk of a new civil war and new actors. Only Atticus is for Cicero a trusted person: Atticus has been his friend since his youth and studies cultivated together in Athens. Atticus is a solid base, beyond the different life choices: Atticus a convinced Epicurean, Cicero opposing Epicureanism; Atticus open to the dimension of the world of private affairs, Cicero completely suited to politics; Atticus a great admirer of Greek culture, Cicero an ambitious strategist

---

99 Atkins 2013 argues that these dialogues together probe the limits of reason in political affairs and explore the resources available to the statesman, given these limitations. But on the other hand (47–79) the role of utopia is evident: how it can help illuminate human nature.

100 See Lévy 2012b, 71–76.

101 *Att.* 14.14.4 (Puteoli, 28 or 29 April of 44): "If so, I shall be happy to see our freedom restored. If not, what shall I have gained by this change of masters, except the joy of gazing on the just death of a tyrant?".

of Roman culture; Atticus an antiquarian, Cicero an orator. The tasks of one were no less demanding than those of the other, as Cicero willingly points out.[102] On 11 May 44, in Puteoli, in a letter to his friend in which he takes stock of some aspects of the political situation and announces his intentions, he writes (*Att.* 14.20.4):

> *Epicuri mentionem facis et audes dicere* μὴ πολιτεύεσθαι?

That is to say: in a situation of this type, so dramatic, so full of historical, social and political implications, when the tyrannicides and the hopes of a return to republican liberties are at stake, "you dare to mention Epicurus and tell me to *keep out of politics*?"

Obviously, it's just a joke, but an important one. The whole weight of the Epicurean philosophical theory appears for a moment and in a moment is discarded for its inadequacy.

On the contrary, the ethical drive that supports Cicero's political commitment takes on a new strength, in a sort of longed for reconciliation between theory and political practice.

It is clear from this that whether Cicero's political faith was intelligently manifested in the organization of his political philosophical thought, in a complementary way the philosophical research (and in particular the study method developed) had important repercussions in the practical performed choices, even in the most delicate historical moments. Unfortunately, Cicero never came up with a real system and an integrated political project. Therefore, if we want to talk about coherence, we will find it exclusively in the moral tension animating his philosophical experience and political life.

---

102 See *Att.* 1.17.5; cf. *supra*, p. 74.

5 Cicero's Philosophical Vocabulary

As we have seen, Cicero devotes great attention to developing a philosophical vocabulary in the Latin language. Powell (1995b), 273–300, dedicates an important essay to Cicero's translation from Greek. He studies the approach, the different contexts, the methods, the strategy, and the aim. He reflects on Ciceronian complaints about the poverty of Latin and on the limits of the so-called literal translation, which Cicero attributes to *interpretes indiserti* (*Fin.* 3.15). He concludes with this shared observation (297): "His project was not, as commonly thought, to create a new philosophical language in Latin, but rather to show that the Latin language as it was, with a few additions here and there, could function as a philosophical language in its own right."

Here, we focus on some technical words, with respect to which he has shown particular awareness and caution in deciding on a possible translation. Almost always, his choices have been welcomed by later philosophical literature in Latin.

5.1 ἀδιάφορα – *indifferentia*

In the framework of Stoic philosophy, ἀδιάφορα ('indifferent things') indicates all the data of natural reality that interfere with the subject's experience and therefore should influence it. In this sense they are neither good nor bad, but they are in the middle, as we read in Stob., *Ecl.* 2.7.7a.4–9, p. 79 W. [*SVF* 3.118]:

> Stoics say that those things that stand in the way between good and evil things are indifferent (ἀδιάφορα τὰ μεταξὺ τῶν ἀγαθῶν καὶ τῶν κακῶν). The *indifferentia* are of two types: in the first sense they do not qualify either as good or as evil (μήτε αἱρετὸν μήτε φευκτόν) and, therefore, they must neither be chosen nor avoided; in a second sense, they are unable to determine either an impulse of acceptance or one of repulsion (τὸ μήτε ὁρμῆς μήτε ἀφορμῆς κινητικόν).[1]

According to Chrysippus, virtue must be at the centre and must guide man in leading his life; as a consequence, the true Stoic will not give space to what might influence him and that, instead, should remain 'indifferent' to him. Concerning the evolution of the Stoic doctrine on this topic, see Inwood–Donini (1999), 692–697. In any case, Kidd (1971), 150–172, observes that the status of the *indifferens* is clearly the bare core of Stoic ethics and the crux of the debate between the

---

1 See also Diog. Laert. 7.102–104; Sext. Emp., *Adv. Math.* 11.59. See L&S 58 B-F.

https://doi.org/10.1515/9783110661835-005

Stoics and rival schools. Kidd (166) thinks that we are faced with a single doctrine, but with different internal developments, connected to the three different stages of progress that can be related to the human conditions on which the analyses are focusing: (1) the child, governed by πρῶτον οἰκεῖον – τὰ πρῶτα κατὰ φύσιν (i.e. the first natural experiences); (2) the adult, governed by καθήκοντα – τὰ κατὰ φύσιν (i.e. what must be done according to nature); (3) the *sapiens* governed by λόγος–ἀρετή–φύσις (i.e. what depends on reason, virtue, nature).

However, especially in the later Stoa, the distinction between what 'is preferable' (τὸ προηγμένον) and what 'is not preferable' (τὸ ἀποπροηγμένον) appears with reference to the *indifferentia*. In this way, once it has been understood what the virtuous path to follow is, the specific decisions to be taken are relative: that is to say, they are more or less preferable. According to Barney (2003), 303–304, the issue remains problematic. Klein (2015), 227–282, argues that, for the earlier Stoa, the indifferents are indispensable to deliberation, because an agent must consider their status to ascertain the action that should be carried out. But they are not a source of value or normative justification in their own right. The value of the promoted indifferents is neither instrumental nor final.

We read in Stob., *Ecl.* 2.7.7g.7–13, pp. 84–85 W. [*SVF* 3.128]:

> They therefore define as preferred (προηγμένον) the *indifferens* that we choose on the basis of a reasoning which is crucial for the choice (κατὰ προηγούμενον λόγον). The same applies to what is rejected ... No good is preferred because good has an absolute value (διὰ τὸ τὴν μέγιστην ἀξίαν); instead, favourite things, which are such as they have a relative value (τὴν δευτέραν χώραν καὶ ἀξίαν ἔχον), are akin to the nature of good things.

Cicero is perfectly aware of this evolution of the concept of ἀδιάφορον; in fact, he underlines that *in principle* the Stoics made the radical distinction between what is good and what is bad. Only what is good is *honestum*, that is to say 'virtuous'; only what is dishonest – that is, foul – is bad. But then they wanted to establish a difference (*aliquid tamen quod differret esse voluerunt*) between the elements that, in themselves, have no real power (*quae nihil valerent*) to give happiness or unhappiness in life. Cicero (*Fin.* 3.50) distinguishes, among these worthless elements, those which he defines as *aestimabilia* (that is, to be taken into consideration), those which are not (*contra*) and those which are neither (*neutrum*). The last ones are the indifferents in an absolute sense.

Undoubtedly Cicero takes up this distinction that goes back, according to him, already to Zeno. In fact, the ἀδιάφορα (*indifferentia*) can be distinguished in τὰ ἀξίαν ἔχοντα (*aestimabilia*), τὰ ἀπαξίαν ἔχοντα (not *aestimabilia*), τὰ οὐδετέρως ἔχοντα (*neutrum*). We reconstruct this, as always, thanks to Stobaeus who reports, in *Ecl.* 2.7, pp. 79–85 W., the classification of the indifferents as developed by the Augustan philosopher Arius Didymus[2] [see in particular *SVF* 3.131].

Cicero knows that the Stoics proceeded further, specifying a gradation for both the *aestimabilia* and the *non-aestimabilia*. So here, *Fin.* 3.51:

a) those who provide sufficient reason (*satis esse causae* / *satis habere causae*) to be preferred (*quam ob rem anteponentur*) or not preferred (*quam ob rem reicerentur*) to others. Among the former: health, good functioning of the senses, lack of pain, glory, wealth; among the latter: pain, illness, loss of consciousness, poverty, ignominy;

b) those that are different from these, because they do not provide sufficient reason: *alia autem non esse eius modi* / *partim non item*.

At this point Cicero notes:

> This is the source of Zeno's term προηγμένον, and its contrary ἀποπροηγμένον. For all the abundance of the Greek language (*lingua copiosa*), he still availed himself of new and artificial words, something we are not allowed, despite our threadbare Latin tongue (*in hac inopi lingua*) – though you are in the habit of saying that Latin is actually more abundant than Greek. None the less, it will not be out of place to explain Zeno's reason for adopting the term προηγμένον, since this will make its meaning more readily understood.[3]

Cicero recognizes the terminological inadequacy of the Latin language to express the key concepts of Greek philosophy. He applies himself to showing the etymological background of προηγμένον and ἀποπροηγμένον, from which he derives the value of *pro-ductus*: 'what is led to pre-eminence', 'what is high' and therefore is 'preferred':

> This is the term (i.e. *producta*) we may use – it is literal. Alternatively, 'pro-moted' (*promota*) and 'demoted' (*remota*), or as we have long said, 'advantageous' (*praeposita*) or 'superior' (*praecipua*), and 'to be rejected' (*reiecta*) for the opposite. If the meaning is understood, we should be relaxed about the words we use.[4]

---

2 Arius' classification distinguishes, among other things, the 'indifferents' (a) on the basis of the context which the 'preference' criterion belongs to: psychic, corporeal, external (Stob., *Ecl.* 2.7.7b.9–16, pp. 80–81 W.; cf. Diog. Laert. 7.106); (b) as a consequence of their rousing the impulse towards something / rousing the impulse away from something / rousing neither one nor the other impulse (Stob., *Ecl.* 2.7.7c.5–10, p. 82 W.). See Long 1983, 41–51 [= Long 1996, 107–133].
3 *Fin.* 3.51.
4 *Fin.* 3.52. See also *Fin.* 3.15: "προηγμένα and ἀποπροηγμένα should certainly be allowed too, even though they may correctly be rendered as preferred (*praeposita*) and rejected (*reiecta*)."

Cicero does not offer a single word to reproduce the meaning of the original. Within the proposed constellation, each interpreter can move emphasizing one aspect rather than another. In any case, he shows that he has fully understood the meaning of the concept expressed in the Greek language.

And here, in conclusion, Cicero arrives at the definition of ἀδιάφορον:

> Now everything that is good, we say, occupies the first rank. So what we call advantageous or superior (*praepositum vel praecipuum*) must be what is neither good nor bad (*nec bonum esse nec malum*). Hence we define this as 'indifferent' (*indifferens*). It occurs to me that I should render their term ἀδιάφορον as 'indifferent', but with a moderate value (*idque ita definimus: quod sit indifferens cum aestimatione mediocri*). It had to be the case that there were some things left in the middle (*in mediis*) that would be either in accordance with nature or not. This being so, there were bound to be included among the former category items of some value. And given this, there had to be some things that were advantageous.[5]

The Stoic ἀδιάφορον is therefore interpreted as that which "does not carry (the Greek verb φέρειν, 'to carry', is present in the root) advantage or disadvantage" in an evident way: that is, it is *indifferent* to the actual outcome of a choice or action. According to Cicero, we cannot think that the median things (between good and evil), which belong to the natural reality and the life of man, are not constituted in such a way as not to be worthy of any evaluation, and therefore we can prefer or not prefer them;[6] another thing, however, is to think that, for this reason, they have an effective importance: this is what the Stoics would warn us about.

The Stoic Seneca[7] would definitively welcome Cicero's proposal. The translation of ἀδιάφορα with *indifferentia* would no longer be questioned.

5.2 βούλησις – *voluntas*

The meaning of βούλησις is not easy to express in modern terms: translations range across 'willing', 'purpose', and 'will'.[8]

What is more interesting, however, is to attempt to carry out a retroversion of 'willing' in the classical Greek language; we will thus discover that the very

---

5 *Fin.* 3.53.
6 Fin. 3.53: *nihil in his poni quod satis aestimabile esset, nec, hoc posito, non aliqua esset praeposita.*
7 *Epp.* 82.10; 14; 117.9; *Vit. b.* 22.4. See Barney 2003, 304–319, regarding Seneca's solution in relation to that offered by Cicero.
8 See LSJ and *TLG*. For Latin *voluntas*, see *OLD*.

conception of what we now mean by 'willing / will' is much more detailed and complex:[9] it is as if the 'passage' in the Latin philosophical language (= *voluntas*) constitutes a sort of funnel where a lot has been simplified.

The Greeks used:

- βούλησις to refer to 'willing' as Aristotle does, for example in *De an.* 433a 23 or in *EN* 1111b 19; it should be borne in mind that Aristotle, *De an.* 414b 2 and 433a 13, considers ὄρεξις ('appetency') the general word including ἐπιθυμία ('desire'), θυμός ('spirit', 'strength', 'impulse', 'temper', 'will'), and βούλησις;
- βούλεσθαι to refer to 'will' or 'wish' or 'be willing' when choice or preference were implied;[10]
- αἵρεσις expressly indicates the choice; in a figurative sense it also indicates the school, the system of philosophic principles that someone professes;
- προαίρεσις to refer to the resolution, to the deliberately choosing that follows the evaluation, as in Arist., *EE* 1226b 17 ss.; *EN* 1139a 23–25;[11] 1103a 10–11; 1139a 23; *GE* 1189a 31–32;
- ἐθέλειν / θέλειν alludes to the willingness, referred to 'consent' rather than 'desire'; in this sense it is different from βούλεσθαι, cf. Plat., *Grg.* 522ε: εἰ δὲ βούλει, σοὶ ἐγὼ ... ἐθέλω λόγον λέξαι, "If you want, I agree to tell you this with a speech."

Trying to summarize, for the Greek philosophers the 'will' is a kind of 'appetite' that pushes to rational 'decision'. Furthermore, when a decision is made voluntarily (i.e. it occurs of *one's own free will*), the attribute ἑκών is used, which means 'wittingly', 'purposely' 'of one's own motion', 'spontaneous' and, therefore, 'willingly'.[12] Aristotle studies what willingness depends on and is defined by (*EE* 2.9): whether from appetite (τῇ ὀρέξει), from decision (τῇ προαιρέσει) or from the ability to think (τὸ κατὰ τὴν διάνοιαν). In the

---

9 See Kenny 1975; Dihle 1982; Frede 2011.

10 Βούλησις, although having the same root, does not coincide with βούλευσις, which, in judicial technical language, refers to the deliberation. There is a similar distinction between βούλεσθαι (to will) and βουλεύεσθαι (to deliberate).

11 To keep in mind *EN* 1139a 23–25: "Since virtue (ἡ ἠθικὴ ἀρετὴ) is a habitual state that produces choices (ἕξις προαιρετική), and choice (προαίρεσις) is a deliberate desire (ὄρεξις βουλευτική), precisely for this reason, if the choice is the best (εἴπερ ἡ προαίρεσις σπουδαία), the reasoning must be true (τόν τε λόγον ἀληθῆ εἶναι) and the desire correct (τὴν ὄρεξιν ὀρθήν)."

12 In the philosophical field, the pages of Aristotle in *Book* III of the *Nicomachean Ethics* and in *Book* II of the *Eudemian Ethics* are fundamental in this regard. In particular, in *EE* 2.7–8, Aristotle analysed themes such as the 'voluntary' and the 'involuntary' (τὸ ἑκούσιον / τὸ ἀκούσιον), 'what is done by force' (βίῳ) or 'by necessity' (ἀναγκαζόμενον).

fundamental *chap.* 10, he focuses on the 'decision'; it is first related to the will (βούλησις); then, however, it is clearly distinct not only from will, but also from opinion (δόξα) and from conjecture (ὑπόληψις). All this implies, in Aristotle, a reflection on the concept of choice (αἵρεσις); for this reason he specifies the centrality of deliberating (τὸ βουλεύσασθαι), that is, of arriving at a deliberate opinion (δόξα βουλευτική). To what extent the one who deliberates, deliberates out of ignorance or with awareness, is ultimately the reason why the deliberation is correlated to the aim that the deliberating man proposes. Therefore, whoever deliberates consciously will be, according to Aristotle, precisely the one who has examined the end (τέλος) towards which it tends and who is able to decide what tends towards it (ὅ τι ἐκεῖ συντείνει). Aristotle concludes his examination (*chap.* 11) by reiterating the link between reason and action thanks to their relationship precisely to the end: on the one hand, the end is the principle of reflection (*EE* 1227b 32–33: τῆς μὲν οὖν νοήσεως ἀρχὴ τὸ τέλος), that is, what allows the rational being to grasp the objective and identify the means that allow him to reach his own state of perfection and equilibrium in the becoming world; on the other hand, it is "that in view of which" (36: τέλος δ' ἐστὶ τὸ οὗ ἔνεκα) decisions are made (38: τὸ προαιρεῖσθαι οὗ ἔνεκα) and then man acts; that is to say: that in view of which we carry out the various steps to achieve the end (36: τὰ πρὸς τὸ τέλος).

In *Nicomachean Ethics*, Aristotle broadly confirms the basic theses supported in the *Eudemian Ethics*. The analysis relating to the involuntary actions we undertake out of ignorance and compulsion is very accurate (*chapters* 1 and 2); in *chap.* 3 Aristotle focuses on the error and wonders what it depends on. In the crucial *chapters* 4 and 5 he studies the προαίρεσις and its relationship with virtue. Hence the end (*chap.* 6) and the decisions to be made with respect to the end (*chap.* 7). Lastly, the approach to the issue of responsibility (*chap.* 7); this problem is what Aristotle re-discusses in *Book* V, *chap.* 10–13, in relation to justice and the law, which should have codified the character of justice in its universality (*EN* 1137b 27: διὰ τὸ καθόλου).

Precisely the issue of responsibility (*chap.* 7) is addressed in a more detailed way than is the case in the *Eudemian Ethics*.[13]

---

13 In the latter, Aristotle limited himself to arguing: "It is clear that all those actions of which man is the principle and master can happen or not, and that it is in his power that those things happen or not, of which he is master whether they are or not. For all those things which it is in his power to do or not to do he himself is responsible; and those things for which he is responsible are in his power", *EE* 1223a 4–9. See Cooper 2013, 265–312; Bobzien 2014, 81–109.

As is evident, all this implies that the possibility of deciding something actually belongs to a certain 'individual' capable of knowing and then carrying out a consequent action. This is the modern problem of 'free will'.[14]

This problem is faced in a very different way by Aristotle (and his commentators) than Stoicism: according to the latter philosophy, it seems problematic to try to combine freedom of will within a deterministic perspective.[15]

Only in the Hellenistic period and in the Roman and Late Antiquity did 'will' begin to be understood *directly* as the principle of 'action', as the 'tendency' and at the same time the 'tension' to achieve a certain result.[16] According to Stoicism, 'will' ends up by conjugating itself with the rational nature of man and becomes the determining element of his morality. According to Epicureanism, on the other hand, it becomes essential to understand what really belongs to man, conceived as an individual being passive and active at the same time with respect to the physical world that surrounds him and that he is able to 'perceive'; this is because autonomy and freedom of will derive only from here. This is attested by not only Lucretius, a faithful interpreter of Epicurus, but by Cicero himself, in his explicit reference to τὸ ἐφ' ἡμῖν: to what depends on us.[17]

The term *voluntas* occurs very frequently in Cicero. A quick check of *Lexikon zu den philosophischen Schriften Cicero's* (Merguet 1877) and *Lexikon zu den Reden des Cicero* (Merguet 1877–1884), allows us not only to verify the frequency and variety of use, but also to ascertain some differentiation between the use in philosophically oriented writings and that in the orations.

Obviously in the background there is the verb *velle*, and the inherent intentional value transpires in expressions in which the 'voluntariness' of an action is opposed to its 'necessity', that is to say not so much to 'non-dependence' from the agent's decision, but rather to the inevitability of an external constraint.

---

14 List 2019 offers an overview of the modern concept of free will. Unfortunately, and inexplicably, he does not consider the Greco-Roman philosophical tradition and, in particular, Aristotle.

15 Both schools explicitly addressed the topic: Cicero's testimony has reached us (see *On Fate*) about the Stoics, and the testimony of Alexander of Aphrodisias (also author of another *On Fate*) about the Aristotelian doctrine.

16 In this direction, in addition to Cicero, see Chrysippus and especially the Stoic Seneca. See Voelke 1973, 161–190; Inwood 2005, 132–156; Gómez 2014, 121–139.

17 See *Fat.* 46–48; Maso 2014a, 235–250. A definitive assessment of the linguistic use of ἐφ' ἡμῖν, παρ' ἡμᾶς, ἐξ ἡμῶν and *in nostra potestate* is impossible, due to the lack of evidence: in the 'original' texts of Chrysippus and Epicurus, ἐφ' ἡμῖν is not confirmed (although both Ancients and Moderns agree that this use is absolutely plausible); and, most importantly, Cicero's Latin expression (*in nostra potestate*) leaves open the question of the Greek source text. By his famous expression *innata potestas*, Lucretius 2.286 seems to assume παρ' ἡμᾶς.

This is a clearly defined aspect in *Top.* 63, in a work that echoes Aristotle's researches in logic, but in a context where the question is inserted in the topic concerning the causality of an action:

> But in some of these causes there is a uniform operation (*constantia*), and in others there is not. In nature and in art there is uniformity (*constantia*); but in the others there is none. But still of those causes which are not uniform, some are evident, others are concealed. Those are evident which touch the desire or judgment of the mind (*appetitionem animi iudiciumque*); those are concealed which are subject to fortune: for as nothing is done without some cause, this very obscure cause, which works in a concealed manner, is the issue of fortune. Again, the produced results are partly unintended (*ignorata*), partly intentional (*voluntaria*). Those are unintended which are produced by necessity; those are intentional (*voluntaria*) which are produced by design. For to shoot an arrow is an act of intention (*voluntatis est*); to hit a man whom you did not mean to hit is the result of fortune. And this is the topic which you use like a battering-ram in your forensic pleadings; if a weapon has flown from the man's hand rather than been thrown by him. Also agitation of mind may be divided into absence of knowledge and absence of intention (*in ignorationem atque imprudentiam*). And although they are to a certain extent voluntary (*quamquam sunt voluntariae*) – for they are diverted from their course by reproof or by admonition –, still they are liable to such emotions that even those acts of theirs which are intentional (*ea quae voluntaria sunt*) sometimes seem either unavoidable (*necessaria*), or at all events unintentional (*certe ignorata*).

According to Cicero, something may happen without us knowing it (*ignorata*), though we see its effects; something else happens, instead, because we wanted it (*voluntaria*). In the first case, Cicero does not hesitate to define the outcome of the event as *necessaria effecta*; in the second, it introduces the concept of *consilium*, that is the responsible decision of whoever is the cause of a certain effect.

Voluntas is also present in the Ciceronian correspondence. In *Epistulae ad familiares* the word appears almost 150 times, with meanings that allude both to its psychological value[18] and to its intrinsic intensity deriving from awareness.[19]

But in conclusion, what is *voluntas* for Cicero?

---

18 See *Fam.* 5.2.10: "That kindly disposition I still maintain (*maneo in voluntate*), and so long as it is your pleasure (*quoad voles tu*), I shall continue to maintain it; and I shall sooner cease to resent your brother's conduct because I love you, than because of that resentment permit our mutual goodwill (*nostra benevolentia*) to be in the slightest degree impaired."

19 See *Fam.* 6.4.2: "I mean that the best possible consolation in trouble is the consciousness of a right purpose (*conscientiam rectae voluntatis*), and that there is no serious evil other than wrong conduct"; *Fam.* 3.9.1: "And so, conscious as I was (*conscientia*) of my unswerving goodwill towards you (*meae constantis erga te voluntatis*), I replied with a touch of temper".

As we said, in the background there is the comparison with Aristotle and with Stoicism,[20] as well as with Antiochus of Ascalon.

We have a passage in which Cicero tries to make explicit the literal meaning of *voluntas* and reports the word that, he supposes, in Greek could better convey its meaning:

> By nature, all people pursue those things which they think to be good and avoid their opposites. Therefore, as soon as a person receives an impression of some thing which he thinks is good, nature itself urges him to reach out after it (*ad id adipiscendum impellit ipsa natura*). When this is done prudently and in accordance with consistency (*id cum constanter prudenterque fit*), it is the sort of reaching which the Stoics call a βούλησις, and which I shall term 'volition' (*nos appellemus voluntatem*). They think that volition, which they define as 'a wish for some object in accordance with reason' (*voluntas est, quae quid cum ratione desiderat*), is found only in the wise person. But the sort of reaching which is aroused too vigorously and in a manner opposed to reason is called 'desire' or 'unbridled longing' (*ea libido est vel cupiditas effrenata*), and this is what is found in all who are foolish.[21]

Cicero therefore decides to translate βούλησις with *voluntas*: he seems to hesitate, but in fact his hesitation depends on the awareness of how much the Latin word is inclusive of many distinct meanings in the Greek language. A confirmation comes from the fifth book of *On the Ends of Good and Evil*, in which Cicero, after concluding the comparison between the Epicurean doctrine presented by Torquatus and the Stoic doctrine presented by Cato, confronts the Academy of Antiochus and the Roman Peripatetic entourage.[22] The subject is the relationship between body and mind. According to Cicero, the body has its own natural activity (*est autem etiam actio quaedam corporis*, *Fin.* 5.35), which gathers and coordinates its various parts; like the body, the soul must also be perfectly intact: that is, it must profit from all its virtues. But these ones can be innate and not voluntary (*non voluntariae*), like cleverness, or voluntary (*quae in voluntate positae*): the latter are more properly virtues.

---

20 However, for Stoicism, it is not easy to define what will is. See Stob., *Ecl.* 2.7.9a.1–9, p. 87 W. [= *SVF* 3.173]: "There are several kinds of practical impulse (τῆς δὲ πρακτικῆς ὁρμῆς), among which: intention (πρόθεσιν), determination (ἐπιβολήν), disposition (παρασκευήν), resolution (ἐγχείρησιν), <choice> (αἵρεσιν), deliberation (προαίρεσιν), will (βούλησιν), volition (θέλησιν). [...] Choice is an act of will due to reasoning (αἵρεσιν δὲ βούλησιν ἐξ ἀναλογισμοῦ); deliberation is a kind of choice preceding choice (προαίρεσιν δὲ αἵρεσιν πρὸ αἱρέσεως); will is a reasonable impulse (βούλησιν δὲ εὔλογον ὄρεξιν); volition is an act of autonomous will (θέλησιν δὲ ἑκούσιον βούλησιν)."
21 *Tusc.* 4.12 = *SVF* 3.438.
22 Staseas from Naples, come to Rome in 92 BCE, was probably the first Roman Peripatetic philosopher. See *Fin.* 5.8; 5.75; *De Or.* 1.104–105.

This is a description and explanation of the parts of the body and soul that cannot be attributed to Aristotle. While here we distinguish the voluntary virtues from the involuntary ones, in Aristotle we distinguish, instead, between ethical virtues and dianoetic virtues. It is not clear whether this distinction can be traced back to Antiochus of Ascalon.

Keeping mind and body together is the strategy that Cicero proposes. We also find this purpose in the reply to Balbus' Stoicizing theses, developed by the Academic Cotta in the third book of *On the Nature of the Gods*:

> For you yourselves (i.e. the Stoics) are fond of saying that there is nothing that a god cannot accomplish, and that without any toil; as man's limbs are effortlessly moved merely by his mind and will (*ut enim hominum membra nulla contentione mente ipsa ac voluntate moveantur*), so, as you say, gods' power can mould and move and alter all things. Nor do you say this as some superstitious fable or old wives' tale, but you give a scientific and systematic account (*sed physica constantique ratione*) of it.[23]

From this passage we understand that reason (*ratio*) and tension (*contentio*) can be considered the forms in which will (*voluntas*) is translated in its generality; beside it Cicero puts (but in practice opposes) the subjective perspective of those who have their task to carry out responsibly anyway.

Self-control and the right balance certainly characterize the way in which Cicero interprets right will. In *Tusc.* 4.12 (see above), he specified accurately that the act of willing is to be understood as tending towards something (or desiring something) in such a way that *id cum constanter prudenterque fit*, that is, that it takes place in a balanced (i.e. not according to variations in excess or failing) and rational way: obviously by this Cicero means the rationality expressed in applying to action.

5.3 εἱμαρμένη – *fatum*

According to the Stoic school, fate is the principle everything is guided by and everything is subject.[24] We know, thanks to Aulus Gellius,[25] a key passage from the fourth book of Chrysippus' Περὶ προνοίας which, in addition to the Latin translation, presents us with the original Greek:

---

23 *ND* 3.92.
24 As for the definitions of εἱμαρμένη see *SVF* 2.912–927; L&S 55 K-S.
25 Aulus Gellius (2nd century CE), Roman scholar and grammarian, studied rhetoric, law and philosophy in Athens and Rome. He was close to the Middle Platonic stance.

Fate (εἱμαρμένην) is a certain everlasting natural ordering of the whole (φυσικήν τινα σύνταξιν τῶν ὅλων ἐξ ἀϊδίου): one set of things follows another (τῶν ἑτέρων τοῖς ἑτέροις ἐπακολουθούντων) and together finds its destruction (μεταπολουμένων), since the interconnection (ἐπιπλοκῆς) is inevitable (ἀπαραβάτου).[26]

The fundamental elements of the Stoic doctrine relating to destiny are practically all there: the natural order, its eternity and its evolution / cyclicality, the inevitable interconnection of all entities. Moreover, since this passage belongs to Περὶ προνοίας (i.e. to a work on 'foreseeing' with respect to what happens), it allows us to imagine the causal relationship between entities, in relation to the future. As we have previously observed, Cicero dedicates a specific work (*On Fate*) to studying the Stoic meaning of εἱμαρμένη.[27] We must turn to this work in order to derive the distance between Cicero's conception of nature and that of the Stoic school.

However, we must here highlight at least two definitions that Cicero proposes, so as to grasp the meaning of his interpretation and, therefore, of his translation:

a) the definition of fate reported in a fragment – which finds confirmation in *Div.* 1.125 – and which is attributable to *On Fate*:

Fate is the interconnection of events for eternity, which changes by order and by its law, in such a way, however, that this variation is eternal;[28]

b) the definition that Cicero says he takes from the first book of Chryippus *On the Nature of the Gods*, in *ND* 1.40:

[Chrysippus] also identifies Jupiter with the mighty Law, everlasting and eternal, which is our guide of life and instructress in duty, and which he entitles Fatal Necessity, and Everlasting Truth of future events.[29]

In the first quotation, Cicero strictly adheres to the Stoic doctrine: he emphasizes that we are faced with an internal law (*suo ordine et lege*) that eternally governs (*per aeternitatem*) the concatenation (*conexio*) and the variation (*varietas*) of what happens. In the second quotation, Cicero shows that he is perfectly close to

---

26 *N.A.* 7.2.1 = *SVF* 2.1000, L&S 55 K.

27 See *supra*, p. 83, as regards the meaning of destiny, *fatum*, and εἱμαρμένη.

28 See Servius, *in Verg. Aen.* 3.376 (= *Fat., fr.* 2 Ax): *Fatum est conexio rerum per aeternitatem se invicem tenens, quae suo ordine et lege variatur, ita tamen ut ipsa varietas habeat aeternitatem.*

29 *Idemque etiam legis perpetuae et aeternae vim, quae quasi dux vitae et magistra officiorum sit, Iovem dicit* (i.e. Chrysippus) *esse, eandemque fatalem necessitatem appellat sempiternam rerum futurarum veritatem.*

the immanentistic conception of the world that Stoicism, and Chrysippus in particular, professes. The 'whole' is divine and, in the 'whole', the eternal force of the law is manifested (*legis perpetuae et aeternae*); from this emerges – and this is a further element that Cicero grasps – the paidetic dimension of destiny: it indicates and teaches what man must do (*magistra officiorum*). Finally, since fate – as fate – must necessarily be fulfilled, the problem of truth is involved: what happens in the future is certainly true, if the relationship of cause and effect has a logical basis (*sempiternam rerum futurarum veritatem*).

Here we see the entire topic addressed in *On Fate*, where the meaning of Stoic determinism lies precisely in the combination between the logical and physical dimensions of the cause-effect relationship. It is a thesis which, as we know, Cicero does not share but which he cleverly proposes and discusses.

Concerning the limits (and also the complexity) of Cicero's conception of εἱμαρμένη (which more generally involves the problem of causality), Susanne Bobzien's work dedicated to determinism is recommended. The scholar focuses on the 'framework story' in Cicero's *Fat.* 39–40 and 44–45.[30] She considers Cicero responsible for the overall 'scenario': a scenario, however, based on works drawing on Chrysippus and his conception of fate. Rival theories are compared, one necessitarian, the other libertarian. Bobzien believes that, regardless of the objectivity of what Cicero claims, he fabricates his tale, presumably with some doxographic support, without worrying much about the historicity. Beyond Bobzien's considerations, the way in which the 'scenario' is constructed remains an important fact: Cicero does not mention any source (although his frequentation of the works of the Stoics close to him and of the Academics is indubitable); he manages and arranges the various arguments in defence of his own moral conception; it grasps the sense of stoic εἱμαρμένη, but does not accept the many implications inherent in the behaviour that each man independently decides to adopt.

5.4 καθῆκον – *officium*

As we have already seen,[31] Cicero, with regard to the moral theory on 'duty', first of all relates to Panaetius. Cicero is persuaded of the goodness of his Latin translation of καθῆκον with *officium*; however, some detailed analysis is convenient, precisely because in this case Cicero neither relies on an innovative

---

30 See Bobzien 1998, 314–324.
31 See *supra*, pp. 45–47.

semantic calque nor opts for *munus*, a word he already knows, but which he seems to use in more practical-operational[32] than theoretical-moral contexts.

In the fifth book of *On the Ends of Good and Evil*, Cicero approaches the problem of the *summum bonum* with reference to the doctrine of the 'Old Academy' (i.e. the views advanced by Antiochus as common to the Academics and Peripatetics). He points out the great difference with respect to Epicureanism and, also, to Stoicism. However, he specifies that the *summum bonum* is based on our natural instincts. The ways in which the different schools interpret the τέλος to be aimed for may diverge, but it is certain that the foundation of the procedures we adopt to achieve it (i.e. our task / duty, as being animated) rests directly on nature. It follows that, conversely, in nature itself (and in its way of organizing) men, too, must find the way to understand what their duty is:

> When we have ascertained the ends of things, knowing the ultimate good and ultimate evil, we have discovered a map of life (*inventa vitae via est*), a chart of all the duties (*conformatio omnium officiorum*); and therefore have discovered a standard to which each action may be referred; and from this we can discover and construct that rule of happiness (*beate vivendi ratio*) which all are aiming for (*id quod omnes expetunt*).[33]

We note that Cicero strictly connects duty (that is, what each man as an agent does) to two precise and indisputable elements: a) duty is 'appropriate' to nature (*accommodatum naturae*), so it depends on it; b) duty rests and receives strength from the appetitive faculty of the soul (*appetitum animi*), that is, from what is the ὁρμή of the Greek philosophers.[34]

In short: beyond the τέλος that each philosophical school proposes (and on the basis of which it will stand out and 'fight'), the theory remains that there is, on the one hand, the anchoring of 'duty' to nature and its proactive drive,[35] while,

---

32 See, *Mil.* 22: "The task / duty (*munus*) of the most authoritative citizens is to resist"; *Off.* 1.20: "The first function / duty (*primum munus*) of justice is that no one harm anyone"; *Fin.* 3.31: "The supreme duty (*summum munus*) of the wise man is to resist appearances and resolutely withhold his assents".

33 *Fin.* 5.15–16.

34 Cicero translates ὁρμή with *appetitio animi* in *Fin.* 3.23; therefore, in 4.32 and 39, he uses the term *naturalis appetitio*. In 5.17 he writes that: "Now practically all have agreed that the subject with which Prudence is occupied and the end which it desires to attain (*quod assequi vellet*) is bound to be something intimately adapted (*aptum et accommodatum*) to our nature; it must be capable of directly arousing and awakening an impulse of desire (*appetitum animi*), what in Greek is called ὁρμή."

35 Note that, later on, the Stoic Seneca would translate, unlike Cicero, ὁρμή with *impetum*; see *Ep.* 113.18: "No animated creature endowed with reason does anything unless, first, it has been

on the other, the submission of 'duty' to the *ratio* characterizing a particular animal: man.

For man, in fact, living according to nature means living according to reason; and, in turn, life according to reason is the virtuous life, as Aristotle indicated. Aristotle, as is known, intended to refer both to the *ratio*, governing the virtuous method of acting (and which is identified in the so-called *ethical virtue*); and to the *ratio perfecta*, which implies self-realization (and which is identified in the so-called *dianoetic virtue*).

5.5 κατάληψις, καταληπτικὴ φαντασία – *comprehensio, visum comprehendibile*

By κατάληψις the Stoics mean the act of understanding. It is something that lies between science and non-science (i.e. opinion). In this sense κατάληψις is also a criterion of truth.

Cicero is perfectly aware of this, since he correctly combines the act with the content of understanding, which consists not so much in the real object itself, but in the representation (φαντασία) of it as formed in the mind.[36]

So he writes in *Varr.* 41–42 [*SVF* 1.60]:

'Zeno held that not all presentations (*visis non omnibus*)[37] are trustworthy, but only those that have a manifestation, peculiar to themselves, (*propriam declarationem*)[38] of the objects

---

prompted by the impression of some particular thing; next, it has entertained an impulse (*impetum cepit*); and finally, assent has confirmed this impulse (*impetum*)", (transl. by Graver 2015). On the characters and centrality of the concept of impulse in Stoic thought, see Brennan 2003, 265–269.

36 Sandbach 1971a, 11–15, gives us some clarification on Cicero's interpretation.

37 To translate φαντασία Cicero adopts *visum*. See *Varr.* 40: "Here first all he (i.e. Zeno) made some new pronouncements about sensation itself, which he held to be a combination of a sort of impact offered from outside, which he called φαντασίαν and we may call a presentation (*visum*), and let us retain this term at all events, for we shall have to employ it several times in the remainder of my discourse"; *Luc.* 18: "*visum*: for we have by this time sufficiently get accustomed – by our yesterday's conversation – to this rendering of φαντασία." Reinhardt 2018, 305–325, however, takes back *percipere visum* to the Stoic concept of 'cataleptic impression'. In his opinion, Cicero thought that it is the impression, not what it is an impression of, that is securely grasped.

38 Most likely Cicero is here alluding to a technical term of Hellenistic philosophy both in the Stoic and Epicurean fields: ἐνάργεια. This defines 'clear evidence' for the senses: that is, the conformity of what is perceived to external reality (see Epic., *Hrd.* 48; 52; 71). See immediately below.

presented; and a trustworthy presentation, being perceived as such by its own intrinsic nature, he termed 'comprehensible' (*comprehendibile*) – will you endure this coinage?' 'Indeed we will,' said Atticus, 'for how else could you express καταληπτόν?' 'But after it had been received and accepted as true, he termed it a "comprehension", (*comprehensionem*) resembling objects contained in the hand – and in fact he had derived the actual term from manual "prehension", nobody before having used the word in such a sense, and he also used a number of new terms, for his doctrines were new. Well, a thing grasped through sensation (*sensu comprensum*) he called itself a sensation (*sensum*), and a sensation so firmly grasped through reasoning (*si ita erat comprensum*) as to be irremovable he termed knowledge (*scientia*), while a sensation not so well grasped he termed ignorance (*inscentiam*), and this was the source also of opinion, an unstable (*inbecilla*) impression akin to falsehood and ignorance. At a stage between knowledge and ignorance he placed that 'comprehension' (*comprehensionem*) of which I have spoken, and he reckoned it neither as a right nor as a wrong impression, but said that it was only 'credible' (*ei credendum esse*).'

The translation of κατάληψις with *comprehensio* that Cicero proposes is a real morphological calque[39] and appears inevitable, thanks also to the figurative reference that its etymology, both in Greek and in Latin, explicitly evokes. We are dealing with what later, but with great accuracy, would be described by Sextus Empiricus, referring to Zeno and to what the Stoics called καταληπτικὴ φαντασία:

An apprehensive presentation is one caused by an existing object in accordance with that object and imaged and stamped in the subject, such as could not be derived from a non-existent object.[40]

Cicero was well aware of this aspect of the Stoic doctrine and knew that a *kataleptic representation* could be considered as such, only if it received a firm and permanent assent: this agreement is many-sided, because it complies to the following three requirements: a) it comes from a real object ; b) it conforms to a real object and faithfully captures and preserves all its characters: i.e. its precise configuration; c) it is clear and evident, so that it cannot come from something that does not exist, but from that certain precise object which is represented.[41] This last requirement is interesting, both because it excludes the possibility that

---

39 See Powell 1995b, 228.

40 *Adv. Math.* 7.248.

41 See Cic., *Luc.* 18 and 77 [= *SVF* 1.59]; Diog. Laert. 7.46 and 50 [= *SVF* 2.53 and 60]; Sext. Emp., *Adv. Math.* 7.426 [= *SVF* 2.69]. The later Stoics introduced a further requirement, according to which "there must be no adverse circumstances", Sext. Emp., *Adv. Math.* 7.253–257; see Alesse 2018, 152–158. Cic., *Luc.* 104, points out that, according to the Academic philosopher Clithomacus, for the representations to be probable, they must not have any impediment: *neque tamen omnia eius modi visa adprobari, sed ea quae nulla re inpedirentur.*

the *kataleptic representation* is pure imagination, and because it evokes 'evidence', another technical word that Cicero tries to translate:

> There was nothing clearer than ἐνάργεια, as the Greeks call it; let us term it 'transparency' (*perspicuitatem*) or 'evidence' (*evidentiam*), if you will, and let us manufacture terms if necessary.[42]

For the Stoics, however, the *kataleptic representation*, which is necessarily determined by something existing, consists in a real act of understanding that pertains to the ἡγεμονικόν. This aspect is strongly highlighted by the 'externalist' interpretations (see Frede 1976, 151–176; Alesse 2018, 145–151). On the contrary, the 'internalist' interpretation highlights the role of the mind in recognizing the features of evidence and clarity in the representation it receives (see Annas 1990, 184–203).

As a consequence of the *kataleptic representation*, the ἡγημονικόν[43] itself proceeds to the *adsensus / adsensio*: a word Cicero translates συγκατάθεσις. We know that Diocles of Magnesias (2nd or 1st century BCE) specified that: "the speeches on assent (περὶ συγκαταθέσεως), on comprehension (περὶ καταλήψεως) and on intelligence (περὶ νοήσεως) do not hold up without representation (ἄνευ φαντασίας)."[44] Now Cicero, in *Fat.* 42, points out that: "Assenting could not occur, unless aroused by a sense-impression (*adsensio non possit fieri nisi commota viso*)"; and in *Varr.* 40 he writes: "To these presentations received by the senses he (i.e. Zeno) joins the act of mental assent (*assensionem adiungit animorum*), which he makes out to reside within us and to be a voluntary act (*quam esse vult in nobis positam et voluntariam*)."

In agreement with Zeno, Cicero specifies that assent (*adsensio*) is an act of approval (*adprobatio*) and remembers that it is in our power:

> For while we were explaining the power (*vim*) residing in the senses, it was at same time disclosed that many things are grasped and perceived by the senses (*comprendi multa et percipi sensibus*), which cannot happen without the act of assent (*sine adsensione*). Again, as the greatest difference between an inanimate and an animate object is that an animate object performs some action (...), either it must be denied the possession of sensation or it

---

42 *Luc.* 17.
43 Cicero disregards the ἡγεμονικόν of the Stoics; the translation into Latin of this fundamental element of physical doctrine is due to Seneca, who adopts the word *principale*. See *Ep.* 113.23 [= *SVF* 2.836].
44 Diog. Laert. 7.49.

must be assigned a faculty of assenting (*adsensio*) as a voluntary act (*quae est in nostra potestate*).[45]

Cicero adds that without assent neither memory (*memoria*) nor the notions of objects (*notitiae rerum*) nor the arts and sciences (*artes*) can exist. And the man, who will not give consent to anything, will not even have the possibility of existing as a man, because he will have nothing that depends on him.

Therefore:

> Speaking generally, before we act it is essential for us to experience some representation (*ante videri aliquid quam agamus necesse est*), and our assent to be given to the representation (*eique quod visum sit adsentiatur*); therefore one who abolishes either representation or assent (*visum aut adsensum*) abolishes all action out of life.[46]

As a result of the *kataleptic representation* and the assent given to it, we have action (as we have already explained), but also the formation of the notions of things: what Zeno called ἔννοια[47] and Cicero translates as *notio*.[48] We must imagine the ἡγεμονικόν as a sheet of paper prepared for writing, on which the notions of the things we acquire are progressively transcribed, following the repeated experiences of a large number of representations.[49] It is obviously a result, on the one hand, deriving from the fact that, following the sensation (*e sensibus*), the notions of things are imprinted in the soul (*notiones rerum in animis imprimerentur*); on the other hand, it depends on the fact that the ἡγεμονικόν is

---

45 *Luc.* 37.
46 *Luc.* 39.
47 On this, see Plut., *Comm. not.* 1084f [= *SVF* 2.847], who does not hesitate to define the ἔννοιαι "a certain type of representation (φαντασία γάρ τις ἡ ἔννοιά ἐστι)."
48 See *Fin.* 3.21: "As soon as man has understanding, or rather becomes capable of 'conception' (*notionem*) – in Stoic phraseology ἔννοια ..."; *Top.* 31: "I mean by notion (*notionem*) what the Greeks call sometimes ἔννοιαν, and sometimes πρόληψιν. It is knowledge implanted and previously acquired of each separate thing, but one which requires development." Only a paragraph earlier (30) Cicero had been concerned with finding the correct way to render another key word of Greek metaphysics into Latin: "In partition, there are as it were members; as of a body – head, shoulders, hands, sides, legs, feet, and so on. In division there are forms (*formae*) which the Greeks call εἴδη; our countrymen who treat of such subjects call them *species*. And it is not a bad name, though it is an inconvenient one, if we want to use it in different cases. For even if it were Latin to use such words, I should not like to say *specierum* and *speciebus*. And we have often occasion to use these cases. But I have no such objection to saying *formis* and *formarum*; and as the meaning of each word is the same, I do not think that convenience of sound (*commoditatem in dicendo*) is wholly to be neglected." As is evident, Cicero here follows an aesthetic-formal linguistic criterion applied to the grammar rules.
49 See *SVF* 2.83.

active in establishing, through a firm and constant assent, that one is not faced with an approximation, an error or, simply, an *a-kataleptic representation* (i.e. devoid of evidence and that may come from something that does not exist).

5.6 οἰκείωσις – *conciliatio*

According to the Stoic school, the doctrine of οἰκείωσις is fundamental. It alludes to the process through which an entity becomes itself by *appropriating* its natural *characteristics*: οἶκος (the 'home') is 'what we live in' and, therefore, is what is most proper to us. It is a real 'conciliation' with nature. This is a general founding process not only of Physics, but also of Ethics, since it allows the affirmation of each man, within a precise structure of social interaction.

According to one of the most typical interpretative lines of ancient Physics, 'attraction' and therefore 'conciliation' derive from similarity / affinity – and therefore from 'appropriateness.'

Cicero, Seneca, and Hierocles[50] are the philosophers who provide us with the most authoritative evidences.

Today we obtain a reliable updated statement on the doctrine thanks to four specific works:

- *The Stoic Theory of Oikeiōsis: Moral Development and Social Interaction in Early Stoic Philosophy*, by Troels Engberg-Pedersen, Aarhus 1990;
- *«Oikeiōsis». Ricerche sul fondamento del pensiero stoico e sulla sua genesi*, by Roberto Radice, Milano 2000;
- *Oikeiōsis. Stoische Ethik in naturphilosophischer Perspektive*, by Chang-Uh Lee, Freiburg 2002;
- *Die Oikeiōsislehre der Stoa. I. Rekonstruktion ihres Inhalts*, by Robert Bees, Würzburg 2004.

The works of Engberg-Pedersen and Radice aim to give a general and systematic historical-philosophical portrait, trying to reconstruct the problematic background from which the birth and development of the doctrine of οἰκείωσις comes. In the background we find the Ethics of the Cynics and the centrality of

---

50 Concerning this Stoic philosopher, who lived in the 2nd century CE, we received quotations thanks to Stobaeus' *Anthology* (5th century CE), and a fragment of 300 lines from Papyrus Berolinensis 9780, discovered in 1901, probably deriving from Hermopoulis (Egypt). In it, self-perception and self-ownership, which are both the primary and the most basic faculties of animals, are discussed. See Inwood 1984, 151–184; Long 1996, 250–263. As for the evidences, see Bastianini-Long 1992, 268–451, and Ramelli 2009. See also L&S 53B, 57C–D.

the concept of nature; then the reconsideration of the Platonic/Aristotelian tradition. Lee's work analyses the peculiar aspects of Stoic 'appropriation' and places them in a general cosmological-theological perspective. Bees's work focuses above all on the three major sources: Cicero's *On the Ends of Good and Evil* and *On the Nature of the Gods*, and Seneca's *Letter* 121. As in Radice's, we note a particular attention to the scientific-biological, medical and psychological background and to the contribution probably made to the doctrine by the Stoic Posidonius. Coming to the major witnesses, however, we observe that Seneca offers his Stoic interpretation of the οἰκείωσις with great clarity; Cicero, on the other hand, especially in the third book of *On the Ends of Good and Evil*, exposes the Stoic position almost as a response to the Epicurean interpretation; similarly we can grasp, in the second book of *On the Nature of the Gods*, an answer to the Epicurean theological perspective offered in the first book. In this regard, a comparison between Epicureanism and Stoicism as regards the 'cradle argument' is offered by Brunschwig (1986), 138–144.

As for the translation, Cicero has no doubts.[51] He uses the verb *conciliari* and the noun *conciliatio*, both alluding to the state of agreement, between two or more elements or situations, due to specific features of 'appropriateness' characterizing them.[52] Seneca certainly follows him, underlining the close connection established between the constitution of the human being and his actions.[53]

---

51 Striker 1996, 281, is convinced, instead, of the untranslatability of this word. She interprets οἰκείωσις in this way: "Recognition and appreciation of something as belonging to one".

52 Pembroke 1971, 120, in his pioneering study on οἰκείωσις, points out that Cicero alternates *conciliatio* and *commendatio*. However, the evidences we possess do not confirm this. See *Fin.* 3.23, where in *commendatus / commendari* we must rather note the meaning: "to introduce to someone."

53 See *Ep.* 121.14–16: "You say that every animal from the outset is attached to its own constitution (*constitutioni suae conciliari*), but also that the human constitution is a rational one. Therefore, the human being is attached (*conciliari*) to itself not as an animate creature but as a rational creature, for the human being is dear to itself by virtue of that part that makes it human. How, then, can a baby be attached (*conciliari*) to a rational constitution when it is not yet rational? Each stage of life has its own constitution: one for the baby, another for the child, another for the young person, and another for the mature. Each is attached to the constitution it is in (*ei constitutioni conciliantur in qua sunt*) ... So, although each thing's constitution changes, the attachment to its constitution (*conciliatio constitutionis suae*) occurs in the same way". In Graver's translation the verb 'to attach' expresses the concept of adaptation and joining. Gill 2016, 221, proposes 'familiarization'. We find an analysis of this passage in reference to both Cicero and Hierocles in Striker 1996, 286–290.

But here is the key passage in which Cicero, through Cato, presents the doctrine of οἰκείωσις:

> Every animal, as soon as it is born (this is where one should start), is concerned with itself (*sibi conciliari*), and takes care to preserve itself. It favours its constitution and whatever preserves its constitution, whereas it recoils from its destruction and whatever appears to promote its destruction. In support of this thesis, the Stoics point out that babies seek what is good for them (*salutaria*) and avoid the opposite before they ever feel pleasure or pain (*antequam voluptas aut dolor attigerit*). This would not happen, unless they valued their own constitution and feared destruction. But neither could it happen that they would seek anything at all, unless they had self-awareness and thereby self-love. So one must realise that it is self-love (*principium ductum esse a se diligendo*), which provides the primary motivation. Most Stoics do not believe that pleasure should be ranked among the natural principles – I passionately agree. If it were otherwise, if nature were thought to have included pleasure (*si voluptatem natura posuisse*) amongst the primary objects of desire, then a host of loathsome consequences would follow. As to why we love (*diligamus*) those objects which by nature we first take up (*quae prima sunt adscita natura*), the following is sufficient explanation: anyone, given the choice, would prefer all the parts of their body to be well adapted (*apta malit*) and sound rather than of equal utility but impaired and twisted.[54]

Coming into the world – and, consequently, existence – is a natural occurrence; it is therefore instinctive that every living creature tends to the preservation of itself. This means: "to maintain one's state" (*suum statum*).[55] Once this is established, the presentation offered by the Stoic Cato takes on a less Stoic colour: in the background Cicero reveals the Cyrenaic/Epicurean conception, clearly underlining that the perception of one's body – and therefore the pleasure of oneself as felt through the senses – is the foundation of οἰκείωσις.[56] From an early age we seek well-being: *salutaria*. Then, animated beings proceed preferring pleasure (*voluptas*) and avoiding pain (*dolor*). Finally, in man, reason intervenes and, according to Epicurean doctrine, the enhancement of stable pleasure depends on it: the so-called *katastēmatic pleasure*. Obviously Cato, as a Stoic, believes that pleasure cannot be part of the natural principles. The very concept of virtue would be at risk. However, according to the way in which Cicero

---

54 *Fin.* 3.16–17.

55 Cicero explicitly reiterates this in *Fin.* 2.33: "In fact the young are not moved by nature to seek pleasure, but simply to love themselves (*se ipse diligat*) and to wish to keep themselves safe and sound (*ut integrum se salvumque velit*). Every living creature, as soon as it is born, loves both itself and all its parts".

56 The double matrix – Epicurean on the one hand and Stoic on the other – that characterizes the οἰκείωσις is also evident in the cursory exposition made by Diog. Laert. 7.85 [= *SVF* 1.178].

presents the οἰκείωσις, the strong continuity between the physical and psychological dimensions remains central. The good of the body and the good of the soul are not opposed and virtue makes sense because it is a source of pleasure. According to Cicero, no virtue in itself would be desirable.[57]

However, beyond this approach to some aspects of the Epicurean conception, the primary foundation of the οἰκείωσις remains, the one perfectly corresponding to the Stoic perspective: the self-preservative impulse. In the name of it, we choose what is convenient and decide our action: in this sense, each one takes upon himself the task that, in the unfolding of the life of the universe, everyone has. In practice: everyone embraces their duty, *officium*:

> The initial 'appropriate action' (this is what I call the Greek καθῆκον) is to preserve oneself in one's natural constitution (*primum est officium ut se conservet in naturae statu*). The next one is to take what is in accordance with nature and reject its opposite.[58]

Keeping true to one's nature and, therefore, preserving oneself: this is the task that every living creature (and above all man) must accept. Cicero takes up the Stoic concept of ὁμολογία to refer to that good everything must be related to. Though hesitating, he proposes the Latin term *convenientia*.[59] It is the concept that guides all Stoic Ethics and that refers to the idea of 'agreement': "living in accordance with nature", ὁμολογουμένως τῇ φύσει ζῆν.[60] It is what the Stoic doctrine demands.

In the fifth book of *On the Ends of Good and Evil* we can see the intervention of the Peripatetic M. Pupius Piso, who in his youth was a friend of Cicero and with him was in Athens to listen to Antiochus. Maybe the entire exposition of Pupius Piso (§§ 5.24–76) reflects the teaching of his master Antiochus.[61] We can certainly detect an approach that aims to combine the Epicurean and Stoic perspectives, within a background of a Platonic/Peripatetic matrix. In *Fin.* 5.59–60 we read that

---

57 In *Fin.* 1.46–50, Cicero reviews wisdom, temperance, fortitude and justice to demonstrate that all virtues are joined with pleasure and cannot in any way be torn from it: *copulata esse ... cum voluptate, ut ab ea nullo modo nec divelli nec distrahi posse* (50).

58 *Fin.* 3.20.

59 *Fin.* 3.21: "This good lies in what the Stoics call ὁμολογία. Let us use the term 'consistency' (*convenientiam*), if you approve. Herein lies that good, namely moral action and morality itself, at which everything else ought to be directed."

60 See *SVF* 3.5–12.

61 See Gill 2016, 222–225. Cicero exposes this part as derived from the 'Old Academy': in this way he refers not only to Plato and his pupils as Speusippus, Xenocrates, Polemon, Crantor, but also to Aristotle, see *Fin.* 5.2 and 7. Striker 1996, 283–285, explains the reason for the proximity of the Ciceronian perspective to the Peripatetic one.

nature generated the human body so that some parts were perfect from birth, while others took shape during the progress of age, with no particular contributions from outside. Nature then made the soul perfect too, so that it could obtain its own consolidation by itself (*suam confirmationem*). However, man is master of himself and can decide what he wants, although he has a mind capable of avoiding evil and accepting the virtues without resorting to particular forms of education. This is the task of everyone: "to build on the foundations we were given until we reach our desired goal."[62]

Nature seems to provide the basis and the tool (i.e. reason) for men to truly become themselves. Because of the love we bring towards ourselves, what we consider honest by nature must be sought in itself.[63] According to Cicero, οἰκείωσις thus finds its most correct enhancement.

However, we can ask whether Cicero's interpretation of this fundamental Stoic doctrine entails a coherent outcome also in the framework of the ethical-political doctrine and the physical / metaphysical perspective.

Precisely the possible influence of Aristotelian thought could allow a positive answer with respect to the first side of the question.[64] In *Fin.* 5.65–66 the virtue of man gradually opens up to humanity (*societas*), to alliance of shared interests (*communicatio utilitatum*), to mutual affection (*charitas generis humani*). Each man is assigned his task, and human nature is so constituted as to have an innately civic and social character: *quod Graeci* πολιτικόν *vocant*. This arises already from the moment of procreation, but it gradually develops and becomes manifest in the adult man. We can ask whether this political bias is purely ideal: according to the Stoics, their approach is certainly elitist, especially if we consider that only *sapiens* can reach the truth and therefore the awareness of their own role. But, in fact, Cicero goes beyond the Stoic perspective and seems to proceed from *amor sui* (and therefore from individual ethics) to *amor omnium*, and therefore to the συμπάθεια which animates the world: in fact, the key to founding the concept of 'social justice'.[65]

---

62 Fin. 5.60: *Ad ea principia quae accepimus consequentia exquirere, quoad sit id quod volumus effectum.*

63 *Fin.* 5.61: *Haec honesta quae dico, praeterquam quod nosmet ipsos diligamus, praeterea suapte natura per se esse expetenda,* "The things that I call honest must be sought for themselves, for their nature, as well as for the love we bring to ourselves" (I turn away here from Annas' translation, which I usually follow).

64 See Gill 2016, 229–233.

65 Not all interpreters agree on this point; according to Lee 2002, 126–129, it is a question of grasping the ideal, not so real, value of Cicero's suggestion.

As for the other side, together with that of συμπάθεια, the concept of κόσμος comes into play.[66] By συμπάθεια, the Stoic school refers to the experience that every living being (but not only: all entities as substantiated by the πνεῦμα) has of 'belonging' to the κόσμος; it is the consequence of the unity of the κόσμος.[67] By κόσμος the Stoics refer both to the system composed of the sky, the earth and their nature (that is to say, their being constituted by gods, men and what they produce), and to the divine order and perfection reigning there.[68] The Stoics then introduce the concept of ἡγεμονικόν, to define the principle that internally governs every natural being and that, in the cosmos, coincides with god.[69] In its realization the κόσμος expresses both its divine nature and its artistic and providential activity.[70] Cicero believes that what the Greeks indicate with πρόνοια can be translated with *prudentia* or *providentia*.[71]

Also in this case, while referring to the Stoic masters, Cicero shows that he is also looking at the Platonic/Aristotelian tradition. It is not accidental that he pays particular attention to the anthropocentric perspective in which he places the conclusion of Lucilius Balbus' speech. The thesis around which the third book of *On the Nature of the Gods* is built is based on the role of men, their rationality and responsibility (in opposition to the providence of the Stoics).

---

66 Cic., *ND* 2.19, shows that he appreciates the exposition that Lucilius Balbus makes of Stoic theology. The following question confirms this: "Consider the sympathetic agreement, interconnexion, and affinity of things (*tanta rerum consentiens conspirans continuata cognatio*): whom will this not compel to approve the truth of what I say?"

67 In Pseudo-Plutarch's *On Fate* 547d [= *SVF* 2.912], we read: "This cosmos is directed by nature, crossed by a single pneuma and in itself held by a relationship of sympathy."

68 See *SVF* 2.527. We could probably imagine a cosmobiological model of reality and becoming. See Bees 2004, 248–257.

69 See *ND* 2.29–30 and 36–39. Cicero, here, translates the Greek ἡγεμονικόν with *principatum*. Since it contains all things and therefore is supremely good, the world must possess wisdom and divinity. It is perfect, and virtuous.

70 See *ND* 2.58: "The nature of the world is styled by Zeno not merely 'craftsmanlike' (*non artificiosa solum*), but actually as a 'craftsman', (*sed plane artifex*) capable of foreseeing and providing (*consultrix et provida*) for all needs in every detail".

71 *ND* 2.58. On the function and importance of πρόνοια in this context, see §§ 73–75, 81–84, 127–134, and 154–161. In the plant world, in the animal world, in man, in the organs of the body: wherever we can see the presence of providence. It appears in the modalities of 'adaptation', that is, οἰκείωσις. Of particular note the mention of *prudentia*: it is the technical word with which Aristotle's φρόνησις is translated into Latin. See *Off.* 1.153: ... *prudentiam, quam Graeci* φρόνησιν *dicunt*; see also *De Or.* 3.95.

5.7 πιθανόν – *probabile*

This word alludes to something that is more or less credible but of which there is no sure opinion. In the Greek term there is an evident reference to the verb πείθειν, which means 'to persuade', 'to make believe', 'to influence'; the Latin one indicates that we are dealing with something that must be 'proved', 'confirmed.' A global conception of the world follows from this different approach (*probabilism* and, more generally, *scepticism*), according to which we cannot arrive at certain and definitive knowledge, but only 'probable' and endowed with 'verisimilitude.'

The 'probable', however, becomes an indispensable criterion for action. Especially the Stoic philosophy – which had placed the doctrine of καταληπτικὴ φαντασία (that is the *kataleptic representation*, the 'comprehensive representation' of all possible physical aspects) at the centre of epistemology – then gave considerable importance, in the process of knowledge, to the *persuasive* or *non-persuasive* 'representation' of reality, in view of the 'assent' that the subject must then give.

Hence πιθανὴ φαντασία, that is, the *probabilis visio* or *probabile visum*: the 'probable representation', since it persuades us.[72] It is exactly on this that Cicero focuses his attention; in dialogue with Lucullus, he discusses the position of Antiochus, referring to the arguments of Carneades and Clitomachus.[73]

Cicero writes at *Luc.* 99:

> Carneades holds that there are two classifications of representations (*visorum*),[74] which under one are divided into those that can be perceived (*quae percipi possint*) and those that cannot, and under the other into those that are probable (*probabilia*) and those that are not probable; and that accordingly those representations that are styled by Academia contrary to the senses and contrary to perspicuity belong to the former division, whereas the latter division must not be impugned; and that consequently his view is that there is no representation of such a sort as to result in perception (*visum nullum esse ut perceptio consequeretur*), but many that result in a judgement of probability (*probatio multa*). For it

---

72 As is evident, *probabile* (i.e. πιθανόν) has nothing to do with statistical frequency.

73 Clitomachus was acquainted with Stoic and Peripatetic philosophy; he studied principally with Carneades, whom he succeeded as chief of the New Academy in 129 BCE. See *supra*, p. 55. Ioppolo 2017, 192–197 and 209–215, considers Cicero's testimony important to trace a precise divergence between Carneades and Clitomachus with regard to the theory of probability and the consequent way of understanding the ἐποχή. Clitomachus seems to move away from Carneades' distinctive ontological intentionality, displaying the epistemological detachment implicit in adherence to the probable.

74 Here and later I slightly readjust the translation of Rackham 1933, proposing 'representation' instead of 'presentation.'

is contrary to nature for nothing to be probable (*probabile nihil esset*), and entails that entire subversion of life of which you, Lucullus, were speaking; accordingly even many sense – percepts must be deemed probable (*probanda multa sunt*), if only it be held in mind that no sense-representation has such a character as a false representation could not also have without differing from it at all. Thus the wise man will make use of whatever apparently probable representation (*specie probabile*) he encounters, if nothing presents itself that is contrary to that probability (*quod sit probabilitati illi contrarium*), and his whole plan of life will be charted out in this manner.

We are not interested in establishing how much the argument here developed actually depends on Carneades through Antiochus or by other means: on this we can see Allen (1997), 217–254, and Cappello (2019), 221–225; in particular Görler (1997), 36–57, attempts to establish Cicero's philosophical stance in *Lucullus*. We dedicate our attention to the use of the verb *probare*, of the adjective *probabile*, and of the noun *probabilitas*. These Latin words inevitably evoke the modern conception of 'probability', and opinions are very diverse on the absence or emergence of this physical / mathematical concept in the ancient world. See Obdrzalek (2006), 264–268, who disagrees with Sambursky (1956), 35–48, and Hacking (1975), 1–10. Recently, Reinhardt (2019), 243–249, has emphasized that the technical meaning (i.e. the etymological connection with *ap-probare*) and the eminently rhetorical one (which refers to something plausible, 'not impeded', and therefore suitable for persuasion) are, in Cicero, very close to each other.

In the passage quoted above we deduce that Cicero keeps the verb *probare* as a reference: in fact, what comes from the outside – and which as such is attested by the senses and perceived by the subject – must not only be admitted, but its *non-validity* cannot be declared, unless after an examination based on a logical, reliable criterion. Therefore what is perceived waits to be validated (*probatum*): it is true – or rather, it is plausible – and valid until proven otherwise. Therefore the wise man, according to Cicero, cannot and must not exclude the *probabile*. Indeed: he recognizes as probable also what he does not understand, what he does not perceive, what he has not yet given his consent to, but which is similar to the truth: *multa sequitur probabilia non conprehensa neque percepta neque adsensa sed similia veri* (*Luc.* 99). Exactly for this reason, the whole life seems to be based on the probable (obviously to be proven). Indeed: *quae nisi probet omnis vita tollatur*, "If he were not to approve them, all life would be done away with."

The strong weight that Cicero places on the moment of *adprobatio*[75] means that attention is diverted from the risk of an absolute ἐποχή. So, we are not faced with an indefinite postponement of assent or decision and, therefore, a situation involving abstention; we are faced with the demonstration that everything is possible, in the sense that everything can really be true. Very concretely Cicero exemplifies:

> When a wise man is going on board a ship, surely he has not got the knowledge already grasped in his mind (*conprehensum animo habet*) and perceived (*perceptum*) that he will make the voyage as he intends: how can he have it? But if, for instance, he were setting out from here to Puteoli, a distance of four miles (*stadia triginta*), with a relaible crew and a good helmsman and in present calm weather, it would appear probable (*probabile videatur*) that he would get there safe. He will therefore be guided by representations (*visis consilia*) of this sort to adopt plans of action and inaction and will be readier at proving (*probet*) that snow is white than Anaxagoras was.[76]

Cicero then declares that he refers to Clitomachus in specifying the difference between what is perceptible and what is probable. In fact, "many false objects are probable (*probabilia*) but nothing false can be perceived and known (*perceptum et cognitum*)", *Luc.* 103. As is evident, also in this case the existence of what is real goes far beyond what is perceived and known, but not beyond what one can think of 'feeling' (and that for this reason we consider probable).

All this allows Cicero not to fall into the trap of those who might object to him that we should also *probare* this same argument. In fact, he concludes:

> If we do not win your approval (*non probamus*) for these doctrines, they may no doubt be false, but certainly they are not detestable. For, we don't rob you of daylight, but, whereas you speak of things as being 'perceived' and 'grasped' (*percipi comprehendique*), we describe the same things, provided they are probable (*si modo probabilia sint*), as 'appearing' (*videri dicimus*).[77]

Therefore, according to Cicero, what is probable does not prevent the decision or the action. What we do not perceive or do not know, is not for this not probable. Only dogmatists (and Epicureans and Stoics can be counted among them) deny this.

---

75 Cicero, in *Academica*, uses *adprobatio* as a synonym of *adsensum* / *adsensio*. See *Luc.* 37: "Let us say a few words on the subject of 'assent' (*adsensione*) or 'approval' (*adprobatione*), termed in Greek συγκατάθεσιν."

76 *Luc.* 100. Anaxagoras denied that snow was white because he knew that it was made of water solidified, and this water was black.

77 *Luc.* 105.

What is probable becomes fundamental thanks to the fact that it combines with the plausible (i.e. *similia veri*), and this prevents it from completely abolishing the truth:

> We do not (i.e. abolish truth altogether), for we observe some things that are true just as we observe some that are false. But there is 'appareance' as a basis of approval (*sed probandi species est*), whereas we have no mark as a basis of perception (*percipiendi signum nullum habemus*).[78]

As it appears (true or false it is), something not only appears but also *exists* as apparent, and therefore 'truly' *appears* true or false.

One last consideration: Cicero is aware that this approach to what is probable and what is plausible is also useful in reference to the other value of πιθανός / πιθανότης: the one that refers to the art of persuading.[79] Just because there is no denying the actual possibility of what is probable, the wise man (and in this case the rhetorician) can intervene to transform the possibility into verisimilitude and, ultimately, into personal conviction.

5.8 πρόληψις – *anticipatio, praenotio, praesensio*

In *ND* 1.43–45 the Epicurean Velleius proposes *anticipatio* and *praenotio* as a translation of πρόληψις:

> For what nation or what tribe of men is there but possesses untaught some 'preconception' (*anticipationem quandam*) of the gods? Such notions Epicurus designates by the word πρόληψιν, that is, a sort of preconceived (*anteceptam*) mental picture of a thing, without which nothing can be understood or investigated or discussed. [...] We must admit it as also being an accepted truth that we possess a 'preconception,' (*anticipationem*) as I called it above, or 'prior notion,' (*praenotionem*) of the gods. For we are bound to employ novel terms

---

78 *Luc.* 111.

79 Already Chrysippus [*SVF* 3.229a] alluded to the seductive character of certain representations (τὴν πιθανότητα τῶν φαντασιῶν); Diog. Laert. 7.89 [= *SVF* 3.228] recalls how, even in the Stoic doctrine, rational being can be influenced by external factors (διὰ τὰς τῶν ἔξωθεν πραγμάτων πιθανότητας). Epicurus, *fr.* [29].23.14 [Arrighetti], alluded to the 'convincing' character (πιθανόν) that makes certain data 'plausible'. In *Pyth.* 87, he used the noun τὸ πιθανολογούμενον to define 'what is convincing.' Moreover, the verb πιθανολογεῖν already belongs to Aristotle who uses it to indicate the use of persuasive arguments, see *EN* 1049b: "It is obviously absurd both to accept that a mathematician appeals to *persuasion* (πιθανολογοῦντος), and to expect *scientific proofs* (ἀποδείξεις) from a rhetorician." Plato, in *Theaet.* 162ε, uses the noun πιθανολογία, to refer to a persuasive and plausible argument.

to denote novel ideas, just as Epicurus himself employed the word πρόληψιν in a sense in which no one had ever used it before.

Anticipatio and *praenotio* are absent in almost all classical Latin literature. We find only one other attestation of *anticipatio* in Servius' commentary *in Verg. Aen. 6.359.4*; *praenotio* is, instead, a real *unicum*.

In Lucretius, 4.1057, we find an interesting *praesagire*:[80] *Namque voluptatem praesagit muta cupido*, "Silent craving presages pleasure." Cicero does not disdain this opportunity: so, for example, he writes in *Div.* 1.65: "One who has knowledge of a thing before it happens (*qui ante sagit, quam oblata res est*) is said to 'presage' (*praesagire*), that is, to perceive the future in advance (*futura ante sentire*)." This juxtaposition of *praesagire* and *ante sentire* leads us in the direction of *praesentire* and *praesensio*. *Praesensio* is precisely the technical term that Cicero preferably adopts, probably because the purely logical / functional aspect of *anticipatio* or *praenotio* responds less to the authentic sense of Greek.

According to Chrysippus, προλήψεις ('anticipations') are to be understood together with the ἔννοιαι (i.e. 'concepts') as parts of reasoning, as "particular activities of the soul" for which the soul itself can be considered "a set of concepts and of πρόληψις."[81] And since a concept is an imagination of the mind, the same can be said of προλήψεις; more precisely: if in concepts a programmatic logical design is evident, in προλήψεις everything happens occasionally, without a design.[82] The origin of a πρόληψις is obviously material. Reasonably, it is due to the experience of the accumulation of representations that are all the same:

> Perceiving something like white, once it disappears, the memory remains; when there are more similar memories, then let's say we have an experience. Experience (ἐμπειρία) is indeed a large number of similar representations (τῶν ὁμοειδῶν φαντασιῶν).[83]

The experiences we have in childhood are what, due to their natural referring to things in their generality, we consider προλήψεις.[84] They are 'natural προλήψεις, but this does not mean they can be thought of as innate ideas of the Platonic type. They are formed in connection with the development of ἡγεμονικόν. Precisely through the ability to reason on what we feel the rational animal knows reality: at the same time, however, the possibility of generalizing is decisive, that is, of

---

80 See also 4.1106: *praesagit gaudia corpus*, "The body presages pleasure".
81 *SVF* 2.841 (= Gal., *PHP* 5.3).
82 *SVF* 2.83 (= Aët., *Plac.* 4.11).
83 *SVF* 2.83.
84 Diog. Laert. 7.54: "*prolēpsis* is the natural intelligence (ἔννοια φυσική) of things in their generality."

conceiving on the basis of προλήψεις. In fact, as Chrysippus writes in the first book *On reasoning*, the criteria of truth are 'sensation' and προλήψεις, intending to emphasize that the ἡγεμονικόν must use them, in a continuous changing game between *representations* (φαντασίαι), *assent* (συγκαταθέσεις), *sensations* (αἰσθήσεις), and *impulses* (ὁρμαί).[85] Combined with the 'sensation' and the 'concept', the Stoic προλήψεις unequivocally manifests its instrumental role in reason, while not clearly revealing its nature. Indeed, it is not only the simple result of physical connections: as an object of thought, it can be formed following purely mental operations such as 'similitude' (καθ᾽ ὁμοιότητα), 'analogy' (κατ᾽ ἀναλογίαν), 'displacement' (κατὰ μετάθεσιν), 'composition' (κατὰ σύνθεσιν), 'opposition' (κατ᾽ ἐναντίωσιν), and 'transposition' (κατὰ μετάβασιν).[86]

The contrast with the Epicurean doctrine becomes evident at this point. This doctrine attributes the ἐπίνοιαι (i.e. the 'notions', the 'foreknowledge') to similar mechanisms, but strictly refers the latter to physical sensation. Therefore, we can hardly shelve the hypothesis that the πρόληψις is a tool borrowed first of all from the Epicurean doctrine and only later adapted to a physical conception of the universe and of knowledge such as that of Stoicism.[87]

Indeed, Epicurus seems to have better specified the role and status of the πρόληψις. Firstly, it must not be confused with the feeling or passion. In *Canon* Epicurus states that there are three criteria of truth: τὰς αἰσθήσεις (sensations), τὰς προλήψεις and τὰ πάθη (passions).[88] We must therefore distinguish its traits and first of all connect the πρόληψις to the memory of sensation, that is, to the persistence of the physical trace (ἐγκατάλειμμα)[89] of what has happened and which has been confirmed several times in subsequent experiences. It is a kind of:

> Acquisition (κατάληψις) or correct opinion (δόξα ὀρθή) or idea (ἔννοια) or general notion (καθολικὴ νόησις) accumulated in us (ἐναποκειμένη), that is the memory (μνήμη) of what often appeared from the outside. Like, for example, that thing that turns out to be a 'man'. Together, in fact, in saying 'man', thanks to πρόληψις we immediately think about his figure based on the previously experienced feelings.[90]

---

85 *SVF* 2.836 [= Aët., *Plac.* 4.21].
86 *SVF* 2.87 [= Diog. Laert. 7.52].
87 See Sandbach 1971b, 22–37, in particular 30–31. According to Dyson 2009, 1–22, in the Stoic conception, instead, a form of innatism should be seen; based on it, προλήψεις and ἔννοιαι (i.e. 'anticipations' and 'concepts') would end up coinciding.
88 Diog. Laert. 10.31.
89 See Epic., *Hrd.* 50.
90 Diog. Laert. 10.33.

At this point, not only the doctrine of the 'noun' – based on πρόληψις – can develop; primarily, a very strong relationship will be established between the "notions that derive from an act of the mind" (τὰς φανταστικὰς ἐπιβολὰς τῆς διανοίας)[91] and πρόληψις. This is essential if we want to connect the experience already acquired with the prefiguration of the future, without the latter being considered a pure and simple 'hypothesis', 'presupposition' (ὑπόληψις). Προλήψεις are clear and evident by virtue of their anchoring to the original sensation and their being an instrument for the experience and comprehension of the present.[92] According to the Epicurean doctrine, only in the present time do we have the experience of ourselves and of our 'being aggregates of atoms': it is an evident experience for which man appreciates his being in life, the absence of pain, the pleasure free from terror and anguish. In the present time we know what surrounds us, the entire universe, and we even come to deduce the existence of the atom and that of the gods. But that's not usually the case, common people have only 'fallacious presuppositions' of both: in practice, they are a sort of 'weak πρόληψις', as the Stoics probably postulate; and in this way, πρόληψις coincides with ὑπόληψις.[93]

Cicero, however, seems to refer to scientific πρόληψις. Hence, he prefers the word *praesensio*. He uses *praesensio* mostly in *On the Nature of the Gods* and in *On Divination*. To *praesensio* he attributes a precise scientific value, since on the one hand, with it, it would refer to the different forms and possibilities of divination;[94] on the other, *praesensio* would attest to the existence of the surrounding reality, of its becoming, and of the gods:

> Assuming that we have a definite and preconceived idea (*certa notione animi praesentiamus*) of a deity as, first, a living being, and, secondly, a being unsurpassed in excellence by anything else in the whole of nature, I can see nothing that satisfies this preconception or idea (*praesensionem notionemque*) of ours more fully than, first, the judgement that this world, which must necessitarily be most excellent of all things, is itself a living being and a god.[95]

---

91 See Diog. Laert. 10.31. In L&S 17 A, Epicurus' technical expression is translated as follows: "focusings of thought into an impression."

92 See Diog. Laert. 10.33–34.

93 On this see Seneca, *Ep.* 117.6; he uses the technical word *praesumptio* to indicate the man's knowledge of the gods.

94 See Div. 1.1: *praesensionem et scientiam rerum futurarum*; 1.105: *praesensio aut scientia veritatis futurae*. Because of that: *praesensio divinatio est* (2.14).

95 *ND* 2.45.

However Cicero then associates the *praesensio rerum futurarum* indifferently to Stoicism (e.g. to Cleanthes, in *ND* 2.13; 3.16) and to Atomism (*Div.* 1.5; 2.31–32); this means that the word does not seem to have, for him, any connotation of school. *Praesensio*, therefore, simply but incontrovertibly refers to the opportunity (and necessity) of overcoming the conjectural moment on the basis of a correct interpretation of the signals and their adequate explanation. As examples, see the physician foreseeing the progress of a disease, the general anticipating the plan of the enemy, the pilot forecasting the approach of bad weather.[96] They are based on the logical rationality that seems to dominate the succession of events. It is a rationality that both the peasant and the augur presuppose;[97] in fact, they continue to make predictions, too, despite the risk of error, because "They make their conclusions only if based on some reasonable and probable conjecture."[98] In this way the cause/effect relationship, observed in the succession of phenomena, becomes the cornerstone of the scientific 'hypothesis / prediction': "How can anything be foreseen (*provideri*) that has no cause and no distinguishing mark of its coming?"[99]

According to Cicero, πρόληψις (interpreted as *praesensio*) is therefore a prediction based on the validity of the cause/effect relationship; the cogency of the latter, in turn, acquires consistency by virtue of the gradually confirmed outcome of the forecast. This is an authentic 'circle' that finds its surest attestation in the manifestation of the cosmos:

> Eclipses of the sun and also of the moon are predicted (*praedicuntur*) for many years in advance by men who employ mathematics in studying the courses and movements of heavenly bodies; and the unvarying laws of nature will bring their predictions to pass (*ea praedicunt enim quae naturae necessitas perfectura est*).[100]

In conclusion: the 'weak' form of the πρόληψις (scientifically correct and based on pure conjecture) both belongs to Cicero (*praesensio*, but also *anticipatio* and *praenotio*) and – later – to the Stoic Seneca (*praesumptio*);[101] the 'hard' form of πρόληψις (which is also scientifically correct, but based on the immediate connection of sensitive perception and construction of reality) belongs only to

---

96 *Div.* 2.16.
97 *Div.* 2.15: "Can there, then, be any foreknowledge (*praesensio*) of things for whose happening no reason exists?".
98 *Div.* 2.16.
99 *Div.* 2.17.
100 *Div.* 2.17.
101 Cicero never uses the word *praesumptio* or the forms of the respective verb *praesumere*.

some traits of Ciceronian thought (*praesensio*) and testifies to the permanence of an Epicurean tone strongly anchored to the evidence (ἐνάργεια) of the experience, for which the subsequent confirmation or the contrary attestation will be inevitable.[102]

---

102 See Epic., *Hrd.* 51. In relation to the method of inference, see Philodemus, *De signis* fr. 1 (De Lacy & De Lacy 1987).

6 Epilogue

By means of this foray into Cicero's philosophical vocabulary, we can appreciate two important points:

(a) Cicero's commitment to understanding the issues addressed by the Greek philosophers. Every single word requires prudence and accuracy, but, at the same time, decision. Establishing the clear meaning of Greek philosophical terminology is essential; such meaning then becomes the starting for a complex form of reconstruction of concepts and arguments, based on a different linguistic code, but focused on reproducing the originals;

(b) Cicero goes beyond the goals of an interpreter and translator. His knowledge of the Greek and Latin languages enables his original re-examination of Greek/Hellenistic philosophical topics. Hence their actualization in the context of republican Rome, with the aim of favouring the formation of the ideal *orator* and, more generally, of the man engaged in political and cultural life.

It is clear, at this point, that Cicero's role shifts from that of a simple mediator of Greek tradition and culture to that of the philosopher intending to pursue an educational, moral and civic project. This is why the topics investigated in chapters 1 and 2 – namely the Ciceronian philosophical apprenticeship and his philosophical commitment – constitute the premise and, at the same time, the foundation of what we later recognized to be Cicero's civic and moral engagement. However, since Cicero does not present himself as a theorist, thus leading many scholars to deny his stature as a 'philosopher', chapter 3 then highlighted the philosophical quality of his approach to the Academic school and then, with the correct competence, to the Stoic and Epicurean doctrines. In this way, his strategy of arguing both sides of a question (*in utramque partem disserere*) certainly stands out, and, at the same time, his intention of combining philosophical content with the language that transmits it – i.e. the union of philosophy and rhetorical technique – becomes evident.

Many issues remain open, despite having received a very careful treatment from Cicero (see chapter 4): for example, the question of determinism (and, therefore, of destiny) in relation to the direct responsibility of agents, the problem of coherence between theoretical-philosophical thought and political action, and the meaning, then and today, of 'eclecticism' and 'probabilism'.

Certainly, the volume of surviving works by Cicero remains astonishing; even more striking is the commitment to philosophical studies developed in the most difficult and extreme moments of his political engagement, especially in his last year of life. Unfortunately, we lack any correspondence from the last five months of Cicero's life. We would certainly have benefited from such further information

https://doi.org/10.1515/9783110661835-006

to understand better how Cicero judged, from a philosophical point of view, the political choices he had made in the face of the crisis overwhelming the Republic – a crisis he himself acknowledged, in relation to both his private and public situation, in his last surviving words to Atticus: *consenti hac cura, ubi sum, ut me expediam*, «Help me to get free from the tiresome position I am in» (*Att.* 16.15.6: November 44).

Bibliography

Editions of Ciceronian works

(For the Latin texts and for the translations I have consulted the works listed below. I slightly modified the translations when necessary. The translations for the works not listed here are mine.)

1933. *The Poems of Cicero*, Ewbank, W.W. (ed.). London: University of London Press.

1972. *Aratea: Fragments poétiques*, ed. Soubiran, Jean. Paris: Les Belles Lettres.

1962. *Hortensius*, ed. Grilli, A. Milano: Istituto Editoriale Cisalpino (2010[2], Bologna: Patron).

1976. *Ciceros Hortensius*, ed. L. Straume-Zimmermann. Bern: Lang.

1976 (1949[1]). *De inventione ; De optimo genere oratorum ; Topica*. Translated by H.M. Hubbell. Cambridge Mass., London: Harvard University Press, W. Heinemann.

1960. *De oratore book 3. Together with De fato, Paradoxa stoicorum, De partitione oratoria*. Ed. Rackham, H. London: W. Heinemann Ltd.

1990. *De oratore libri tres*. Ed. by Wilkins, A.S. Hildesheim [etc.]: Georg Olms.

2001. *On the ideal orator (De oratore)*. Transl. by J. Wisse and J.M. May. New York: Oxford University Press.

1971. *Brutus,* with an English Translation by Hendrickson, G.L. / *Orator,* with an English Translation by Hubbell, H.M. London: W. Heinemann Ltd.

1960 (1915[1]). *De re publica,* ed. Ziegler, K. Lipsiae: Teubner.

1998. *The Republic and the Laws*. Translated by N. Rudd, with Introduction and Notes by J. Powell and N. Rudd. Oxford: Oxford University.

1999. *On the Commonwealth and On the Laws*. Edited by James E.G. Zetzel. Cambridge: Cambridge University Press.

2006. *De re publica; De Legibus; Cato maior De Senectute; Laelius De Amicitia,* ed. Powell, J.G.F. Oxonii: e typographeo Claredoniano.

1992. *Cicero: On Stoic Good and Evil: De Finibus III and Paradoxa Stoicorum*. Edited with introduction, translation and commentary by M.R. Wright. Warminster: Aris & Phillips Ltd.

1839. *M. Tullii Ciceronis De finibus bonorum et malorum libri quinque*. Io. Nicolaus Madvigius recensuit et enarravit. Kopenhagen. Repr. Hildesheim: Olms 1965.

1971 (1914[1]). *De finibus bonorum et malorum,* with an English Translation by H.M.A. Rackham. Cambridge Mass., London: Harvard University Press, W. Heinemann.

1998. *De finibus bonorum et malorum libri quinque,* ed. L.D. Reynolds. Oxonii: e typographeo Claredoniano.

2001. *On Moral Ends*. Edited by J. Annas; transl. by R. Woolf. Cambridge: Cambridge University Press.

1853. *The Academic Questions, Treatise De finibus, and Tusculan disputations of M. T. Cicero,* with a Sketch of the Greek Philosophers Mentioned by Cicero, Literally Translated by C.D. Yonge. London: Henry G. Bohn.

1908. *Paradoxa Stoicorum. Academicorum Reliquiae cum Lucullo, Timaeus, de Natura Deorum, de Divinatione, de Fato,* ed. O. Plasberg. Lipsiae: Teubner.

2006. *On Academic Scepticism*. Translated with Introduction and Notes by Ch. Brittain. Indianapolis: Hackett Publishing Co.

https://doi.org/10.1515/9783110661835-007

1966 (1927¹). *Tusculan Disputations*. Translated by King, J.E. London: Heinemann – Cambridge, MA: Harvard University Press.

1985. *Tusculan disputations* 1. Edited with Translation and Notes by Douglas, A.E. Warminster: Aris & Phillips.

1990. *Tusculan Disputation* 2. & 5. Edited with Translation and Notes by Douglas, A.E. Warminster: Aris & Phillips.

2002. *Cicero on the Emotions: Tusculan Disputations* 3. & 4. Translated and with Commentary by Graver, M. Chicago: Chicago University Press.

1955. *De natura deorum libri III*. Ed. by A.S. Pease. Cambridge, Mass. (U.S.): The Harvard University Press (repr. Darmstadt: Wissenschaftliche Buchgesellschaft, 1968).

1967 (1933¹). *De natura deorum, Academica*. Ed. with an Enghlish Translation by Rackham H.M.A. Cambridge, Mass., London: Harvard University Press, W. Heinemann.

1998. *The Nature of the Gods*. Translated with Introduction and Notes by P.G. Walsh. Oxford: Oxford University Press.

1963. *De divinatione*, A.S. Pease (ed.). Darmstadt: Wissenschaftliche Buchgesellschaft.

1963. *De fato, Über das fatum*, hrsg. von K. Bayer. München: Heimeran Verlag.

1991. *Cicero: 'On Fate' (De Fato) & Boethius: 'The Consolation of Philosophy' (Philosophiae Consolationis) iv.5–7, v*, ed. R.W. Sharples. Warminster: Aris & Phillips.

2014. *Cicerone. Il fato*. Introduzione, edizione, traduzione e commento di S. Maso. Roma: Carocci.

2019. *Über das Schicksal*, Lateinisch–deutsch, herausgegeben, übersetzt und erläutert von H. Weidemann. Berlin/Boston: De Gruyter.

1968 (1928¹). *De officiis*. With an English Translation by W. Miller. Cambridge, Mass., London: Harvard University Press, W. Heinemann.

1991. *On Duties*. Edited by M.T. Griffin and E.M. Atkins. Cambridge: Cambridge University Press.

1994. *De Officiis*, ed. M. Winterbottom. Oxonii: e Typographeo Clarendoniano.

1971 (1923¹). *De Senectute; De Amicitia; De Divinatione*. With an English Translation by W.A. Falconer. Cambridge, Mass., London: Harvard University Press, W. Heinemann, Ltd.

1988. *Cato Maior, De senectute*. Powell, J.G.F., ed. Cambridge: Cambridge University Press.

1990. *Laelius, on Friendship & the Dream of Scipio*. Edited with an Introduction, Translation & Commentary by J.G.F. Powell. Warminster: Aris & Phillips Ltd.

2003. *Topica*, ed. T. Reinhardt. Oxford: Oxford University Press.

1918. *Letters to Atticus*. With an English Translation by Winstedt E.O. London: Heinemann – New York: Putnam.

1987. *Epistulae ad Atticum*, 1–2, ed. D.R. Shackleton Bailey. Stuttgart: Teubner.

1988. *Epistulae ad familiares*, libri 1–16, ed. D.R. Shackleton Bailey. Stuttgart: Teubner.

2004. *Epistulae ad familiares*, 1–2, ed. D.R. Shackleton Bailey. Cambridge: Cambridge University Press.

1980. *Epistulae ad Quintum fratrem et M. Brutum*, ed. D.R. Shackleton Bailey. Cambridge: Cambridge University Press.

Ancient work's editions

Alesse, F. (a cura di) (1997). *Panezio di Rodi. Testimonianze. Edizione, traduzione e commento.* Napoli: Bibliopolis.

Arrighetti, G. (a cura di) (1973). *Epicuro opere.* Torino: Einaudi.

De Lacy, H. & E.A. De Lacy (eds.) (1987). *Philodemus. On Method of Inference,* ed. with Transl. and Comm. Napoli: Bibliopolis.

Edelstein, L. and I.G. Kidd (eds.) 1972 (1989²). *Posidonius. The Fragments.* Cambridge: Cambridge University Press.

Theiler, W. (ed.) (1982). *Posidonius. Die Fragmente.* Berlin/New York: de Gruyter.

Van Straaten, M. (ed.) (1946). *Panétius, sa vie, ses écrits et sa doctrine.* Amsterdam: H.J. Paris.

Van Straaten, M. (ed.) (1962³). *Panetii Rhodii Fragmenta.* Leiden: Brill.

Vimercati, E. (a cura di) (2002). *Panezio. Testimonianze e frammenti.* Milano: Bompiani.

Vimercati, E. (a cura di) (2004). *Posidonio. Testimonianze e frammenti.* Milano: Bompiani.

Secondary literature

Alesse, F. (1994). *Panezio di Rodi e la tradizione stoica.* Napoli: Bibliopolis.

Alesse, F. (2018). 'La rappresentazione catalettica nella Stoa post-crisippea', in: *Lexikon Philosophicum,* special issue: *Hellenistic Theories of Knowledge,* F. Verde e M. Catapano (eds.), 145–167.

Algra, K.A. (1997). 'Chrysippus, Carneades, Cicero. The Ethical Divisiones in Cicero's *Lucullus',* in: Inwood–Mansfeld 1997, 107–139.

Allen, J. (1997). 'Carneadean Argument in Cicero's *Academic Books',* in: Inwood–Mansfeld 1997, 217–256.

Altman, W.H.F. (ed.) (2015). *Brill's Companion to the Reception of Cicero.* Leiden/Boston: Brill.

Altman, W.H.F. (2016). *The Revival of Platonism in Cicero's Late Philosophy: Platonis aemulus and the Invention of Cicero.* Lanham, MD/London: Lexington Books.

André, J.-M. (1966). *L'otium dans la vie moral et intellectuelle romaine, des origines à l'époque augustéenne.* Paris: Université de Paris.

Annas, J. (1989). 'Cicero on Stoic Moral Philosophy and Private Property', in: Griffin–Barnes 1989, 151–173.

Annas, J. (1990). 'Stoic Epistemology', in: Everson 1990, 184–203.

Annas, J. (1993). *The Morality of Happiness.* Oxford: University Press.

Annas, J. (2007). *Carneades' Classification of Ethical Theories,* in: Ioppolo–Sedley 2007, 187–223.

Annas, J. and G. Betegh (eds.) (2016). *Cicero' De finibus. Philosophical Approaches.* Cambridge: Cambridge University Press.

Arenson, K. (ed.) (2020). *The Routledge Handbook of Hellenistic Philosophy.* New York/London: Routledge.

Asmis, E. (1990). 'Free Action and the Swerve: Review of W.G. Englert, *Epicurus on the Swerve and Voluntary Action',* in: *Oxford Studies in Ancient Philosophy* 8, 275–291.

Atkins, J.W. (2013). *Cicero on Politics and the Limits of Reason. The Republic and Laws.* Cambridge: Cambridge University Press.

Aubert-Baillot, S. (2019). 'Terminology and Practice of Dialectic in Cicero's Letters', in: Bénatouïl–Ierodiakonou 2019, 254–282.

Barnes, J. (1989b). 'Antiochus of Ascalon', in: Griffin–Barnes 1989, 51–96.

Barnes, J. (1997). 'Roman Aristotle', in: Barnes–Griffin 1997, 1–69.

Barnes, J. and M. Griffin (eds.) (1997). *Philosophia togata II. Plato and Aristotle at Rome*. Oxford: Clarendon Press.

Barney, R. (2003). 'A Puzzle in Stoic Ethics', in: *OSAPh* 24, 303–340.

Bastianini, G. and Long, A.A. (1992). 'Hierocles', in: *Corpus dei Papiri Filosofici Greci e Latini (CFP)* I, vol. I**, Firenze: Olschki, 268–451.

Beard, M. (1986). 'Cicero and Divination: the Formation of a Latin Discourse', in: *The Journal of Roman Studies* 76, 33–46.

Bees, R. (2004). *Die Oikeiōsislehre der Stoa. 1: Rekonstruktion ihres Inhalts*. Würzburg: Königshausen & Neumann.

Bellincioni, M. (1970). *Struttura e pensiero del 'Laelius' ciceroniano*. Brescia: Paideia.

Bénatouïl, T. & K. Ierodiakonou (eds.) (2019). *Dialectic after Plato and Aristotle*. Cambridge: Cambridge University Press.

Bett, R. (ed.) (2010a). *The Cambridge Companion to Ancient Scepticism*. Cambridge: Cambridge University Press.

Bett, R. (2010b). 'Beauty and its Relation to Goodness in Stoicism', in: Nightingale–Sedley 2010, 130–152.

Bishop, C. (2019). *Cicero, Greek Learning, and the Making of a Roman Classic*. Oxford/New York: Oxford University Press.

Blom, H. van der (2010). *Cicero's Role Models: the Political Strategy of a Newcomer*. New York: Oxford University Press.

Bobonich, C. (ed.) (2017). *The Cambridge Companion to Ancient Ethics*. Cambridge: Cambridge University Press.

Bobzien, S. (1998). *Determinism and Freedom in Stoic Philosophy*. Oxford: Clarendon Press.

Bobzien, S. (1999). 'Chrysippus' Theory of Causes', in: Ierodiakonou 1999, 196–242.

Bobzien, S. (2014). 'Choice and Moral Responsibility', in: Polansky 2014, 81–109.

Boissier, G. (1865). *Cicéron et ses amis*. Paris: Hachette.

Bonazzi, M. (2012a). 'Antiochus and Platonism', in: Sedley 2012, 307–333.

Bonazzi, M. (2012b). 'Plutarch on the Difference between Academics and Pyrrhonists', in: *Oxford Studies in Ancient Philosophy* 43, 271–298.

Bonazzi, M. (2017). 'The Platonist Appropriation of Stoic Epistemology', in: Engeberg–Pedersen 2017, 120–141.

Bonazzi, M. and C. Helmig (eds.) (2007), *Platonic Stoicism – Stoic Platonism: the Dialogue between Platonism and Stoicism in Antiquity*. Leuven: Leuven University Press.

Boyancé, P. (1936a). *Études sur le Songe de Scipion*. Paris: E. de Boccard.

Boyancé, P. (1936b). 'Les Mèthodes de l'histoire litteraire. Cicéron et son oeuvre philosophique', in: *Revue des études latines* 14, 288–309.

Brennan, T. (2003). 'Stoic Moral Psychology', in: Inwood 2003, 257–294.

Brennan, T. (2005). *The Stoic Life. Emotion, Duties, and Fate*. Oxford: Clarendon Press.

Bringmann, K. (1971). *Untersuchungen zum späten Cicero*. Göttingen: Vandenhoeck and Ruprecht.

Brittain, Ch. (2001). *Philo of Larissa: the Last of the Academic Sceptics*. Oxford: Oxford University Press.

Brittain, Ch. (2012). 'Antiochus' Epistemology', in: Sedley 2012, 104–130.

Brittain, Ch. (2016). 'Cicero' Sceptical Methods: the Exemple of the *De finibus*', in: Annas–Betegh 2016, 12–40.

Brunschwig, J. (1986). 'The Cradle Argument in Epicureanism and Stoicism', in: Schofield–Striker 1986, 113–145.

Brunt, P.A. (2013). *Studies in Stoicism*. Oxford: Oxford University Press.

Bruwaene van den, M. (1937). *La théologie de Cicéron*. Louvain: Bibliothèque de l'Université.

Büchner, K. (1964). *Cicero. Bestand und Wandel seiner geistige Welt*. Heidelberg: C. Winter Universitätsverlag.

Büchner, K. (1976). *Somnium Scipionis. Quellen, Gesthalt, Sinn*. Wiesbaden: F. Steiner Verlag.

Cappello, O. (2019), *The School of Doubt: Skepticism, History and Politics in Cicero's 'Academica'*. Leiden: Brill.

Carcopino, J. (1947). *Les secrets de la Correspondance de Cicéron*. Paris: L'Artisan du livre.

Classen, J. (1989). 'Die Peripatetiker in Cicero's *Tuskulanen*', in: Fortenbaugh–Steinmetz 1989, 186–200.

Cooper, J. (2013), 'Aristotelian Responsibility', *Oxford Studies in Ancient Philosophy* 45, 265–312.

Davies, J. (1721). *M. Tullii Ciceronis De diuinatione et De fato. Recensuit, et suis animadversionibus illustravit ac emendavit Joannes Davisius Coll. Regin. Cantab. Præsidens. Accedunt integræ notæ Paulli Manucii, Petri Victorii, Joachimi Camerarii, Dionys. Lambini, et Fulv. Ursini. Una cum Hadriani Turnebi Commentario in Librum de Fato*, sumptibus C. Crownfield: Cantabrigiæ.

Destrée, P., R. Salles, and M. Zingano (eds.) (2014). *What is Up to Us? Studies on Agency and Responsibility in Ancient Philosophy*. Sankt Augustin: Academia Verlag.

Dihle, A. (1982). *The Theory of the Will in Classical Antiquity*. Berkeley: University of California Press.

Dillon, J.M. and A.A. Long (eds.) (1988). *The Question of 'Eclecticism'. Studies in Later Greek Philosophy*. Berkeley: University of California Press.

Dirlmeier, F. (1937). *Die Oikeiosis–Lehre Theophrasts*. Leipzig: Dieterich'sche Verlagsbuchhandlung.

Donini, P.L. (1988). 'The History of the Concept of Eclecticism', in: Dillon–Long 1988, 15–33.

Donini, P.L. (1989). *Ethos. Aristotele e il determinismo*, Torino: Edizioni dell'Orso.

Dorandi, T. (2008). 'Chronology', in: *CHHP*, 31–54.

Dugan, J. (2005). *Making a New Man. Ciceronian Self-fashioning in the Rhetorical Works*. Oxford: Oxford University Press.

Dyck, A. (2020). *A commentary on Cicero, De Divinatione II*. Ann Arbor: University of Michigan Press.

Dyson, H. (2009). *Prolēpsis and Ennoia in the Early Stoa*. Berlin/New York: De Gruyter.

Eliasson, E. (2008). *The Notion of that Which Depends on Us in Plotinus and Its Background*. Leiden/Boston: Brill.

Engberg-Pedersen, T. (1990). *The Stoic Theory of Oikeiōsis: Moral Development and Social Interaction in Early Stoic Philosophy*. Aarhus: Aarhus University Press.

Engberg-Pedersen, T. (ed.) (2017). *From Stoicism to Platonism. The Development of Philosophy 100 BCE – 100 CE*. Cambridge: Cambridge University Press.

Englert, W.G. (1987). *Epicurus on the Swerve and Voluntary Action*. Atlanta, GA: Scholar Press.

Essler, H. (2011). 'Cicero's Use and Abuse of Epicurean Theology', in: Fish–Sanders 2011, 129–151.

Everson, S. (ed.) (1990), *Epistemology*. Cambridge: Cambridge University Press.

Fantham, E. (2004). *The Roman World of Cicero's De oratore*. Oxford/New York: Oxford University Press.

Ferrary, J.-L. (1995). 'The Statesman and the Law in Cicero', in: Laks–Schofield 1995, 48–73.

Fish, J. and K.R. Sanders (eds.) (2011). *Epicurus and the Epicurean Tradition*. Cambridge: Cambridge University Press.

Fortenbaugh, W.W. (ed.) (1983). *On Stoic and Peripatetic Ethics: The Work of Arius Didymus*. London: Transaction Publishers; (2017) London/New York: Routledge.

Fortenbaugh, W.W. and P. Steinmetz (eds.) (1989). *Cicero's Knowledge of the Peripatos*. New Brunswick/London: Transaction.

Fortenbaugh, W.W. (ed.) (2018). *Arius Didymus on Peripatetic Ethics, Household Management, and Politics: Text, Translation, and Discussion*. London: Routledge.

Frede, M. (1980). 'The Original Notion of Cause', in: Schofield *et al.* 1980, 217–249.

Frede, M. (1987), 'Stoic and Skeptics on Clear and Distinct Impressions', in: M. Frede, *Essays in Ancient Philosophy*. Minneapolis: Minnesota University Press, 1987, 151–176.

Frede, M. (2011). *A Free Will: Origins of the Notion in Ancient Thought*, edited by A.A. Long with a foreword by D. Sedley. Berkeley/Los Angeles/London: University of California Press.

Freeman, Ph. (2016). *How to Grow Old: Ancient Wisdom for the Second Half of Life Marcus Tullius Cicero*. Princeton: Princeton University Press.

Furley, D.J. (1989). 'Aristotelian Material in Cicero's *De natura deorum*', in: Fortenbaugh–Steinmetz 1989, 201–219.

Galli, D. (2019). *Cicero's* Paradoxa Stoicorum. *Text and Philological Commentary*. Roma: Carocci.

Gaskin, R. (1995). *The Sea Battle and the Master Argument: Aristotle and Diodorus Cronus on the Metaphysics of the Future*. Berlin: De Gruyter.

Gawlick, G. and W. Görler (1994). 'Cicero', in: *Die Philosophie der Antike*, IV: *Die hellenistische Philosophie*, hrsg. von M. Erler, H. Flashar, Basel: Schwabe (Überweg, 4/2), 1054–1168.

Gelzer, M. (1939). 'M. Tullius Cicero', in: *Paulys Realencyclopädie der classischen Altertumswissenschaft*, München: Druckenmüller Verlag, II Reihe XIII Halbband = Band VII, A1, coll. 827–1091.

Gelzer, M. (1969). *Cicero. Ein biographischer Versuch*. Wiesbaden: F. Steiner Verlag.

Gigon, O. (1989). 'Theophrast in Cicero's *De finibus*', in: Fortenbaugh–Steinmetz 1989, 159–185.

Gildenhard, I. (2011). *Creative Eloquence: The Construction of Reality in Cicero's Speeches*. Oxford/New York: Oxford University Press.

Gildenhard, I., Whitmarsh T., Warren, J. (2007). *Paideia romana. Cicero's 'Tusculan Disputations'*. Cambridge: The Cambridge Philological Society.

Gill, C. (2016). 'Antiochus' Theory of *oikeiōsis*', in: Annas–Betegh 2016, 221–247.

Giusta, M. (1964/1967). *I dossografi di etica*, 1/2. Torino: Giappichelli.

Glucker, J. (1978). *Antiochus and the Late Academy*. Göttingen: Vandenhoeck & Ruprecht.

Glucker, J. (1988). *Cicero's Philosophical Affiliations*, in: Dillon–Long 1988, 34–69.

Glucker, J. (1995). 'Probabile, *Veri Simile*, and Related Terms', in: Powell 1995a, 115–143.

Gómez, L.L. (2014). 'Chrysippean compatibilistic Theory of Fate, What Is up to us, and Moral Responsibility', in: Destrée–Salles–Zingano 2014, 121–139.

Görler, W. (1974). *Untersuchungen zur Cicero's Philosophie*. Heidelberg: Winter.

Görler, W. (1988). 'From Athens to Tusculum. Gleaning the background of Cicero's *De oratore*', in: *Rhetorica* VI, 215–235.

Görler, W. (1994). *Philon aus Larissa*, in: *PHA*, 915–37.

Görler, W. (1997). 'Cicero's Philosophical Stance in the *Lucullus*', in: Inwood–Mansfeld 1997, 36–57.

Gorman, R. (2005). *The Socratic Method in the Dialogues of Cicero*. Stuttgart: F. Steiner.

Goulet-Cazé, M.-O. (éd.) (2011). *Études sur la théorie stoïcienne de l'action*. Paris: Vrin.

Graver, M. (2007). *Stoicism and Emotions*. Chicago/London: The University of Chicago Press.

Graver, M. (2017). 'The Stoics' Ethical Psychology', in: Bobonich 2017, 200–217.

Griffin, M. (1997a). 'The Composition of the 'Academica'. Motives and Versions', in: Inwood–Mansfeld 1997, 1–27.

Griffin, M. (1997b). 'From Aristotle to Atticus: Cicero and Matius on Friendship', in: Griffin–Barnes 1997, 86–109.

Griffin, M. and J. Barnes (eds.) (1989). *Philosophia togata I, Essays on Philosophy and Roman Society*. Oxford: Clarendon Press.

Grilli, A. (1971). *I proemi del* De re publica *di Cicerone*. Brescia: Paideia.

Grimal, P. (1986). *Cicéron*. Paris: Fayard.

Habinek, T.N. (1990). 'Towards a History of Friendly Advice: the Politics of Candor in Cicero's *De amicitia*', in: *Apeiron* 23, 165–186.

Hacking, I. (1975). *The Emergence of Probability: A Philosophical Study of Early Ideas about Probability, Induction and Statistical Inference*. Cambridge: Cambridge University Press.

Hall, J. (2009). *Politeness and Politics in Cicero's Letters*. Oxford/New York: Oxford University Press.

Hamelin, O. (1978). *Sur le 'De fato'*, éd. par M. Conche. Paris: Éditions de Mégare.

Hankinson, R.J. (1997). *Natural Criteria and the Transparency of Judgement: Antiochus, Philo and Galen on Epistemological Justification*, in: Inwood–Mansfeld 1997, 161–216.

Hankinson, R.J. (1999). 'Explanation and Causation', in: *CHHP*, 479–512.

Harries, J. (2004). 'Cicero and the Law', in: Powell–Paterson 2004, 147–163.

Harries, J. (2013). 'The Law in Cicero's Writings', in: Steel 2013, 107–137.

Hirzel, R. (1871–1883). *Untersuchungen zu Cicero's philosophischen Schriften*. Leipzig: Hirzel.

Ierodiakonou, K. (ed.) (1999). *Topics in Stoic Philosophy*. Oxford: Oxford University Press.

Inwood, B. (1984). 'Hierocles: Theory and Argument in the 2nd Century A. D.', in: *OSAP* 2, 151–184.

Inwood, B. (ed.) (2003). *The Cambridge Companion to the Stoics*. Cambridge: Cambridge University Press.

Inwood, B. (2005). 'The Will in Seneca the Younger', in: B. Inwood, *Reading Seneca. Stoic Philosophy at Rome*. Oxford: Clarendon Press, 2005, 132–156.

Inwood, B. and P. Donini (1999). 'Stoic Ethics', in: *CHHP*, 675–738.

Inwood, B. and J. Mansfeld (eds.) (1997). *Assent & Argument. Studies in Cicero's "Academic Books"*. Leiden: Brill.

Ioppolo, A.M. (1986). *Opinione e scienza. Il dibattito tra Stoici e Accademici nel III e II secolo a. C.*. Napoli: Bibliopolis.

Ioppolo, A.M. (1994). 'Il concetto di causa nella filosofia ellenistica e romana', in: *Aufstieg und Niedergang der römischen Welt* 36, 7, 4491–4545.

Ioppolo, A.M. (2009). *La testimonianza di Sesto Empirico sull'Accademia scettica*. Napoli: Bibliopolis.

Ioppolo, A.M. (2016). '*Sententia explosa*. Criticism of Stoic Ethics in *De finibus* 4', in: Annas–Betegh 2016, 167–197.

Ioppolo, A.M. (2017). 'Clitomachus on what it means to follow the 'probable'', in: Lieberson–Ludlam–Edelheit 2017, 192–217.

Ioppolo, A.M. and D.N. Sedley (eds.) (2007). *Pyrrhonists, Patricians, Platonizers. Hellenistic Philosophy in the Period 155–86 BC*. Napoli: Bibliopolis.

Irwin, T.H. (2012). 'Antiochus, Aristotle and the Stoics on Degree of Happiness', in: Sedley 2012, 151–172.

Kennedy, G.A. (1963). *The Art of Persuasion in Greece*. Princeton, N.Y: Princeton University Press.

Kennedy, G.A. (1972). *The Art of Rhetoric in the Roman World: 300 B.C. – A.D. 300*. Princeton, N.Y.: Princeton University Press.

Kenny, A. (1975). *Will, Freedom and power*. London: Blackwell.

Kidd, I.G. (1971). 'Stoic Intermediates and the End for Man', in: Long 1971, 150–172.

Klein, J. (2015). 'Making Sense of Stoic Indifferents', in: *OSAPh* 49, 227–281.

Klein, R. (herausgeg. von) (1980). *Das Staatsdenken der Römer*. Darmstadt: Wissenschaftliche Buchgesellschaft.

Knoche, U. (1959). 'Cicero: Ein Mittler griechischer Geisteskultur', in: *Hermes. Zeitschrift für Klassische Philologie*, 87, 57–74; see Maurach 1976, 118–141.

Knoche, U. (1968). 'Ciceros Verbindung der Lehre vom Naturrecht mit dem römischen Recht und Gesetz', in: Radke 1968, 38–60.

Koch, B. (2006). *Philosophie als Medizin für die Seele: Untersuchungen zu Ciceros* Tusculanae Disputationes. Stuttgart: Steiner.

Kumaniecki, K. (1959). *Cyceron i jego współcześni*. Warszawa: Czytelnik; ital. transl. (1972): *Cicerone e la crisi della repubblica romana*. Roma: Centro Studi Ciceroniani Editore.

Laks, A. and M. Schofield (1995). *Justice and Generosity: Studies in Hellenistic Social and Political Philosophy: Proceedings of the Sixth Symposium Hellenisticum* (1992). Cambridge: Cambridge University Press.

Lee, C.-U. (2002). *Oikeiōsis. Stoische Ethik in naturphilosophischer Perspektive*, Freiburg/München: Alber.

Leeman, A.D., H. Pinkster *et al.* (1981–2008). *M. Tullius Cicero De oratore libri 3. Kommentar*. Heidelberg: Universitätsverlag Winter.

Lefèvre, E. (2001). *Panaitios und Ciceros Pflichtenlehre. Von philosophischen Traktat zum politischen Lehrbuch*. Stuttgart: Steiner.

Lévy, C. (1992). *Cicero Academicus. Recherches sur les* Académiques *et sur la philosophie cicéronienne*. Rome: École française de Rome.

Lévy, C. (1994). 'Source de la philosophie cicéronienne', in: *Dictionnaire des philosophes antiques*. I, éd. R. Goulet, Paris, 373–386.

Lévy, C. (2003). 'De finibus' and 'Tusculanae disputationes', in: *Dictionnaire des philosophes antiques. Supplément*, 666–675.

Lévy, C. (2012a). 'Michelangelo Giusta et la doxographie du souverain bien: esquisse de bilan', in: *Vestigia notitiai. Scritti in memoria di Michelangelo Giusta*, a cura di E. Bona, C. Lévy, G. Magnaldi. Alessandria: ed. dell'Orso, 1–12.

Lévy, C. (2012b). 'Philosophical Life versus Political Life. An Impossible Choice for Cicero', in: Nicgorsky 2012, 58–78.

Lévy, C. (2017). 'Cicéron, était-il un 'Roman Sceptic'?', in: *Ciceroniana On Line* 1.1, 9–24.

Lieberson, Y.Z., I. Ludlam, A. Edelheit (eds.) (2017). *For a Skeptical Peripatetic. Festschrift in Honour of John Glucker*. Sankt Augustin: Academia Verlag.

Lintott, A. (1997). 'The Theory of the Mixed Constitution at Rom', in: Barnes–Griffin 1997, 70–85.

Lintott, A. (2008). *Cicero as Evidence. A Historian's Companion*. Oxford: Oxford University Press.

Lintott, A. (2013). *Plutarch: Demosthenes and Cicero*, Translated with Introduction and Commentary. Oxford: Oxford University Press.

List, C. (2019). *Why Free Will Is Real.* Cambridge MA (USA)/London: Harvard University Press.

Lockwood Jr., T.C. (2020). 'Documenting Hellenistic Philosophy: Cicero as a Source and Philosopher', in: Arenson 2020, 46–57.

Long, A.A. (ed.) (1971). *Problems in Stoicism.* London: The Athlone Press.

Long, A.A. (1983). 'Arius Didymus and the Exposition of Stoic Ethics', in: Fortenbaugh 1983, 41–68 = Long 1996, 107–133.

Long, A.A. (1995a). 'Cicero's Politics in *De officiis*', in: Laks–Schofield 1995, 213–240.

Long, A.A. (1995b). 'Cicero's Plato and Aristotle', in: Powell 1995a, 37–61.

Long, A.A. (ed.) (1996). *Stoic Studies.* Cambridge: Cambridge University Press.

Long, A.A. and D. Sedley (1987). *The Hellenistic philosophers*, i: *Translation of the Principal Sources with Philosophicals Commentary*; ii: *Greek and Latin Texts with Notes and Bibliography.* Cambridge: Cambridge University Press.

Madvig, N. (1839) = Cicero 1839

Maso, S. (2009). '«Dignitatem tueri» in Cicerone: dalla dimensione civile all'istanza filosofica', in: *Méthexis* 22, 77–100.

Maso, S. (2014a). '*Motus animi voluntarius.* The Ciceronian Epicurus from Libertarian Free Will to Free Choice', in: Destrée *et al.* 2014, 235–250.

Maso, S. (2014b) = Cicero 2014.

Maso, S. (2015). *Grasp and Dissent. Cicero and Epicurean Philosophy.* Turnhout: Brepols.

Maurach, G. (herausgeg. von) (1976). *Römische Philosophie.* Darmstadt: Wissenschaftliche Buchgesellschaft.

May, J.M. (ed.) (2002a). *Brill's Companion to Cicero: Oratory and Rhetoric*, Leiden/Boston/Köln: Brill.

May, J.M. (2002b). 'Ciceronian Oratory in Context', in: May 2002a, 49–70.

McConnell, S. (2014). *Philosophical Life in Cicero's Letters.* Cambridge: Cambridge University Press.

Meier, Ch. (1968). 'Cicero Consulat', in: Radke 1968, 61–116.

Merguet, H. (1877). *Lexikon zu den philosophischen Schriften Cicero's.* Jena: Fischer; repr. 1971, Hildesheim – New York: Olms.

Merguet, H. (1877–1884), *Lexikon zu den Reden des Cicero.* Jena: Fischer; repr. 1971, Hildesheim – New York: Olms.

Michel, A. (1960). *Rhétorique et philosophie chez Cicéron. Essai sur les fondements de l'art de persuader.* Paris: Presses Universitaires de France.

Mitchell, T.N. (1979). *The Ascending Years.* New Haven: Yale University Press.

Mitchell, T.N. (1991). *Cicero the Senior Statesman.* New Haven/London: Yale University Press.

Müller, G.M. (2016). 'Cicero', in: *Brill's New Pauly Supplements II* – Volume 7: *Figures of Antiquity and their Reception in Art, Literature and Music.* Brill Online.

Müller, G.M. & F. Mariani Zini (eds.) 2018. *Philosophie in Rom – Römische Philosophie?* Berlin/Boston: De Gruyter.

Narducci, E. (2002). '*Orator* and the Definition of the Ideal Orator', in: May 2002, 427–444.

Narducci, E. (2009). *Cicerone. La parola e la politica.* Roma/Bari: Laterza.

Nicgorski, W. (ed.) (2012). *Cicero's Practical Philosophy.* Notre Dame (IN): University of Notre Dame Press.

Nicgorski, W. (2016). *Cicero's Skepticism and His Recovery of Political Philosophy.* London/New York: Palgrave Macmillan.

Nightingale, A.W. and D. Sedley (eds.) (2010). *Ancient Models of Minds. Studies in Roman and Divine Rationality*. Cambridge: Cambridge University Press.

North, J.A. and J.G.F. Powell (eds.) (2001). *Cicero's Republic*. In: *Bulletin of the Institute of Classical Studies*. Suppl. 76. London: University of London.

Obbink, D. (1996). *Philodemus. On Piety 1*, part 1. Oxford: Clarendon Press.

Obdrzalek, S. (2006). 'Living in Doubt: Carneades' *Pithanon* Reconsidered', in: *Oxford Studies in Ancient Philosophy* 31, 243–279.

O'Keefe, T. (2005). *Epicurus on Freedom*. Cambridge: Cambridge University Press.

Oppermann, H. (herausgeg. von) (1976). *Römische Wertbegriffe*. Darmstadt: Wissenschaftliche Buchgesellschaft.

Pease, A.S. (1955) = Cicero 1955.

Pembroke, S.G. (1971). '*Oikeiōsis*', in: Long 1971, 114–149.

Perelman, C. and L. Olbrechts-Tyteca (1958). *Traité de l'argumentation. La nouvelle rhétorique*. Paris: Presses Universitaires de France.

Petersson, T. (1920). *Cicero. A Biography*. Berkeley: University of California Press.

Pohlenz, M. (1934). *Antikes Führertum. Cicero 'de officiis' und das Lebensideal des Panaitios*. Leipzig/Berlin: Teubner. (1967) Amsterdam: Hakkert.

Pohlenz, M. (1940). *Grundfragen der stoischen Philosophie*. Göttingen: Vandenhoeck & Ruprecht.

Polansky, R. (ed.) (2014). *The Cambridge Companion to Aristotle's* Nicomachean Ethics. Cambridge: Cambridge University Press.

Powell, J.G.F. (ed.) (1995a). *Cicero the Philosopher*. Oxford: Clarendon Press.

Powell, J.G.F. (1995b). 'Cicero's Translations from Greek', in: Powell 1995a, 273–300.

Powell, J.G.F. (2001). 'Were Cicero's *Laws* the Laws of Cicero's *Republic*?', in: North–Powell 2001, 17–39.

Powell, J. (2012). 'Cicero's *De Re Publica* and the Virtues of the Statesman', in: Nicgorski 2012, 14–42.

Powell, J. and J. Paterson (eds.) (2004). *Cicero the Advocate*. Oxford: Oxford University Press.

Prost, F. (2001). 'La psychologie de Panétius: réflexions sur l'évolution du stoïcisme à Rome et la valeur du témoignage de Cicéron', in: *REL 79*, 37–53.

Purinton, J.S. (1999). 'Epicurus on 'Free Volition' and the Atomic Swerve', in: *Phronesis 44*, 253–299.

Radice, R. (2000). «*Oikeiōsis*». *Ricerche sul fondamento del pensiero stoico e sulla sua genesi*. Milano: Vita e Pensiero.

Radke, G. (ed.) (1968). *Cicero, ein Mensch seiner Zeit*. Berlin: De Gruyter.

Ramelli, I. (2009). *Hierocles the Stoic: Elements of Ethics, Fragments, and Excerpts*, translated by D. Konstan. Leiden/Boston: Brill.

Remer, G.A. (2017). *Ethics and the Orator: The Ciceronian Tradition of Political Morality*. Chicago/London: The University of Chicago Press.

Reinhardt, T. (2016). 'To See and to Be See: On Vision and Perception in Lucretius and Cicero', in: Williams–Volk 2016, 63–90.

Reinhardt, T. (2018). 'Cicero and Augustine on Grasping the Truth', in: Müller–Mariani Zini 2018, 305–323.

Reinhardt, T. (2019). '*Pithana* and *probabilia*', in: Bénatouïl–Ierodiakonou 2019, 218–253.

Reydams–Schils, G. (2016). 'Teaching Pericles. Cicero on the Study of Nature', in: Williams–Volk 2016, 91–107.

Rühl, M. (2018). *Ciceros Korrespondenz als Medium literarischen und gesellschaftlichen Handelns*. Leiden: Brill.

Runia, D.T. (1989). 'Aristotle and Theophrastus Conjoined in the Writings of Cicero', in: Fortenbaugh–Steinmetz 1989, 23–38.

Salles, R. (2005). *The Stoics on Determinism and Compatibilism*. Aldershot: Ashgate.

Sambursky, S. (1956). 'On the Possible and the Probable in Ancient Greek', in: *Osiris* 12, 35–48.

Sandbach, F.H. (1971a). 'Phantasia kataleptike', in: Long 1971, 9–21.

Sandbach, F.H. (1971b). 'Ennoia and Prolepsis in the Stoic Theory of Knowledge', in: Long 1971, 22–37.

Schallenberg, M. (2008). *Freiheit und Determinismus. Eine philosophischer Kommentar zu Ciceros Schrift 'De fato'*. Berlin/New York: De Gruyter.

Schofield, M. (1986). 'Cicero for and against Divination', in: *The Journal of Roman Studies* 76, 47–65.

Schofield, M. (2012a). 'The Fourth Virtue', in: Nicgorsky 2012, 43–57.

Schofield, M. (2012b). 'Antiochus on Social Virtue', in: Sedley 2012, 173–187.

Schofield, M. (2013). 'Writing Philosophy', in: Steel 2013, 73–87.

Schofield, M. (2021). *Cicero: Political Philosophy*. Oxford/New York: Oxford University Press.

Schofield, M., M. Burnyeat, and J. Barnes (eds.) (1980). *Doubt and Dogmatism. Studies in Hellenistic Epistemology*. Oxford: Clarendon Press.

Schofield, M. and Striker, G. (eds.) (1986). *Norms of Nature: Studies in Hellenistic Ethics*. Cambridge/Paris: Cambridge University Press.

Sedley, D. (1983). 'Epicurus' Refutation of Determinism', in: ΣΥΖΗΤΗΣΙΣ, *Studi sull'Epicureismo greco e romano offerti a Marcello Gigante*. Napoli: Macchiaroli, 11–51.

Sedley, D. (1995). 'Philosophical Allegiance in the Greco-Roman World', in: Powell 1995a, 97–119.

Sedley, D. (1997). 'The Ethics of Brutus and Cassius', in: *The Journal of Roman Studies*, 87, 41–53.

Sedley, D. (ed.) (2012). *The Philosophy of Antiochus*. Cambridge: Cambridge University Press.

Seel, O. (1968). 'Cicero und das Problem des römischen Philosophierens', in: Radke 1968, 136–160.

Shackleton Bailey, D.R. (1971). *Cicero*. London: Duckworth.

Sharples, R.W. (1995). 'Causes and Necessary Conditions in the *'Topica'* and *De fato'*, in: Powell 1995a, 247–271.

Sharples, R.W. (1991) = Cicero 1991.

Smith, P.R. (1995). '"A self-indulgent misuse of leisure and writing'? How Not to Write Philosophy: Did Cicero Get it Right?', in: Powell 1995a, 301–323.

Stark, R. (1954). 'Ciceros Staatdefinition', in: Klein 1980, 332–347.

Steel, C. (ed.) (2013). *The Cambridge Companion to Cicero*. Cambridge: Cambridge University Press.

Steinmetz, F.A. (1967). *Die Freundschaftslehre des Panaitios, nach einer Analyse von Cicero*. Wiesbaden: Steiner Verlag.

Stockton, D. (1971). *Cicero. A Political Biography*. Oxford: Oxford University Press.

Striker, G. (1983). 'The Role of *oikeiosis* in Stoic Ethic', in: *Oxford Studies in Ancient Philosophy*, I, 145–167, in: Striker 1996, 281–297.

Striker, G. (1996). *Essays on Hellenistic Epistemology and Ethics*. Cambridge: Cambridge University Press.

Stroh, W. (2008). *Cicero: Redner, Staatsmann, Philosoph*. München: Beck.

Skvirsky, A. (2019). 'Doubt and Dogmatism in Cicero's *Academica*', in: *Archai* 27, 1–21.

Syme, R. (1939). *The Roman Revolution*. Oxford: Clarendon Press.

Syme, R. and F. Santangelo (2016). *Approaching the Roman Revolution: Papers on Republican History*. Oxford: Oxford Scholarship Online.

Tarrant, H. (1985). *Scepticism or Platonism? The Philosophy of the Fourth Academy*. Cambridge: Cambridge University Press.

Tarrant, H. (2011). *From the Old Academy to Later Neo-Platonism*. Farnham: Ashgate.

Testard, M. (1958). *Saint Augustin et Cicéron*. Paris: Études Augustiniennes.

Thorsrud, H. (2009). *Ancient Scepticism*. Stockfield: Acumen; repr. 2014, Routledge.

Thorsrud, H. (2010). 'Arcesilaus and Carneades', in: Bett 2010a, 58–80.

Thorsrud, H. (2012). 'Radical and Mitigated Skepticism in Cicero's *Academica*', in: Nicgorski 2012, 133–151.

Thurn, A. (2018). *Rufmord in der späten römischen Republik: Charakterbezogene Diffamierungsstrategien in Ciceros Reden und Briefen*. Berlin/Boston: De Gruyter.

Tieleman, T. (2007). 'Panaetius' Place in the History of Stoicism, with Special Reference to His Moral Psychology', in: Ioppolo–Sedley 2007, 103–142.

Timpanaro, S. (a cura di) (1988). *Cicerone. Della divinazione*. Milano: Garzanti.

Turkowska, D. (1965). *L'Hortensius de Cicéron et le Protreptique d'Aristote*. Wroclaw: Académie Polonaise des Sciences.

Turnebus, A. (1552) *Marci Tullii Ciceronis Liber De Fato. In eundem commentarius*. Apud Adrianum Turnebum typographum Regium: Paris.

Voelke, A.J. (1973). *L'idée de volonté dans le stoïcisme*. Presses Universitaires de France: Paris.

Vogt, K.M. (2017). 'The Stoics on Virtue and Happiness', in: Bobonich 2017, 183–199.

Warren, J. (2016). 'Epicurean pleasure in Cicero's *De finibus*', in: Annas–Betegh 2016, 41–76.

Weidemann, H. (2019) = Cicero 2019.

White, P. (2010). *Cicero in Letters. Epistolary Relations of the Late Republic*. Oxford: Oxford University Press.

Williams, G.D. and K. Volk (eds.) (2016). *Roman Reflections. Studies in Latin Philosophy*. Oxford: University Press.

Wisse, J. (1988). *Ethos and Pathos from Aristotle to Cicero*. Amsterdam: Hakkert.

Wisse, J. (2002). '*De oratore*: Rhetoric, Philosophy, and the Making of the Ideal Orator', in: May 2002, 375–400.

Woolf, R. (2015). *Cicero: the Philosophy of a Roman Sceptic*. London: Taylor & Francis.

Wynne, J.P.F. (2019). *Cicero on the Philosophy of Religion. On the Nature of the Gods and on Divination*. Cambridge: Cambridge University Press.

Zarecki, J. (2014). *Cicero's Ideal Statesman in Theory and Practice*. New York: Bloomsbury.

Zetzel, J.E.G. (2013). *Political Philosophy*, in: Steel 2013, 181–195.

Zyl, D.H. van (1990). 'Cicero's Eclecticism and Originality', in: *Akroterion* 35, 118–122.

Index Rerum et Nominum Antiquorum

As too frequent, the following items have not been indexed: Academy, Aristotle, duty/*officium*/καθῆκον, Epicureanism, Epicurus, good/ἀγαθόν/*bonum*, knowledge, method, Peripatos/Peripatecics, pleasure/*voluptas*, soul/*animus*, Stoicism, truth/ἀλήθεια, virtue/ἀρετή, wise man/*sapiens*.

https://doi.org/10.1515/9783110661835-008

Index Nominum Recentiorum

https://doi.org/10.1515/9783110661835-009

Index Locorum

https://doi.org/10.1515/9783110661835-010